Integrated Marketing Communication

Integrated Marketing Communication

Series Editor: Jeanne M. Persuit
University of North Carolina Wilmington

Integrated marketing communication (IMC) is a holistic approach to the areas of advertising, public relations, branding, promotions, event and experiential marketing, and related fields of strategic communication. This series seeks to ground IMC with communication ethics in order to take the theory and practice of IMC beyond a critical and deconstructive understanding and into new areas of productive inquiry. We seek to advance the scholarship of IMC in a manner that influences and informs future practice. Submissions may rely on varied methodologies and relate to the study and practice of communication and its theoretical diversity, including but not limited to the areas of rhetoric, visual communication, media ecology, philosophy of communication, mass communication, intercultural communication, and instructional communication. We welcome submissions addressing all facets of IMC and its relationship with communication ethics. While edited volumes will be considered, we encourage the submission of scholarly monographs that explore, in-depth, issues in IMC as related to communication ethics.

Titles in the Series

Integrated Marketing Communication: Creating Spaces for Engagement, edited by Jeanne M. Persuit and Christina L. McDowell Marinchak

Integrated Marketing Communication

Creating Spaces for Engagement

Edited by Jeanne M. Persuit and
Christina L. McDowell Marinchak

LEXINGTON BOOKS
Lanham • Boulder • New York • London

Published by Lexington Books
An imprint of The Rowman & Littlefield Publishing Group, Inc.
4501 Forbes Boulevard, Suite 200, Lanham, Maryland 20706
www.rowman.com

Unit A, Whitacre Mews, 26-34 Stannary Street, London SE11 4AB

British Library Cataloguing in Publication Information Available

Library of Congress Cataloging-in-Publication Data

Names: Persuit, Jeanne M., 1973- editor. | McDowell Marinchak, Christina L., editor.
Title: Integrated marketing communication : creating spaces for engagement / edited by Jeanne M. Persuit & Christina L. McDowell Marinchak.
Description: Lanham : Lexington Books, 2016. | Includes bibliographical references and index.
Identifiers: LCCN 2016033989| ISBN 9781498540025 (cloth : alk. paper) | ISBN 9781498540032 (electronic)
Subjects: LCSH: LCSH: Communication in marketing. | Customer relations.
Classification: LCC HF5415.123 .I5823 2016 | DDC 658.8001/4--dc23 LC record available at https://lccn.loc.gov/2016033989

∞™ The paper used in this publication meets the minimum requirements of American National Standard for Information Sciences Permanence of Paper for Printed Library Materials, ANSI/NISO Z39.48-1992.

Printed in the United States of America

Contents

Acknowledgments

This book is a result of the support, encouragement, and hard work of many people. We only hope the appreciation we offer in this acknowledgement is something we've been expressing throughout the entire process.

First, we would like to thank our editor Nicolette Amstutz, editorial assistant Jimmy Hamill, and former editorial assistant Kasey Beduhn from Lexington Books/Rowman & Littlefield. Your collective support and assistance has made this a wonderful experience, and demonstrates Lexington's commitment to scholarly advancement in integrated marketing communication.

Second, we would like to thank the Scholars' Panelists from the 2015 Integrated Marketing Communication Conference at the University of North Carolina Wilmington (UNCW): Dr. Ronald C. Arnett, Duquesne University; Dr. J. Kevin Barge, Texas A&M University; Dr. Carl M. Cates, Valdosta State University; Dr. Vernon E. Cronen, UNCW; and Dr. Karen M. Russell, University of Georgia. Without their guidance, experience, and support, this volume would not have been possible.

We specifically would like to acknowledge Dr. J. Kevin Barge for his insight, his thoughtful responses, and his fantastic keynote speech at the 2015 IMC Conference. His work on designing spaces for communication inspired both the conference theme and this book, and for that we will always be in his debt.

Our copyeditor and Chicago style expert, Christopher J. (C.J.) Pendergast, an MFA candidate in the Creative Writing Program at UNCW, was an essential part of our team and we are thankful for his dedication and conscientiousness. We were lucky to work with him and we look forward to seeing his future success.

We would also like to thank Dr. Ronald C. Arnett and Dr. Janie M. Harden Fritz for their wise counsel and advice, especially throughout this process.

Last, and most importantly, we would like to thank our contributors. We appreciate your patience, diligence, enthusiasm, and professionalism, and we can only hope we did justice to your ideas. Thank you so much for your work.

Jeanne would like to thank her co-editor, Dr. McDowell Marinchak, for inspiration, moral support, endless amounts of patience, creativity, laughter, and most of all, friendship.

She would also like to thank her department chair, Dr. Richard K. Olsen and her colleagues in the Department of Communication Studies at UNCW for their reassurance and assistance. In addition, she would like to thank Debbie Whiting and Meghan Larson, because without these two women the IMC Conference and this book would not exist. Finally, she thanks her husband, Robert, her son, Jake, and her family, Dan and Cissy Bowman, Amy and Patrick McElhone, and Patrick Bowman and Caitlin Price, for cheering her on, always.

Christina would like to thank her co-editor, Dr. Persuit, for the opportunity to be part of this project, her guidance and inspiration, and, most importantly, a friendship of commitment, sacrifice, trustworthiness, and, more than anything, care.

She would also like to thank her department chair, Dr. Edward J. Forrest and her colleagues in the College of Business and Public Policy at UAA for acknowledging the vital role the communication discipline has in business as a means to creating an emergent space of learning. In addition, she also extends much gratitude and love to her husband, Marc, for always providing an ear, lending a shoulder, and, most of all, giving his heart.

The "end by us"!

Introduction

Communication. A conversation, an e-mail, a newspaper, a magazine, a social media interaction—a "snap," a "tweet," a "share," a "like," a "chat," a "post," a "favorite," a "comment," and so on—we have so many ways today to communicate—not just a billboard. What has opened up the communication possibilities? Technology. Advances in technologies not only offer a variety of communication tools for organizations to reach consumers, but for people to truly be engaged and involved in the brand setting us apart from previous historical moments. *Humans of New York* celebrates for instance, in an image and a short story, unique individuals and their life experiences (or, differences). What began as a photography project is now engaging "over twenty million followers on social media, and provides a worldwide audience with daily glimpses into the lives of strangers of New York City" (humansofnewyork.com). After the attacks on *Charlie Hebdo* in Paris, the slogan *#JeSuisCharlie* ("I am Charlie") engaged supporters of freedom of speech and freedom of the press, who may disagree with the sentiments published by *Charlie Hebdo* but fully defend its right to expression. Without a doubt, communication today is multidimensional and technology is the permitting factor for us to be reached in 360 degrees. However, we see opportunities for engagement by brands, organizations, and institutions everywhere, not just online. Technology is just one example of enabling communication with the world, encouraging the interplay of ideas and narratives, and opening spaces for human communicative engagement.

In today's global society, creating spaces for engagement and collaboration can be a daunting task for scholars and practitioners in the field of marketing. A field traditionally recognized as building a relationship between an organization, a product (brand), and a current as well as potential audience through production (product-based) orientation is part of the past. Integrated marketing communication (IMC) is a response to the needs of contemporary society, placing the consumer at the crux of engagement. IMC is a consumer-based approach, integrating the personal into marketing with the intent of reaching the consumer through connecting marketing practices to everyday life.

IMC is a holistic approach to the areas of advertising, public relations, branding, promotions, event and experiential marketing, and related fields of strategic communication. In this book, we explore how IMC can open up spaces for engagement in our classrooms and our communities.

We seek to advance the scholarship of IMC in a manner that influences and informs future practice by academics and practitioners. Capturing some of the most up-to-date thinking and research on IMC, each author offers a case study through which the reader can engage the ideas. The chapters included emerged from the third biennial IMC conference held at the University of North Carolina Wilmington in May 2015. The conference theme was "IMC: Creating Spaces for Engagement." The authors of the work included in this book all presented at this conference and have situated the scholarship of IMC in the communication discipline. The breadth of the contributors is also in the spirit of IMC: the authors hail from all over the U.S. and Europe, they examine public and private sector organizations that offer products and services, and they rely on various methodologies and theoretical approaches, with particular emphasis on rhetoric, philosophy of communication, qualitative research, and historical perspectives in IMC. Moreover, each chapter considers IMC from a different communicative perspective, including strategic communication, philosophy of communication, rhetorical theory, health communication, crisis and risk communication, communication theory, and mass communication. IMC, at its best, is coordinated, coherent, and persuasive, and although independently written, collectively provides clear insight into why and how IMC can open up spaces for engagement.

The origination of this volume, and indeed, the creation of the biennial IMC Conference itself, came from the need to situate the study of IMC in the communication discipline. The authors in this volume, along with other scholars and professors who examine IMC, believe that the study of human communication can inform the teaching, research, and practice of IMC, leading to more ethical and productive efforts. The study of IMC in the U.S. is relatively new, dating back to the early 1980s at Northwestern University's Medill School of Journalism, but its concepts and insights connect to ideas that are as old as the study of rhetoric itself, beginning over 2,500 years ago (Persuit 2013). In addition, some of the authors in this volume are business school faculty, which creates a fruitful opportunity to study marketing and its related components in a way that truly reflects the necessity of understanding narrative, audience, and meaning in business, and understanding strategic thinking, consumer behavior, and sustainability in communication.

As conference planners, we struggled with identifying the best forum in which to unpack these ideas. Our conference scholars panel—which included directors of graduate programs in IMC and communication, scholars in communication ethics, organizational communication, public relations, and coordinated management of meaning, and leadership of the international, national, and regional communication associations in the U.S.—recommended that we not only unpack these ideas but apply them to cases that could illustrate their power and possibility. This volume emerged from these discussions, and our cases range from the study of one young entrepreneur to the efforts of multinational corporations to non-profit organizational response to government and educational institutions in transition. We hope that this volume, like IMC itself, serves both a pragmatic and idealistic purpose: to inspire others to think about these ideas and how they could translate to real, productive action.

As editors of this volume, our goal was to explore how IMC, as grounded in the communication discipline, enables community engagement, with a focus on creating spaces for community engagement and collaboration. This book responds to questions that guided and arose from the conference, including: How can IMC encourage engagement with a variety of audiences, including voters, customers, volunteers, students, non-profits and government organizations, and other stakeholders? How can a theoretical approach to IMC encourage ethical practice? How can we theorize IMC to help build vibrant, productive communities? How is the use of "big data" in IMC encouraging or discouraging community engagement? How can various IMC contexts, including social media, public relations, advertising, event planning, marketing communication, and promotions, be more deeply understood through communication and rhetorical theory approaches? While each chapter is anchored by a case study, this text goes beyond a collection of case studies for analysis; the authors navigate new and groundbreaking theoretical ideas.

In the opening chapter, a foundation for understanding IMC and engagement is set through an exploration of how IMC campaigns generate a space for civic conversation. In our current capitalistic society, where vernacular civic discourse is deteriorating, IMC campaigns can generate civically engaged conversations among citizen consumers. This chapter investigates what these conversations look like, and what this type of communication does by using vernacular civic discourse as a benchmark. Applying Starbucks' "Fair Trade Coffee" campaign as a case study, the idea of engaged communicative consumption is proposed as a means to recognizing consumers' communicative action as the driving force of consumption involving thoughtful choices that are related to civic ideas.

In chapter 2, IMC and consumers' engagement with brands through social media is addressed as a response elicited by a mass media stimulus, in particular commercial advertising through an examination of a 2014 Coca-Cola commercial "It's Beautiful," which aired during the Super Bowl, the Winter Olympics, and the FIFA World Cup tournament that year. The main focus is on the dilemma of communicating a brand image consistently over time to achieve and maintain a desired positioning in the consumer's mind on the one hand, and the principles of stimulating consumer engagement in social media, corporate citizenship, and rejuvenating the brand on the other.

Chapter 3 moves to focus on applying the research and theory in the field of communication to the craft of event planning through the lens of

IMC. The authors take a praxis approach in which theory informs action during the event planning process. The theory applied examines the research in the fields of communication, event planning, and IMC, making connections among the scholarship, and informing the analysis of the event planning process of the 2010 Eastern Communication Association (ECA) convention in Baltimore, Maryland, nicknamed the Charm City.

Chapter 4 addresses IMC and advertising, specifically the generating of persuasive tactics that lead consumers to feel like kids again. The author finds this a powerful way to allow a temporary escape into appreciating and anticipating purchase decisions in life once more. The chapter investigates within IMC and branding frameworks, why and how the marketing practices should show consumers that they can look to their brands and products as socially constructed reminders of childhood.

In chapter 5, the author conducts an examination of the "Vote Yes!" campaign in the Republic of Ireland in 2015, where the issue of marriage equality was put to a popular vote and ultimately succeeded. In public relations, audiences are often referred to as *publics*, with whom an organization must engage to produce short- and long-term success. The orientation of public relations is often to generate awareness, but public relations with an IMC orientation aims to effect behavioral change, not just attitudinal change. The chapter explores how PR with an IMC orientation can be informed by two ideas from ancient rhetorical theory: epideictic rhetoric and *kairos*, and that this theoretical ground can enable an ethical and effective approach to IMC.

A study of a young entrepreneur who follows principles of IMC without formal training is presented in chapter 6. In this qualitative investigation, the entrepreneur created a new business, a vintage furniture and accessories shop, in the former location of a flea market. While studies of IMC usually focus on larger organizations, the study in this chapter offers a microcosmic perspective. The conclusion discusses responses to the research questions posed and implications for values, identities, and organizational learning.

Chapter 7 then explores how IMC represents an impactful strategic approach to build loyalty among consumers in health communication. In 2014, CVS unveiled their "Let's Quit Together" campaign concurrently with a name change from CVS Caremark to CVS Health. To fully appreciate the intersection of IMC and organizational ethics, this author explores CVS's approach through the intersection of smoker identity and principles of IMC.

In chapter 8, the interplay of IMC and disaster preparedness offers one lens for exploring these questions and creates a space that gives voice to marginalized publics. By using the American Red Cross as a case study, this author follows a metaphorical perspective for connecting IMC and disaster response. The chapter includes a detailed analysis of how the American Red Cross seeks to better understand the populations it serves and how the organization engages the community in disaster preparedness and response.

Chapter 9 analyzes the practice of discouraging customers from the purchase of a product or service which has become known as "demarketing" (Kotler and Levy 1971). Initially perceived as a contradiction, demarketing offers a formidable organizational strategy to counteract market forces detrimental to the viability of a product, service, or brand. In this chapter the author uses the work of Max Weber as a way to ground demarketing a critical and economic theory and demonstrate how this type of communication as a rational economic action could help in further explaining the failure/success of the 1985 introduction and subsequent discontinuation of New Coke that ultimately enabled Coca-Cola® to reclaim its position as leader of the cola market.

We conclude with an international perspective on brand management and education, with chapter 10's exploration of the trend documents and recent studies on brand and communication management and organizational management as described in three areas: the history of branding, a changing world from branding 1.0 to branding 3.0 and the 3.0 organization, and the consequences of these trends resulted in redeveloping the study program at HAN University of Applied Sciences/Arnhem Business School in the Netherlands. Both practitioners and faculty can learn from this study of the shift in marketplace expectations, and consider the implications for the future of teaching, practicing, and researching IMC.

The ten chapters in this collection advance IMC scholarship, demonstrating how IMC can open spaces for engagement in our classrooms and communities. A response to our contemporary engaged reality makes this possible. The theme of community engagement and collaboration, which include social, political, and economic issues are exemplified in the case studies. Our intent was to demonstrate the way the ideas in each chapter draw from a variety of works, insights, and reflections and work together to form a gestalt understanding of IMC in theory and in practice. We invite our readers to respond to the call to advance the scholarship of IMC, providing new opportunities for human communicative engagement.

REFERENCES

Persuit, Jeanne M. (2013). *Social Media and Integrated Marketing Communication: A Rhetorical Approach*. Lanham, MD: Lexington Books.

ONE

Engaged Communicative Consumption

How IMC Campaigns Generate a Space for Civic Conversation

Christina L. McDowell Marinchak and Jill K. Burk

Sitting in a corner sipping your venti, peppermint mocha with whip, you glance over your cup to observe two friends sitting on a couch catching up, a group of professionals at a large table devising a business strategy, and students at the countertops with their laptops finishing a group project. In this moment, you realize there is much more going on than a "caffeine fix." You realize that coffee is now part of a larger culture of consumption, and it shapes identity, action, and conversation. Such an act frames what Gerard Hauser wrote in *Vernacular Voices*, "We cannot make sense of our collective selves without understanding how deeply discourse shapes us" (2008, 34). Through exploring the historical and current state of civic discourse; addressing the notion of engaged conversations among citizen-consumers; and offering a preliminary investigation into how these ideas unfold in the marketplace, this chapter brings forth an understanding of how integrated marketing communication (IMC) generates a space for civic conversation.

In an attempt to "make sense of our collective selves," and understand how "deeply discourse shapes us" in relation to IMC, we ask the question: How do IMC campaigns provide insight into the generation and continuation of civic discourse in the public sphere where vernacular civic discourse is deteriorating? In our current capitalistic society, where vernacular civic discourse is deteriorating, IMC campaigns can generate civically engaged conversations among citizen-consumers. But, what do these conversations look like, and what does this type of communication do? A benchmark is vernacular civic discourse.

VERNACULAR CIVIC DISCOURSE

Vernacular civic discourse refers to everyday communication among everyday people about issues that are civic in nature—issues that affect a person's community, town, city, and/or nation. The term *vernacular civic discourse* is explored here as describing this phenomenon and communicative action, and is grounded in Gerard Hauser's theory of vernacular rhetoric. Vernacular communication comes in the form of everyday, run-of-the-mill, informal communication. Hauser, in explaining this type of communication, says, "Mostly these conversations are mundane transactions of words and gestures that allow us to negotiate our way through our quotidian encounters. They are not formal exchanges at the podium; they are vernacular expressions of who we are, what we need and hope for, and what we are willing to accept, and our commitment to reciprocity" (2004, 11). This type of communicative exchange is important, and the nature and quality of these communicative acts make up the core phenomenon for this investigation. While Hauser uses the terminology of vernacular rhetoric, we make a diminutive move to focus only on a specific type of rhetoric that contains distinct themes and issues; *ergo* the term vernacular civic discourse.

Vernacular civic discourse is observed as everyday exchanges among everyday citizens about everyday civic issues as a pertinent part of our contemporary society. In a society where civic engagement and discourse is diminishing it is particularly important to find spaces where this type of discourse may be occurring in different ways than in the past. While everyday citizens may not be attending town meetings in formal institutional settings or listening intently to the State of the Union address or the president's weekly radio address, people are engaging in discourse about civic issues. In contemporary society, citizens communicate with one another in all kinds of forums . . . communication is not limited to formal institutional forums (Hauser 2004, 36). From this perspective, we claim there is reason to believe citizens are learning about issues through IMC campaigns.

STATE OF CIVIC DISCOURSE IN CONTEMPORARY SOCIETY

To grasp the impact IMC campaigns have on civic engagement, it is necessary to consider the current state of civic discourse. In an age driven by information glut, virtual connectivity, and technologically mediated communication, the experience of face-to-face communication and physical interaction takes on renewed importance. Because of technological advancements, we have a vast amount of civic information at our fingertips, yet our attitudes and actions toward community participation seem to be concurrently diminishing. In the 1980s and 1990s, scholarly work began to raise concern about a decline in civic engagement. Scholarship by political philosopher Michael Sandel, political theorist Benjamin Barber, and sociologists Robert Bellah and Robert Putnam discuss the decline of civic engagement in the United States, and have called for further research and discussions surrounding the current state of civic engagement.

Bellah, Madsen, Sullivan, Swidler, and Tipton in *The Good Society* understand active participation is crucial for the health of society, and hold firm that many people believe America is a great democracy, yet democratic participation is absent from our public life (1992, 6; 138). In *Habits of the Heart* (2008), the authors specifically discuss the state of the United States' current culture of individualism, concluding that Americans yearn for a greater sense of connectedness, a greater sense of community, yet the contradictory nature of our socio-political environment and particular cultural narratives lead to confusion about human beings and their need for community, interconnectedness, and support for others (1992, 27). Robert Putnam's research reveals similar trends. Putnam views American history as one full of stories of "collapse and renewal" ebbs and flows, and ups and down. In *Bowling Alone* (2000), he documents American's current apathetic tendency toward issues, ideas, and communicative practices related to civic engagement. According to Putnam, Americans are *not* less likely to talk about politics than our parents and grandparents; however, we *are* less likely to participate in political face-to-face activities—a glimpse into the engaged citizen-consumer in which "actions speak louder than words." Putnam's work summarizes the drastic decline of citizen participation over forty years, thus demonstrating the need for a resurgence in civic engagement.

A major problem is that people are not only disengaged, they are rhetorically reticent (Schudson 1997, 301). Many Americans lack explicit awareness of the rhetorical participation needed for the establishment and maintenance of a thriving democracy. The practical art of rhetoric requires a human dimension; symbols are chosen and communicated to an audience through a human decision-making process. Rhetoric always contains an ethical component because choices always have to be made. Thus, for a citizen's rhetoric to be a fitting response (Bitzer 1968, 9), to coordinate social action (Hauser 2004, 3), and/or find the available means of persuasion (Aristotle 2006, 6) in an ethical manner, the citizen needs to be civically engaged. Therefore, civic engagement is a crucial aspect of democracy. A democracy works because of horizontal networks of people and a culture of participation in civic affairs (Putnam 1993, 102-03).

Civic engagement equals participation, and participation is an essential component of democracy; however, the current state of civic discourse, as previously discussed, is in decline.

Civic engagement is necessary to sustain a vibrant democracy (Aristotle 2013, 1094b; Dewey 1954, 184; Putnam 1995, 336-49). There are numerous kinds of democracy, and the current democratic system in the United States differs from the ancient Greek *polis*. The term democracy originated in the fifth century from the Greek word *demos*, which roughly translates into a common people who live in a particular district. Although there are different types of democracies, two basic forms endure: a direct democracy and a representative democracy. In a direct democracy, sometimes referred to as a pure democracy, people vote directly on policies and initiatives. There is a one-to-one vote. Each vote is counted and the person or policy that garners a majority of the votes wins the election. The ancient Greek system is the only example of direct democracy in history, albeit on a very small scale and with very limited citizenship participation.

In the United States today, examples of direct democracy can be seen in local government elections, and, at times, on policies or referendums depending on the particular municipality in which one lives. However, implementing a pure democracy, at all governmental levels, is nearly impossible in a nation the size of the United States. Currently, the United States has a representative democracy. This means the people or everyday citizens vote for representatives, and the representatives place a vote on behalf of their constituents. Some scholars, such as Benjamin Barber, believe civic engagement and civic activity is lost through this type of democratic system. He posits, "This approach purchased efficiency without sacrificing accountability, but it did so at an enormous cost to participation and to citizenship" (Barber 1984, xiv). To that end, every citizen is not necessarily governing herself because someone else is representing and governing for her.

Whether it be a direct or representative democracy, there are additional attributes to the democratic system which include respecting elections, protecting liberties and freedoms, safeguarding legal entitlements, and guaranteeing free speech for the country's citizens and the country's media (Diamond 2008, 20-22). While it is important to recognize many interpretations of a democratic system that have existed and continue to exist (Diamond 2008, 20), we believe the critical connection is knowing and acknowledging that these communicative acts constitute and shape our social world. Therefore, to be civically engaged means to be an active member of one's community, which is also rhetorical in nature since rhetoric is symbolic action. Our primary intent here is to address the fact that a participatory democratic system involves rhetoric. For instance, voting is the essential communicative action for all eligible citizens.

This perspective is valuable because a majority of the literature assumes an intrinsic relationship between rhetoric, interpersonal communication, and civic engagement. Mitchell S. McKinney, Lynda Lee Kaid, and Dianne G. Bystrom (2005) in their book chapter titled "The Role of Communication in Civic Engagement" work from a similar perspective. The authors call their philosophy "communicative engagement." Communicative engagement sees citizens' communicative action as the driving force of democracy. McKinney, Kaid, and Bystrom assert "the driving force of democracy can be found in individual citizens' many acts of joining, volunteering, serving, attending, meeting, participating, giving and perhaps most importantly, cooperating with others" (2005, 7; 6). Therefore, democracy is constructed through the communicative action of many individuals (2005, 7). To be civically engaged is to be communicatively engaged.

Scholars have used the feel-good, abstract term of civic engagement in a variety of ways. According to Richard P. Adler and Judy Goggin (2005) in their article titled "What Do We Mean by Civic Engagement," there is little agreement on what actions and beliefs constitute civic engagement. They state that scholars working from particular scholarly perspectives contribute to the range of definitional specificity because these scholars narrow their focus; and therefore, their definitions to work within their specific discipline (2005, 237). Furthermore, civic engagement is an interdisciplinary topic that is discussed and researched in many different academic disciplines (Ostrander and Portney 2007, 1).

The interdisciplinary nature of civic engagement contributes to the wide range of definitional understandings and usages. For example, Susan A. Ostrander and Kent E. Portney define civic engagement simply as "individual and collective action to identify and address public issues and to participate in public life" (2007, 1). Thomas Ehrlich provides a more detailed definition in his text *Civic Responsibility and Higher Education*. He defines civic engagement as: "Working to make a difference in the civic life of our communities and developing the combination of knowledge, skills, values, and motivation to make that difference. It means promoting quality of life in a community, through both political and non-political processes" (2000, vi). To further contribute to the array of ideas, civic engagement, as a concept or ideal, is situated in both the political and community arenas, and concerns both individual and collective actions (Adler and Goggin 2005, 240-41). Thus, the act of voting and the act of throwing away trash in a public trashcan embody an act of civic engagement. Both communicative acts constitute and shape our social world. Therefore, to be civically engaged means to be an active member of one's community. To use the metaphor of spectator and participant (Holba 2007, 96), someone who is civically engaged is a participant in his/her community—not a spectator sitting in the bleachers.

However, as stated previously, many contend that civic engagement in America is declining. If Americans are not civically engaged in their local communities, they are not rhetorically engaged in their communities either. On the contrary, some scholars argue that civic engagement is not declining; it is just shifting and changing (Ostrander and Portney 2007, 2-4; Dalton 2016, 4). Russell J. Dalton in his book, *The Good Citizen: How a Younger Generation is Reshaping American Politics*, examines current norms of political and civic engagement and concludes that norms are changing among Millennials (2007). He argues that an "engaged citizenship emphasizes a more assertive role for the citizen and a broader definition of citizenship to include social concerns and the welfare of others" (2007, 6). He continues with "many Americans believe they are fully engaged in society even if they do not vote or conform to traditional definitions of citizenship" (2007, 6). The communicative acts that constitute this model of citizenship include protests (such as Occupy Wall Street), joining Teach for America, being an organ donor, and acts of political consumerism (2007, 181-2). We see an invitational opening in this change. Perhaps, public engagement may be lacking in this historical moment, but traces of such participation can be seen in vernacular civic discourse brought about by acts of citizenship and engagement through IMC.

IMC AND CIVIC ENGAGEMENT

In the late 1980s a discussion of integrated marketing communication (IMC) was initiated and proliferated as an important theoretical idea. The avocation of IMC occurred at this time primarily due to new and rapid technological changes, especially across digital platforms, a new focus on branding and brands, and increased multinationalization and globalization (Schultz and Schultz 2004, 9). According to IMC pioneering advocates Don Schultz and Heidi Schultz, IMC can be understood as a "strategic business process used to plan, develop, execute, and evaluate coordinated, measurable, persuasive brand communication programs over time with consumers, customers, prospects, and other targeted, relevant external and internal audiences" (2004, 20-21). IMC is a holistic approach to understanding how an organization communicates with its publics. Organizational members, who work under an IMC framework, spend time thinking about the near-seamless communication transactions that occur between an organization and its publics while taking into account the perspective and buying considerations of that consumer.

IMC moves from a traditional understanding of marketing—a focus on the four Ps (product, placement, price, promotion)—to a focus on four key elements. These elements include: (1) the recognition and implementation of all marketing communication functions as an essential business strategy, not merely a tactical endeavor; (2) the involvement of the entire organization with marketing communication functions; (3) the ongoing measurement and evaluation of marketing communication messages; and (4) the understanding that desired results may be delivered over time, not instantaneously (Schultz and Schultz 2004, 43-44). The movement from a traditional marketing, product focus to a contemporary marketing, consumer focus allows for greater integration across marketing platforms and greater understanding of the communication interactions that take place between customers and the products they select to support and make the final purchase.

IMC places particular emphasis on communicative messages, making possible the integration of marketing communication efforts that emphasize the necessity of one voice, one message, and one sound in all messages being sent to the intended audience (Schultz and Schultz 2004, 23). Percy states that IMC foregrounds the "two-way communication between marketer and customer" (1997, 3). Moreover, IMC takes into consideration a consumer's perspective toward decision-making and purchasing (Percy 1997, 2), therefore adopting not only a top-down approach in thinking about the product, but a more nuanced understanding of human beings as complex consumers.

In placing particular emphasis on the complexity of consumers (Calder and Malthouse 2003, 8), IMC allows for the movement toward a more ethical and responsive marketing practice. This focus on customers creates an environment that elevates strategy and initiates a holistic consumer brand experience that is customized (2003, 15). The focus is on individuals and not on market segments, and particular attention is paid to how "customers relate to brands" (Schultz and Schultz 2004, xvii). Seeing humans as complex, decision-making creatures diminishes the one-way, top-down communication approach from organization to consumer and elevates the unique communicative capacity held by human beings. IMC understands the dialogical nature and ongoing message exchange between brand and customer, therefore uniquely grounding IMC in the communication discipline. Understanding communication theory as IMC's theoretical ground allows for a more ethical and effective business practice (Persuit 2013, 43), allowing for a practice that is responsive and reflective, creating an enlarged opening for the place and communicative purpose of consumption in a consumer's life.

"ENGAGED COMMUNICATIVE CONSUMPTION"

Civic engagement demands active participation, and traditionally speaking vernacular civic discourse occurred because people took up issues that impacted a person's community, town, city, and/or nation. In the past, the types of communicative acts that constituted civic engagement were clearer cut. Perhaps this was due to a dominant narrative surrounding what it meant to be a citizen. As mentioned previously, many people believe there is a decline in civic engagement today. However, we believe that a "change" has occurred, rather than a decline, in such engaged conversations. In contemporary society if engaged conversations are not initiated by the everyday, neighborly vernacular, then something else *must* be generating civic engagement.

Consumption practices provide an opening for discussing how "something else" must be generating civic engagement. Why do individuals purchase and consume particular brands and products? According to Mary Douglas and Baron Isherwood, in their text *The World of Goods: Towards an Anthropology of Consumption*, the "formal economist" (1996, 3) asserts that the consumer is a rational person, and that her consumption patterns stem from her rationality. But what happens when a person reaches for a product that she does not need or makes a non-rational purchase? As Douglas and Isherwood explain, "Often it is not so much a sense of having made a decision but of having been overtaken by events" (1996, 4). The cutting edge product or technology, with its new and improved promises, becomes a must-have in order to contend with society and compete with consumers. Although a consumer may be overtaken by events at the type of purchase, "the consumer's choice is his free choice" (1996, 36). Regardless of a consumer's mental state when making a purchasing decision, the choice to consume is still her own to make.

Goods also provide a means to "make and maintain social relationship" (1996, 39). Douglas and Isherwood elaborate: "Goods, then, are the visible part of culture. They are arranged in vistas and hierarchies that can give play to the full range of discrimination of which the human mind is capable. The vistas are not fixed; nor are they randomly arranged in a kaleidoscope. Ultimately, their structures are anchored to human social purposes" (1996, 44). The individual is in need of social compliant "fellows" who will engage in reaffirming her consumptive patterns and behaviors. The authors attribute a moral judgment by giving their presence to the individual for specific events. This said, meaning is in the relationship and information of all goods. Therefore, goods carry no meaning unless they are involved in the system as a whole (1996, 51). Goods, then, become "markers" or "the visible bit of the iceberg which is the whole social process" (1996, 50), markers for why consumers buy (e.g., purchasing a product for flavor, natural attributes, or health reasons). This position is of general consumption practice, but in a time that it is difficult to break through the communication clutter something more must be at play to get people buying (and discussing).

The importance of civic engagement in consumption practices is rooted in understanding that the act of buying and consuming takes on more of a role than only buying a product for its use function. In a moment when consumers have too many brand options and choices to select from, consumers make choices about products for many different reasons (and, not necessarily because a product is the lowest priced). Take for instance the act of buying to support local organizations. Under the engaged citizenship model this communicative act constitutes an act of civic engagement. Other acts of civic engagement connected to a consumer's consumption practice could include buying to support environmental sustainability or buying as an act of social justice—to support or raise awareness of fair trade issues—*engaged communicative consumption.*

We posit engaged communicative consumption recognizes consumers' communicative action as the driving force of consumption involving thoughtful choices that are related to civic ideas. Moreover, these decisions are communicative; they communicate something through action and word. In "Integrated Marketing Communication: Anticipating the 'Age of Engaged,'" Groom (2008) explores "marketing's approach to today's situation of interactivity and engagement as strategic integrated communication" (3). To the end that consumers make purchases "characterizes the human condition," which is action-oriented, pointing to "the significance of the values implicit in IMC initiatives. These values come from people—from the human community—and represent a much deeper sense of meaning than any product or service can ever fully embody. This inspires compelling and resonant communication messages" (2008, 15). The crux of such engagement then is that the "values represented in and through IMC impact the way people encounter, interpret, and share their marketplace experiences' (2008, 15). In a time of heightened consumer skepticism, engaged communicative consumption opens up the possibility for consumers to make purchases based on something more than the traditional 4P's of product, price, promotion and place (mass marketing).

While the phenomenological shift to a consumer-oriented approach is not new through the development of IMC, here we are shifting the point of attention of IMC from the company to the consumption standpoint. As previously discussed, this goes back to why we buy and connecting the meaning through a consumer's consumption practices. Working from within an IMC framework, companies can choose to implement an engaged communicative consumption approach, therefore embracing the opportunity for the brand to shape decisions and preferences through civically engaging the consumer. "People ascribe to a way of life, not to products or brands" (2008, 15). IMC is consumer-centric and therefore aligns with this idea, integrating meaning and purpose behind a consumer's purchase. For companies it may be about responding to the "age of engagement" (2008, 13), but for consumers it is about acting in the *moment of engagement.*

Acting in the moment of engagement entails doing much more than simply purchasing a product. It means stopping to think about the purchase—does consumption mean promoting sustainability, giving to a cause, supporting an effort, and so on. In short, the purchasing of goods (such as, buying) provides for a new civic engagement institution. Therefore, the act of purchasing goods then opens up a space for a new venue that allows for conversations to happen. And, more specifically, the act of buying allows for the potential of an engaged conversation between persons on issues that are civic in nature. Consider for a moment you are standing in long line waiting to order a morning coffee. There is nothing that ties the person in front of, beside of, or next to you together, but the fact that you are buying the same goods creates an opening for conversation to occur, more specifically a conversation that is prompted by the adjective on the label about fair trade coffee. The words, chosen by the organization to highlight, describe, and differentiate their product lead to the purchasing of goods and perhaps ultimately lead to greater communication implications—engaged communicative consumption.

IMC CAMPAIGNS: ENGAGED COMMUNICATIVE CONSUMPTION IN PRACTICE

Organizations want to create spaces for discussion in an effort to market and differentiate; however, from an IMC perspective, understanding that communication starts with the customer, the consumer, the audiences and works backward so these organizations are working with their customers and seeing how customers are responding to the IMC strategies, they are not only developing a way to differentiate their products, but also a way to differentiate their consumers. Therefore, the connection between marketing and production is important to have a successful IMC effort. "The marketing strategy must be integrated within the entire value chain from production right down to sales" (Trop 2009, 192). While such an initiative is a top-down plan, it has the potential to create civic change because conversations around the campaign become bottom up. We think IMC campaigns initiate conversations about civic issues, therefore generating vernacular civic discourse. This conversation becomes a by-product as current grassroots efforts gain traction. We consider the shift, then, in civic discourse issues as tied to material things in contemporary society and believe the form of civic discourse has to change, because the needs are greater—creating opportunity for consumer engagement through IMC campaigns. An example of how an IMC campaign generates a space for civic conversation includes Starbucks. A Starbucks IMC campaign brought awareness of a particular issue—fair trade coffee practices—to a greater population of people due to its pervasiveness and reach.

A Case for IMC and Civic Engagement: Starbucks "Fair Trade Coffee" IMC Campaign

In 2000, Starbucks launched its "Fair Trade Coffee" IMC campaign, taking the step to implement "ethical sourcing, using responsible purchasing practices; farmer support; economic, social and environmental standards; industry collaboration and community development programs" through Coffee and Farmer Equity (C.A.F.E.) suitability practices (www.starbucks.com). C.A.F.E. practices have aided Starbucks in ensuring high-quality coffee while positively impacting "the lives and livelihoods of coffee farmers and their communities" (www.starbucks.com). The fair trade movement was a response to "perceived failure of the market and [a] remedy [for] important social issues" (Haight 2011). While fair trade coffee only accounts for a small amount of coffee sales, many lives of growers have been improved over the last decade because of companies implementing fair trade policies. Moreover, fair trade coffee "has evolved from an economic and social justice movement to largely a marketing model for ethical consumerism" (2011). This IMC campaign provides the basis for how Starbucks generated spaces for civic conversation—positive and negative.

By offering fair trade coffee as well as putting in place a C.A.F.E. practice, Starbucks spurred both positive and negative civic conversation about this global social justice issue. People began to take notice of grassroots fair trade activism surrounding coffee. In addition, citizens began demanding products be made under fair labor conditions in global trade system (www.globalexchange.org), and engaging in conversations about these issues. Since Starbucks is a globally pervasive brand and caters not only to the coffee elite, but the Frappuccino-loving teenager, we have reason to believe that fair trade as well as the ethical and social issues the effort addresses have become more of the vernacular civic discourse and more people are aware of these issues than before Starbucks launched this IMC campaign.

IMC is a strategic business practice used by organizations to change people's behaviors, and includes virtually everything an organization says and does and everyone who is affected by the organization's existence and activities" (Trop 2009, 202-203). A form of IMC that aligns with the current discussion is "organic word-of-mouth" (Groeger and Buttle 2014, 1186), which is a form of word-of-mouth that "occurs naturally and is not explicitly aroused and managed by marketers for strategic purposes" (2013, 1186). All it takes is one tweet, a post, or a like. "In many cases, word of mouth marketing isn't actually about marketing at all. It's about great customer service that makes people want to tell their friends about you. It's about fantastic products that people can't resist showing to everyone" (Sernoviz 2010). Organic word-of-mouth marketing then emerges with the company knowing that conversations may go in a positive or negative directions; Starbucks encountered such conversations during the company's fair trade coffee IMC campaign.

By implementing socially responsible buying policies, Starbucks communicated to consumers that the company buys coffee in a responsible, sustainable manner. This action drummed up positive discussions by Starbucks supporters and customers. Since the company has deliberately avoided traditional marketing practices, such as advertisements in magazines, billboards, newspapers, and celebrity endorsements (Knight 2014), a significant amount of communication is on social media (and for the most part continues to be digital). Starbucks is very active on social media, allowing the company to use digital practices to cultivate a sense of community with supporters and customers (2014). Through social media people are made part of the company, which in turn makes people identify themselves with Starbucks and its activities. During the "Fair Trade Coffee" IMC campaign, Starbucks used social media to communicate to customers, specifically through videos that featured details about its fair trade practices. Social media then became a space for discussion (for civic discussion). IMC is "an indefinable concept that can accommodate any innovative idea, theory or practice that promotes a company's brand and customer relations" (Trop 2009, 193). IMC then is a customer-centric approach, which in the Starbucks "Fair Trade Coffee" campaign was exemplified by how customers were able to communicate with the brand. Thus, brand narrative has a role in all different parts of IMC; everything the company said and did during the fair trade coffee IMC campaign had an impact on consumers.

According to the American Association of Advertising Agencies (1989), IMC involves "the seamless integration of discrete messages." Starbucks social media outlets were a place where discussions were held on the issue of the company's fair trade practices. While there were several posts that supported Starbucks' efforts, there were also negative comments that called into question how much the company was doing to promote fair trade practices. The company has been "heavily criticized by some groups for not doing more to promote fair-trade coffee, which pays farmers in developing countries living wages in exchange for their crops" (Frank 2004, 2). IMC works to "counter the negative consequences of comprehensive structural and functional differentiation in organizational communications systems" (Trop 2009, 194). In 2000, As addressed by Bryant Simon, in *Everything but the Coffee: Learning about America from Starbucks,* Starbucks enacted its "Fair Trade Coffee" IMC campaign, however, this was after the company was "blasted" for "serving sweatshop coffee" by the human rights group Global Exchange (2011, 207). "Unless the company [Starbucks] agreed to carry more fair-trade beans," human rights activists would launch a "'Roast Starbucks' campaign" across the United States (2009, 207). IMC considers the "demand for trustworthiness and transparency" (Trop 2009, 195). While the human rights group "won a compromise" it did not gain "total victory," because Starbucks "didn't commit to selling only fair-trade fare, but it did agree to buy a pile of these beans each year" (Simon 2011, 207-208). Starbucks was the world's largest consumer of fair-trade coffee in 2004, but that was only 3.7 percent of the company's yearly purchases (2011). By 2006, 6 percent of the company's purchases were fair trade (2011). In 2015, Starbucks reported, "99 percent of their coffee is now ethically sourced" (Horovitz 2015). Starbucks, recognizing they would need to respond to the activist groups and acknowledged that the actions were to benefit the greater good would not necessarily benefit the company. Knowing that some consumers would disagree that the company was doing all it could to help the "little guy," Starbucks used its website, point of purchases marketing, and public relations to communicate to its supporters and customers their fair trade efforts. This included putting brochures for the fair trade blend, signs, and fair trade bags in stores (Simon 2011). Additionally, Starbucks responded to questions regarding why not all the coffee purchased by the company was not fair trade on its "My Starbucks Idea" site (starbucks.com). View it "greenwashing" (2011, 209) or successful, strategic business practices, the Starbucks "Fair Trade Coffee" IMC campaign generated civic conversations about an important social and economic issue.

The Starbucks "Fair Trade Coffee" campaign served as a catalyst for conversation about the use of fair trade products, but also the greater issue of economic and social justice issues surrounding fair trade, bringing it to the attention of many since the incorporation of this IMC campaign. In February 2016, Fair Trade USA reported that 59 percent of Americans are now aware of fair trade certified products and recognized the Fair Trade Certified™ label, which is supported by consumer consumption (fairtradeusa.org). Since Starbucks (and a variety of other companies) has started labeling their products "fair trade," people have started to discuss the importance of fair trade consumption practices and look for the fair trade label when making a purchase. Moreover, the fair trade label allows companies to meet consumer needs, communicating they are accountable, responsible, and sustainable in their business practices. According to the 2016 State of Sustainability in America Report, "sustainability is not a trend, it is becoming a cultural shift. All organizations, therefore, will need to realize that sustainability is not just a desired activity but a necessary strategy" (nmisolutions.com). Moreover, "consumers are increasingly looking beyond the product and service and show strong interest in companies' sustainable initiatives" and companies must "make sure packaging choices align with company sustainable strategies" (nmisolutions.com). While fair traded goods have been around, the movement has only recently gained traction with consumers (Smith 2014). Thus, through fair trade discussions demand for such products has increased, therefore spurring this act of civic engagement.

CONCLUSION

In sum, if civic engagement is declining, vernacular discourse is in decline too. Civic participation, however, can be seen in vernacular civic discourse brought about through engaged communicative consumption. Specifically, the purchasing of goods (i.e., buying) provides for a new institution for civic engagement—how we engage through buying. Through such engagement, IMC campaigns can generate a space for civic conversation, for vernacular civic discourse. Specifically, IMC campaigns raise awareness of civic and political issues. Coffee, now part of a larger culture of consumption, shapes identity, action, and conversation. Fair trade coffee is not everyday an issue until the IMC campaign is labeled and tells consumers that it is; therefore, becoming part of the everyday, vernacular lexicon.

REFERENCES

Adler, Richard P., and Judy Goggin. 2005. "What Do We Mean by 'Civic Engagement'?" *Journal of Transformative Education* 3: 236-53.

Aristotle. 2006. *Aristotle on Rhetoric : A Theory of Civic Discourse.* 2nd ed. Translated by George A. Kennedy. USA: Oxford University Press.

Barber, Benjamin R. 1984. *Strong Democracy: Participatory Politics for a New Age.* Berkeley: University of California Press.

Bellah, Robert N., Richard Madsen, William M. Sullivan, Ann Swidler, and Steven M. Tipton. 1992. *The Good Society.* New York: Vintage.

———. 2008. *Habits of the Heart: Individualism and Commitment in American Life : with a New Preface.* 3rd ed. Berkeley: University of California Press.

Bitzer, Lloyd F. 1968. "The Rhetorical Situation." *Philosophy & Rhetoric* 1, no. 1: 1-14.

Calder, Bobby J., and Edward C. Malthouse. 2003. "What is Integrated Marketing Communication?" In *Kellog on Integrated Marketing,* edited by Dawn Iacobucci and Bobby J. Calder, 6-15. Hoboken, NJ: John Wiley & Sons, Inc.

Dalton, Russell J. 2007. *The Good Citizen: How a Younger Generation is Reshaping American Politics.* 2nd ed. Los Angeles, CA: Sage.

Dewey, John. 1954. *The Public and its Problems.* Chicago, IL: Swallow.

Diamond, Larry. 2008. *The Spirit of Democracy: The Struggle to Build Free Societies throughout the World.* New York: Time/Henry Holt.

Douglas, Mary, and Baron C. Isherwood. 1996. *The World of Goods: Towards an Anthropology of Consumption.* Rev. ed. London: Routledge.

Ehrlich, Thomas. 2000. *Civic Responsibility and Higher Education.* Westport: Oryx.

"Ethical Sourcing: Coffee." *starbucks.com,* accessed May 23, 2016, http://www.starbucks.com/responsibility/sourcing/coffee.

"Fifty-Nine Percent of Americans Now Aware of Fair Trade Certified Products." *fairtradeusa.org,* last modified February 26, 2016, http://fairtradeusa.org/pressroom/press_release/fifty-nine-percent-americans-now-aware-fair-trade-certified products.

Frank, John. "Starbucks employs Cone for 'fair trade' message. PR Week," *London ed.* June 18, 2004.

Groeger, Lars, and Francis Buttle. 2014. "Word-of-mouth marketing: Towards an improved understanding of multi-generational campaign reach." *European Journal of Marketing* 48, no. 7/8: 1186-1208.

Groom, S. Alyssa. 2008. "Integrated Marketing Communication: Anticipating the 'Age Of Engage.'" Communication Research Trends 27: 3-19.

Haight, Colleen. 2011. "The Problem with Fair Trade Coffee." *Stanford Social Innovation Review*. Summer 2011. http://ssir.org/articles/entry/the_problem_with_fair_trade_coffee

Hauser, Gerard A. 2004. "Rhetorical Democracy and Civic Engagement." 2004. In *Rhetorical Democracy: Discursive Practices of Civic Engagement*, edited by Gerard A. Hauser and Amy Grim, 1-14. Mahwah: Lawrence Erlbaum Associates.

———. 2008. *Vernacular Voices: The Rhetoric of Publics and Public Spheres*. Columbia, S.C.: University of South Carolina Press.

Holba, Annette. 2007. *Philosophical Leisure: Recuperative Practice for Human Communication*. Milwaukee: Marquette University Press.

Horovitz, Bruce. "Starbucks: 99% Ethically Sourced Java." USA Today, April 10, 2015, http://www.usatoday.com/story/money/2015/04/10/starbucks-fast-food-restaurants-dining-coffee-ethically-sourced/25571937/.

Knight, Matt. 2014. "Social Marketing: Word of Mouth Case Studies From Superdry and Starbucks." Social Media Week. January 24, https://socialmediaweek.org/blog/2014/01/social-marketing-word-mouth-case-studies-superdry-starbucks/.

McKinney, Mitchell S., Lynda Lee Kaid, and Dianne G. Bystrom. 2005. "The Role of Communication in Civic Engagement." In *Communicating Politics: Engaging the Public in Democratic Life*, edited by Mitchell S. McKinney, Lynda Lee Kaid, Dianne G. Bystrom, and Diana B. Carlin, 3-26. New York: Peter Lang.

National Marketing Institute. "2016 State of Sustainability in America." Accessed May 23, 2016 http://www.nmisolutions.com/index.php/research-reports/sustainability-reports/14th-annual-consumer-report-2016-state-of-sustainability-in-america#summary.

Ostrander, Susan A., and Kent E. Portney. 2007. "Introduction: Key Issues in Civic Engagement Research Today." In *Acting Civically: From Urban Neighborhoods to Higher Education*, 1-17. Medford: Tufts University Press.

Percy, Larry. 1997. *Strategies for Implementing Integrated Marketing Communications*. Lincolnwood, IL: NTC Business Books.

Persuit, Jeanne M. 2013. *Social Media and Integrated Marketing Communication: A Rhetorical Approach*. Lanham: Lexington Books.

Putnam, Robert D. 1995. "Bowling Alone: America's Declining Social Capital." *Journal of Democracy* 6, no. 1: 65-78.

———. 2000. *Bowling Alone: The Collapse and Revival of American Community*. New York: Simon.

———. 1993. "What Makes Democracy Work?" *National Civic Review* 82, no. 2: 101-07.

Sander, Thomas H., and Robert D. Putnam. 2010. "Still Bowling Alone? The Post 9/11 Split." *Journal of Democracy* 21, no. 1: 9-16.

Simon, Bryant. 2011. *Everything but the Coffee: Learning about America from Starbucks*. Berkley, CA: University of California Press.

Schudson, Michael. 1997. "Why Conversation Is Not the Soul of Democracy." *Critical Studies in Mass Communication* 14, no. 4: 297-310.

Schultz, Don E., and Heidi Schultz. 2004. *IMC-The Next Generation: Five Steps for Delivering Value and Measuring Returns Using Marketing Communication*. Boston, MA: McGraw Hill.

Smith, Martin. "The Rise of the Fair Trade Coffee Movement." The Modern Ape. January 21, 2014, http://themodernape.com/2014/01/21/rise-fair-trade-coffee-movement/.

Trop, Simon. 2009. "Integrated communications: from one look to normative consistency." *Corporate Communication: An International Journal* 14:190-206.

TWO

Integrated Marketing Communication and Customer Engagement

"It's Beautiful"

Daniel U. Assmus

This chapter addresses consumers' engagement with brands through social media as a response elicited by a mass media stimulus, in particular commercial advertising. Crossing communication channel boundaries for continuing and expanding conversations with target audiences is a feasible way to increase breadth of the communication (i.e., reach) as well as its depth (i.e., elaboration). Also, the conversion of a passive mass media broadcast consumer to a social media communication producer creates campaign success on a number of additional, measurable key performance indicators (KPI) in which integrated marketing communications play a vital role in consumer support and customer engagement.

In the following, customer engagement with brands in social media is defined in the context of service-dominant logic and can be illustrated with the case of the Coca-Cola commercial advertisement titled "America is Beautiful" (often referred to just as "It's Beautiful"), which aired during three major sporting events in 2014: It premiered during that year's NFL Super Bowl and was aired again during the Sochi Winter Olympics and the FIFA Soccer World Cup held in Brazil. Not all the customer engagement stimulated by this campaign element was literally beautiful; however, it was certainly effective with regard to integrated marketing communication in some quantitative success metrics.

INTEGRATED MARKETING COMMUNICATION AND CUSTOMER ENGAGEMENT OR "AUDIENCE"

Integrated marketing communication (IMC) is a customer-centric approach, which moves away from the traditional product-oriented communication strategy used throughout much of the twentieth century. According to Schultz and Kitchen, IMC "connects communication, strategy, and business aims: 'IMC is a strategic business process used to plan, develop, execute, and evaluate coordinated, measurable, persuasive brand communication programs over time with consumers, customers, prospects, and other targeted, relevant external and internal audiences" (Persuit 2014, 31; Schultz and Kitchen 2000). The significant audience, then, emerges in IMC, in which the communication focus is placed on communicating with the audience (Persuit 2014). Moreover, IMC focuses on customer behavior and not attitude as traditional marketing does (2009). The idea is that "behavior more clearly indicates what a person will do in the future than do various intention or attitudinal approaches (Schultz and Schultz 2000, 56). Therefore, "focusing on behavior offers a more reliable metric that can actually be measured; it offers an initial approach to aggregating customers and prospective customers" (Persuit 2014, 32). The idea is that IMC has the ability to influence customer behavior, and as a byproduct increase customer engagement (i.e., customer support and purchases).

Customer Engagement and Service-Dominant Logic

For a little over a decade now, the framework of service-dominant (S-D) logic in marketing developed (Vargo & Lusch 2004; Gummesson 2008), which "recognizes that specific consumer behavior outcomes are generated by customers' particular *interactive, value cocreative experiences* with organizations and/or other stakeholders" (emphasis added, Brodie et al. 2011, 253). The focus in S-D logic has shifted away from the product and onto the engagement with the brand.

Managing consumer engagement (CE) and the related CE behaviors—that is, a "customer's behavioral manifestations that have a brand or firm focus, beyond purchase, resulting from motivational drivers" (van Doorn et al. 2010, 254), constitutes a form of relationship marketing. These relationships are also lived through communication in social media. In fact, one goal of this many-to-many network marketing approach is to reap the benefits of consumer advocacy in the form of electronic word-of-mouth (WOM), which makes interactive social media a prime environment for creating and measuring levels of CE.

Levels of engagement in social media are typically gauged quantitatively on the basis of amount of activity in the form of Twitter retweets, Facebook likes, shares, comments, the use of hashtags, and so on, depending on the particular social medium. These engagement activities translate directly into additional reach as the messages spread through the individual consumers' networks, thus providing an additional quantitative KPI of CE management actions. The awareness effect can then be further boosted with the marketing/advertising tools provided by social media platforms, such as "sponsored stories." In short, engaging customers through brand experiences online will enhance exposure of the brand throughout the medium.

However, customer engagement—in the sense of behavior or a behavioral disposition toward brands in an interactive communicative environment—is not limited to positive WOM. As Hollebeek and Chen (2014) point out,

> particular negatively valenced expressions of marketing-based [CE] may incur specific undesirable outcomes (e.g. the dissemination of negative WOM), which managers need to have an awareness of. This observation also exhibits conceptual consistency with [Higgins and Scholer's (2009) 'regulatory engagement theory']-based prediction that higher "engagement" may not only render a consumer's perception of a focal positively perceived object more positive, but also make a focal negatively perceived object appear more negative. (64-65)

Negative co-creative brand experiences will still produce results in line with the quantitative objectives of increased reach, and resulting awareness can be achieved with high engagement levels regardless of its positive or negative nature. However, the online discourse needs to be evaluated qualitatively as well in order to assess possible impact on brand knowledge. Here, new negative brand associations may be formed that can hurt consumers' brand image and which in turn may have an effect on their brand choice.

The question is not only if any publicity is good publicity, but also how to strategically use the triangular "relationships between brand engagement, brand love and consumers' use of brands to enhance self-expression of identity" (Wallace et al. 2014, 33-34) to push visible and, thus, measurable communicative interaction. Brand love is a strong affirmative attitude, or positive emotional predisposition, toward the brand. It is a precursor to attitudinal loyalty, behavioral loyalty, and further brand engagement, and it is largely based on brand knowledge. The Coca-Cola case at hand will display the intricacies and robustness of this triangular connection.

COCA-COLA'S NEED FOR AWARENESS

Until the year 2012, Coca-Cola was valued the top of Interbrand's 100 best global brands for 13 consecutive years (Elliot 2012). That is, in fact, how long the report had existed. Interbrand ratings constitute a reliable reference because the company was not only the first one to have its brand valuation process certified against the international ISO 10668 standard, but was also a strong supporter of and contributor to the standard's draft. A major component of brand strength, according to the standard and, thus, Interbrand's valuation process, is brand awareness. In 2012, according to a study "by Research Now, Coca-Cola scored over 90% in brand awareness among respondents from the US, Canada, UK, France, Germany and Australia" (Frampton 2012). Such scores can only be achieved through a brand's omnipresence in media and distribution channels. Valued at nearly 78 billion USD, 2012 marked the Coca-Cola brand's last year at the top of the ranking. Despite a healthy single-digit growth rate of its financial brand equity, Coca-Cola was already under pressure from comparatively young but striving technology brands Apple (+129 %) and Google (+26%). In an effort to protect brand equity, continued sponsorship of and advertising throughout mass-mediated, high-reach sporting events had been and continue to be Coca-Cola's long-term strategy not only to boost and maintain brand awareness but also to place brand experiences in a highly emotional context to increase the commitment that is brand love.

The Coca-Cola Company Campaign

Traditionally, the Coca-Cola Company works almost exclusively with pathos appeals (that is, emotional appeals) in its advertising campaigns. This emotional heritage is still visible in the brand's current slogan, "Taste the Feeling"—a reprise of the late 1980's "You Can't Beat the Feeling!"—introduced in January of 2016. This regeneration effort is part of the global roll-out of the company's new and pre-tested "one brand" strategy designed to reshape the brand architecture. The strategy focuses on line extensions rather than a multi-brand strategy and tries to trivialize the message (Moye 2016).

While the new campaign intends to refocus on the product rather than the brand (Schultz, 2016), logos appeals (i.e., logical appeals) are still largely absent as there are few commonly accepted rational reasons to consume Coca-Cola products. In fact, the brand is frequently under global public scrutiny with regard to health and environmental issues (Stecklow 2005) such as childhood obesity, diabetes (Hert et al., 2014) or plastic waste (Nestle and Bittman 2015, 279). Therefore, previous campaigns, for instance, featured fuzzy polar bears or a children's choir supporting "reasons to believe in a better world," or taking a stance against online bullying.

The consistent pairing of the brand with stimuli eliciting a positive emotional response can, over time, effectively transform brand elements such as name, logo, or slogan into conditioned stimuli producing similar affective responses in consumers. The 2014 "It's Beautiful" commercial advertisement, at first glance, seems to perfectly continue this feel-good narrative:

The commercial consists of a collage of U.S. scenery, lifestyles, and subcultures highlighting the diversity of the United States of America with imagery of rural and urban settings, straight and gay lifestyles, and a multiplicity of ethnicities. These diverse visuals are complemented with a multi-lingual rendition of the traditional "America the Beautiful" by Katharine Lee Bates (lyrics) and Samuel A. Ward (music). The commercial advertisement does not use actors in its portrayals, but allows American citizens to star in their own stories throughout the sixty seconds. Instead of the customary "Open Happiness" tagline, the hashtag #AmericaIsBeautiful appears next to the iconic Coke bottle trademark at the conclusion of the advertisement.

How does the subdued musical score and peaceful, almost still photography help promote the idea of happiness within the context of a high-action football game? As also obvious with previous advertisements throughout the seven-year "Open Happiness" campaign, the kind of happiness referred to by the brand is not a loud or obnoxious display of thrill and excitement, but in this particular case rather a recollection of one of the United States' core virtues. According to the U.S. Declaration of Independence, the pursuit of happiness is one of the unalienable rights guaranteed to its citizens. While the advertising narrative makes no explicit reference to the document, the message may be interpreted to focus on a fundamental and shared virtue of the American society. In *Democracy in America,* Alexis de Tocqueville calls attention to the importance of focusing on "the mores—the 'habits of the heart'—that includes consciousness, culture, and the daily practices of life" (Bellah et al. 2008, 275). A focus on mores provides insight "into the state of society, its coherence, and its long-term viability" (2008, 275). Virtues are public and agreed upon by multiple people (Arnett and Arneson 1999). Along the same lines, virtue is a public idea of what is right and wrong, and usually are socially acceptable ideas. In today's society, however, there is an inability to agree on what are the virtue structures that guide people. In this historical moment appealing to these types of virtues can be problematic because "incredulity towards meta-narratives" (Lyotard 1984, xxiv) manifests itself in the growing distrust in governments, religions, and corporations, so it is increasingly difficult to find common denominators of culture that define a people. However, the unalienable rights constitute not only remnants of such common grounds but are the ethical foundation of and still a major contributor to self-identity in American society today. With its commercial, Coca-Cola is tapping into these fundamental sentiments.

Syllogistically, if 1) the pursuit of one's happiness is a virtue that every American, regardless of social standing, heritage, or religious affiliation, will consider a unifying hallmark of their culture, and if 2) Coca-

Cola is happiness, then 3) consequently Coca-Cola is what unites the American people amidst all diversity. Accordingly, the Coca-Cola brand was the only visible constant in the commercial advertisement.

An advertisement that calls its U.S. American audience to rediscover common cultural core virtues while celebrating the diversity of its society is highly philosophical and places the brand in a position of a cultural authority. Some may argue this is an over-interpretation of Coca-Cola's intentions. Some may claim that it cannot or must not be the intention of Coca-Cola to act on behalf of morality. However, Coca-Cola's current executives have recently supported such interpretation of the previous marketing strategy by publicly criticizing the "Open Happiness" campaign and its elements for being too "preachy" and concerned "with 'high-level' ideas" that want to "fix happiness" (Schultz 2016). The campaign included many commercial advertisements broaching additional societal issues ranging from tangible (bullying) to abstract (world peace).

PERFORMANCE

During the 2014 NFL Super Bowl, commercial airtime reportedly sold at an average rate of 4 million U.S. Dollars (USD) per thirty-second advertisement (AdAge 2014). In addition to a second Coke ad, the "It's Beautiful" commercial aired for 60 seconds during the televised event, which translates to a total cost of about 8 million dollars for the advertisement (note: these are gross prices not considering volume discounts and others which the Coca-Cola company realized. Therefore, these costs are only an approximation used for illustration).

Reach was at a record-breaking 111.5 million U.S. viewers (approximately 35% of the U.S. population). Consequently, the cost per one thousand contacts (CPM) per 30 seconds was roughly 35 USD and 70 USD for the one-minute advertisement. The 40% CPM increase over other prime time television programming can be explained with the increased demand for the limited supply of advertising time slots (Chemi 2014). Marketers of mass products still like the idea of large audiences. Especially with the fragmentation of media and audiences alike, a mega television event like the NFL Super Bowl, which attracts the largest global audience of all televised single-sport events, is a highly desirable advertising platform for marketers.

In an explicit attempt to stimulate customer engagement behavior in social media, Coke provided the hashtag #AmericaIsBeautiful. Hashtags are used on Twitter and other social media platforms such as Facebook to label or categorize a message. They help to identify which subjects are discussed most frequently (trending topics), to bundle responses, and to measure the success of social media campaigns as an indicator of customer engagement with a brand.

Table 2.1. Campaign Statistics

2014 Super Bowl advertising rate per 30 sec.	4 million USD
Duration of "It's Beautiful" commercial	60 seconds
Total cost	8 million USD
Target audience (U.S. population)	314 million people
Reach	111.5 million people = 35.5%
Cost per thousand contacts (CPM)	71.75 USD (35.87 USD for 30 seconds)
Super Bowl rate premium vs. regular prime time network rates	40%

Note: Table created by Daniel Assmus

According to international statistics, all non-U.S. participants of several master's seminars on global brand management and bachelor's seminars on international marketing communications, the Coca-Cola commercial was a good strategic fit for the brand's long-term positioning as it evoked similar emotions of happiness in them as the other ads of the campaign. The students appreciated the depicted virtues of a pluralistic society and admiration of the beauty of the country as truly American and, only in part, felt the message was a little too patriotic and pathos-laden. This is not, however, how the entire primary target audience, the 111.5 million U.S. television viewers of the 2014 NFL Super Bowl, received the commercial advertisement.

CONSUMER ENGAGEMENT WITH THE BRAND AND COMMERCIAL ADVERTISEMENT

It may seem surprising that immediately after the airing of the advertisement during the NFL Super Bowl, the hashtag "#f*ckcoke" became a trending topic on Twitter. There were 20 percent of users who disliked the advertisement on Coca-Cola's YouTube channel, and according to a representative YouGov/HuffPost survey "only" one fifth of Americans were offended by the ad (Swanson 2014).

Before addressing the "why" of this negative response, it is important to establish the consequences: If the ratios on social media and the survey are true for the television audience as well, then 22.3 million viewers of the Super Bowl would have hated the ad and, consequently, might have formed negative associations with the brand and perhaps even altered behavioral patterns. In addition to sales, the inconsistency of brand image (Coke = happiness) may be hurtful to financial brand equity—the opposite of what Coca-Cola needed to achieve. Additionally, Coca-Cola would have spent 1.6 million USD alienating consumers from its brand. The negative engagement also created a remarkable amount of negative electronic WOM.

Coca-Cola certainly intended some kind of positive discussion of the advertisement in social media. Otherwise, they would not have included a hashtag. It was an invitation to share our own experiences on why "America is beautiful." However, Coca-Cola executives could have also anticipated the controversy that ensued over the advertisement; the negative posts relate mostly to the fact that the song "America the Beautiful" was sung in six languages in addition to the traditional English rendition.

In the United States, there is an ongoing controversial debate over the need to establish English as the official national U.S. American language. To date, the United States is one of only a few countries in the world that have not defined a national language or national languages. As a result of the debate, twenty-eight of the fifty U.S. states have adopted legislation that makes English the official language of their states. Another indicator that Coca-Cola may have been aware of the potential for controversy over its advertisement is the presence of other controversial elements, which were included in the commercial. In comparison to the language discussion, these received little media and popular attention due to their subtlety.

Most strikingly, a gay couple is shown roller-skating with their adoptive child as one of the multiple lifestyles featured in the advertisement. This message of equality regardless of sexual orientation came in response to accusations that Coca-Cola as a sponsor did not take a public stance against the violations of gay rights in Russia, where the Winter Olympics took place that year. Coca-Cola could have expected more of an emotional response to this aspect of its advertisement as well since there was an intensive public debate on the issue of gay marriage in the United States of America during that time. With the commercial advertisement, Coca-Cola positioned itself prior to the eventual Supreme Court ruling. Coca-Cola then decided to prominently air the commercial advertisement again during the opening ceremony of the Olympic Winter Games in Sochi.

After the firestorm regarding the language choice in the advertisement that ensued in social media following the initial NFL Super Bowl

Table 2.2. Negative Impact

Share of target audience reach offended by the commercial	20% = 22.3 million people
Share of total advertising cost spent on alienating customers	1.6 million USD

Note: Table created by Daniel Assmus

airing, Coca-Cola defended the core virtues represented in the advertisement, but did not engage in the social media discussion. Also, despite the controversy, the company decided to present the ad twice again to U.S. audiences in high-reach settings (Olympics and the FIFA Soccer World Cup that summer). In because of by the controversial online discussions, the objective of creating reach in social media far beyond the viewership of the television ad was achieved; hence, the awareness impact was increased and, consequently, the CPM of the campaign overall went down. Also, despite the many verbal threats to boycott Coca-Cola products, consumption behaviors did not change. In other words, sales numbers did not decrease domestically after the campaign. For the first time in 2015, financial brand equity according to Interbrand dropped in 2015. It is impossible to link the significant brand value decrease to the airing(s) of the advertising alone, but since brand valuation is a measure for marketing effectiveness, the decrease reflects negatively on 2014 marketing activities (not limited to communication). Finally, revisiting the idea of the relationship of customer engagement and brand love, the strong negative emotional response to the commercial in social media is indeed a very good indicator of the positive attitude toward the brand. If people did not already love the brand before the commercial advertisement, they would have unlikely reacted with such high customer engagement behavior levels expressing their disappointment and frustration.

WHY NEGATIVITY MAY BE POSITIVE: THE ROLE OF COGNITIVE DISSONANCE

In order to understand the frustration, one has to look at the third component in the relationship triangle of customer engagement, brand love, and consumers' use of brands to enhance self-expression of identity. With a still modern understanding of "the culture of a nation-state [as] one which generally emphasizes cultural homogeneity and integration" (Featherstone 1990, 1), if the consumption of Coca-Cola acts as a virtue-expression of an American identity, because the brand is as much of a symbol of American culture as apple pie, football, and the pursuit of happiness, and if patriotic songs are also a source and expression of identity, and if finally *American* English is seen as the melting pot language result characteristic of American culture, then the advertisement had to create cognitive dissonance.

Cognitive dissonance is the discomfort experienced as a result of the inability to consolidate two simultaneously held, inconsistent beliefs (Harmon-Jones and Harmon-Jones 2007). Consumers try to escape this discomfort by avoiding or rejecting new information or explaining it away. This reaction may manifest itself in a behavior which can be observed already in young children holding and discovering incongruent beliefs about people, namely through "strong overt aggression, hostility, and destructiveness" (Festinger 1962, 23). The CE of a significant portion of the target audience can certainly be described in Festinger's terms.

In relation to the "It's Beautiful" commercial, only a strongly held, relevant belief that the Coca-Cola brand is a symbol of self-expression and a simultaneously similarly strongly held belief that "America the Beautiful" should be performed in English as an expression of identity can cause the level of dissonance that lead to the magnitude of emotional outburst observed in social media. The Coca-Cola Company could have easily avoided putting many consumers in such a dilemma.

The same ad imagery with the song in English or a different song in different languages would probably not have created the same amount of dissonance. However, it also would not have created the same amount of social media buzz. It would have led to less engagement. Organizational behavior theory is praising diversity as promoting innovation and creativity. But it is not promoting efficiency, because diversity is neither easy nor necessarily comfortable. Coca-Cola chose the uncomfortable route for consumers, thereby enhancing CE behavior. Also from a societal standpoint that may be commendable. From a brand positioning standpoint it may be beneficial only in the very long run.

IMPLICATIONS

Among other things, brand image and brand awareness are among the most important determinants of financial brand equity. Consumers have to recall or recognize (that is, know) the brand and also have to prefer the associations with the brand to those with other known brands. Negative valence toward individual messages may certainly create negative brand associations. However, whether it is a sufficient motivator to terminate brand loyalty depends on the prior brand-consumer relationship.

These relationships are grounded in the number and types of bonds developed over time (Arantola 2002). The more bonds there are between consumer and brand, the stronger is the relationship and the lower is the risk of a bond breakdown (Buttle and Maklan 2009). Coca-Cola has fewer economic and structural bonds, even though the market position creates some supplier dependency; instead, the bonds created with its customers are largely social. These social bonds have a strong potential to form a competitive advantage because they are difficult to replicate by competitors despite their apparent fragility. In fact, social bonds create attitudinal loyalty, which is based on a true preference for the brand rather than the potentially compliance-based behavioral loyalty. In this context, the consumers' willingness to engage in a discussion (or confrontation) with Coca-Cola is an indication for both, the strong existing relationship and the desire to maintain or restore this relationship. With strong bonds, Coca-Cola had little to fear.

Additionally, previous examples of emotional outbursts in the form of a firestorm have shown that the negative engagement is typically short-lived. One such case involved Coca-Cola and its sponsorship of the UEFA EURO 2012 soccer championships. Sponsors of the event were accused of not leveraging their power on the soccer association to force one of the host countries to stop alleged acts of animal cruelty. The claim was made that the Ukrainian government killed stray dogs on a large scale to improve the image of the cities during the championships. Contrary to most other sponsors, most notably McDonald's, Coca-Cola did not address the firestorm on its Facebook page. Similarly, Coca-Cola stayed largely out of the online discussions related to its advertisement.

In conclusion, for brands with a loyal customer following based in strong bonds, stimulating customer engagement by initiating controversial discourse is a feasible way of increasing co-creative brand experiences and reaching beyond what is possible through mass media alone. In awareness terms, cost-efficiency can be pushed through this creation of earned media. While the negativity surrounding the Coca-Cola advertisement was explicit and highly visible, the majority of the target audience (80 percent) felt neutral or even positive about it. Many of them joined the discussion and argued on behalf of Coca-Cola's argument.

Such controversy may in the end not change the brand beliefs and brand image (permanently) or only in the long run if the message has been repeated sufficiently. Taking a stance on societal issues may in fact further the personality of the brand and interrelation with the consumer. Less established brands with less brand love should be more cautious as to the controversial nature of their messages. A controversy may not nuance the brand image held by consumers; it may determine the brand image.

REFERENCES

AdAge. 2014. Who Bought What in Super Bowl XLVIII. *AdvertisingAge*, February 3. http://adage.com/article/special-report-super-bowl/super-bowl-ad-chart-buying-super-bowl-2014/244024/

Arantola, Heli. 2002. Consumer bonding - A conceptual exploration. *Journal of Relationship Marketing*, 1(2): 93-107. doi: 10.1300/J366v01n02_06

Arnett, Ronald C. and Arneson, Pat. 1999. *Dialogic Civility*. Albany: State University of New York Press.

Bellah, Robert N., Richard Madsen, William M. Sullivan, Ann Swindler, and Steven M. Tipton. 2008. *Habits of the Heart: Individualism and Commitment in American Life*. 3rd ed. Berkeley: University of California Press.

Brodie, Roderick. J., Linda D. Hollebeek, Biljana Juric, and Ana Ilic. 2011. Customer engagement: conceptual domain, fundamental propositions, and implications for research. *Journal of Service Research*. doi: 1094670511411703

Buttle, Francis, and Stan Maklan. 2009. *Customer relationship management: Concepts and technologies* (2nd ed.). Oxford, UK: Elsevier Butterworth-Heinemann.

Chemi, Eric. 2014. The Network TV Advantage: Advertisers Pay More for Less. *Bloomberg,* March 3. http://www.bloomberg.com/news/articles/2014-03-26/the-network-tv-advantage-advertisers-pay-more-for-less

Elliott, Stuart. 2012. List of Global Brands Keeps Coke on Top, and Apple Jumps Up. *New York Times.* October 1. http://www.nytimes.com/2012/10/02/business/media/best-global-brands-report-has-coca-cola-on-top-and-apple-climbing.html

Festinger, Leon. 1962. *A theory of cognitive dissonance* (Vol. 2). Stanford university press.

Frampton, Jez. 2012. Interbrand CEO: Insights on Coca-Cola Topping Best Global Brands 2012 Rankings. *Coca-Cola Company* October 2. http://www.coca-colacompany.com/coca-cola-unbottled/interbrand-ceo-insights-on-coca-cola-topping-best-global-brands-2012-rankings/

Featherstone, Mike. (1990). *Global culture: Nationalism, globalization and modernity* (Vol. 2). Sage.

Gummesson, Evert. 2008. Extending the service-dominant logic: from customer centricity to balanced centricity. *Journal of the Academy of Marketing Science, 36*(1): 15-17.

Harmon-Jones, Eddie, and Cindy Harmon-Jones. 2007. Cognitive dissonance theory after 50 years of development. *Zeitschrift für Sozialpsychologie, 38*(1): 7-16. doi: 10.1024/0044-3514.38.1.7

Hert, Kerrie. A., Paul. S Fisk II, Yeong S. Rhee, and Ardith R. Brunt. 2014. Decreased consumption of sugar-sweetened beverages improved selected biomarkers of chronic disease risk among US adults: 1999 to 2010. *Nutrition Research, 34*(1): 58-65. doi: 10.1016/j.nutres.2013.10.005

Hollebeek, Linda D., and Tom Chen. 2014. Exploring positively- versus negatively-valenced brand engagement: a conceptual model. *Journal of Product & Brand Management,* 23(1): 62-74. doi: 10.1108/JPBM-06-2013-0332

Lyotard, Jean-François. 1984. *Post-modern condition: A Report on Knowledge.* University of Minnesota Press

Moye, Jay. 2016. Taste the Feeling: Coca-Cola's 'One Brand' Marketing Strategy Goes Global With New Creative Campaign. *Coca-Cola UK.* January 19. http://www.coca-cola.co.uk/stories/taste-the-feeling/

Nestle, Marion, and Mark Bittman. 2015. *Soda Politics: Taking on Big Soda (and Winning).* Oxford University Press, USA.

Persuit, Jeanne M. 2014. *Social Media and Integrated Marketing Communication: A Rhetorical Approach.* Lanham, MD: Lexington Books.

Schultz, E. J. (2016). Coke Replaces 'Open Happiness' With 'Taste the Feeling' in Major Strategic Shift. *Advertising Age.* January 19. http://adage.com/article/cmo-strategy/coke-debuts-taste-feeling-campaign-strategic-shift/302184/

Schultz, Don E. and Philip J. Kitchen. 2000. *Communicating Globablly: An Integrated Marketing Approach.* Chicago: NTC/Contemporary Publishing Group.

Schultz, Don E., and Heidi Schultz. 2004. *IMC-The Next Generation: Five Steps for Delivering Value and Measuring Returns Using Marketing Communication.* Boston, MA: McGraw Hill.

Stecklow, Steve. 2005. How a global web of activists gives Coke problems in India. *Wall Street Journal,* June 7: A1.

Swanson, Emily. 2014. Most Americans OK With Coke's Super Bowl Ad, But Still Think We Should All Speak English. *Huffington Post.* February 9. http://www.huffingtonpost.com/2014/02/08/english-official-language-poll_n_4748094.html

van Doorn, Jenny, Katherine. N. Lemon, Vikas Mittal, Stephen Nass, Doreén Patrick, Peter Pirner, and Peter C. Verhoef. (2010). Customer engagement behavior: Theoretical foundations and research directions. *Journal of Service Research,* 13(3): 253-266. doi: 10.1177/1094670510375599

Vargo, Stephen L., and Robert F. Lusch. 2004. Evolving to a New Dominant Logic for Marketing. *Journal of Marketing,* 68(1): 1-17. doi: 10.1509/jmkg.68.1.1.24036

Wallace, Elaine, Isebel Buil, and Leslie de Chernatony. 2014. Consumer enga
with self-expressive brands: brand love and WOM outcomes. *Journal of Product & Brand Management*, 23(1): 33-42. doi: 10.1108/JPBM-06-2013-0326

THREE

Integrated Marketing Communication and Event Planning

An Academic Conference in the Charm City

Leeanne M. Bell McManus and Chip Rouse

Producing an event requires the ability to navigate various facets of communication. Event planners rely on their interpersonal skills in working with clients, and must be sensitive, flexible, clear, and ethical. As competent communicators, they need to understand language, possess fine-tuned listening skills, and be able to read others' nonverbal cues. In addition, many event planners understand public relations or have a solid knowledge of marketing and advertising, and their success rests on a combination of their communication skills and their industry know-how. However, the most successful events hinge on understanding and implementing foundational principles within the integrated marketing communication (IMC) literature and in the philosophy and application of communication. This chapter focuses on using the research and theory in the field of communication as a foundation for the craft of the event planning process through the lens of IMC. Today, it is not enough for an event planner to send out a few media advisories and hope the event will succeed; a more integrated and thorough plan is essential. The many facets of IMC in combination with a strong toolbox of communication skills will prepare the event planner for just about any event. As Bell McManus, Rouse, and Verni write, the ability to communicate and adapt will offer event planners an advantage that cannot be overlooked, especially when they must react quickly and respond sensitively (2016, 16-17). Using the Eastern Communication Association (ECA) annual convention as a case study, this work will examine how individuals create space for community engagement and collaboration. Planning a large-scale event necessitates teamwork and cooperation from beginning a script to concluding the debriefing, and all of the event players must work together to facilitate success. In this case study example, in combination with their faculty members, the experiences of the teams of student workers who participated in two conventions—2010 and 2016—in order to gain an understanding of how events are successfully planned and managed through the lens of IMC are chronicled.

EVENT PLANNING

The event planning industry is a multibillion-dollar business that continues to grow as events become more commonplace in today's society. Events such as fundraisers, receptions, retreats, recognition dinners, and galas are becoming the norm in the marketplace; as a result, there needs to be a skilled professional who understands how to plan and achieve a certain outcome for a particular event (Allen 2009, 34; Goldblatt 2014, 155). In the postmodern marketplace of diversity and difference, the event planner needs to integrate a plethora of skills that include researching, designing, planning, coordinating, communicating, and evaluating (Goldblatt 2014, 134-39), to name a few, because clients want "everything from site selection to turnkey event management" (Grimaldi 2015, 31), making the options for an event endless. Planning an event can start years in advance of the actual date of the event; the days of organizing a celebration the night before are no longer realistic because of site reservations and catering preparation.

Historically, events are found in all time periods in every location. Take, for example, bear baiting in Shakespearean England, the opening of the Olympic ceremonies, or the American Cancer Society's Relay for Life—all of these events were successful because of a strategic plan that took into consideration not only the client's vision, but also the audience attending the event (Entrepreneur Media 2015, preface). Civic and political festivals have been the domain of public organizations for hundreds of years, and without any formal guidelines, these events have met the needs of those involved. The rise of a class of millionaires, and a strengthened and more public upper class also led to a more lavish display of affluence during events, a shift that was mimicked in the middle class as well. Most of these events were planned and showcased by family members or volunteers, and it was not until the second half of the 20th century that event planning became recognized as an industry (Bureau of Labor Statistics, U.S. Department of Labor 2016).

Events are defined as "temporary and purposive gathering[s] of people" (Bladen, Kennell, Abson, and Wilde 2012, 3), and the origin of the word comes from the Latin word *ēvenīre*, meaning outcome. The outcome of an event needs to be well thought out before it actually takes place, and this responsibility usually falls to an event planner to produce the desired outcome. No matter the type of event, the desired outcome should guide the planning process and be used as the standard by which the event's success is measured. The goal or outcome of events in business settings is to build the brand that will establish credibility with an audience (Fehrnstrom and Rich 2009, 61). If the event is not connected to the brand, those attending may not see the purpose of the event nor its meaning to the organization. The event thus becomes only a celebratory moment in time, disconnected from any purpose or brand. On the other hand, the American Cancer Society's Relay for Life event has become an integral part of the organization's brand, nearly synonymous with the fight against cancer. Relay events are intimately and consistently associated with the brand, predictable in their logistics and outcomes.

Event planning can be defined in multiple ways; however, a definition that thoroughly embraces the importance and power of communication comes from *Event Planning: Communicating Theory and Practice*:

> Event planning is a communicative process whereby a person creates and coordinates the celebration of an occasion or forms a gathering at a specific location where attendees can learn, socialize, conduct business, and/or serve the community. Those who attend the event typically have a specific purpose that coincides with the overall outcome or goal of the event. (Bell McManus, Rouse, and Verni 2016, 6)

This definition highlights the importance of communication as a process that is crafted for each unique event. Moreover, successful event planners realize the absolute necessity of all communication components from verbal to nonverbal and all communication contexts from intrapersonal to organizational. As communication moves in a continuum, being able to derive meaning and context from interactions demands reflecting on exchanges with others. The need for consistent and coherent communication becomes essential in the planning process because communication creates and shapes our social world (Pearce 1994, 1). An understanding of communication interaction allows for greater clarity in implementing a client's vision or objective for the event.

In the marketplace, credibility is gained through effective communication skills. As Smart and Featheringham (2006, 295) note, skilled professionals need effective interpersonal and conversational abilities that allow for one consistent and clear message. In the event planning industry, collaborating with others is vital—working with clients, delegating tasks, coordinating strategies, and supervising people are just a few examples of interpersonal interactions in business. Speaking effectively, listening, and responding to interpersonal interactions in a professional, proficient manner are crucial if event planners are to succeed in the industry.

The quality of communication that takes place has a direct impact on the overall value of the interpersonal relationships (Erozkan 2013, 739-45). Industry experts must be able to create a solid foundation for relationships with other business professionals. According to Halinen, "Evolving relationship bonds incorporate the continuity dimension of business relationships" (2012, 294). Building professional associations with customers and clients will require establishing strong connections with those who work in various industries that are relevant to the field. These connections can act as sources for future business endeavors. Some of these interpersonal relationships will be long-lasting if a strong working relationship can be developed (Halinen 2012, 294; Jain 2012, 109-12). Interpersonal interactions and communication interactions that lead to a clear and consistent message are all seen as imperative in applying IMC strategies in the business world. IMC, which is grounded in communication theory (Fitzpatrick 2005, 94; Kliatchko 2005, 20), moves the planning process to a strategic philosophy that embraces the idea of "why" things get done rather than the traditional "how to" list, allowing for a comprehensive perspective on the event planning process.

IMC CONNECTION

Integrated marketing communication originated at Northwestern University with the work of Don E. Schultz and Phillip J. Kitchen (Kitchen 1993, 15-21; Schultz and Kitchen 2000, 6-8; Schultz, Tannenbaum and Lauterborn 1994, 2). IMC emerged as a way to bridge the gap between the fields of business and communication. IMC is the study of communicative content engaged from a number of differing vantage points within the marketplace, incorporating the functions of advertising, public relations, marketing, promotions, digital media and much more to engage an institution's target audience. No single function has the utmost importance; integration of multiple communication channels is the driving factor behind IMC because it allows one message to be heard (Fehrnstrom and Rich 2009, 32).

The word "integration" assumes the importance of diverse ideas coming together in a unique way that creates a whole that is more than the combination of its parts (Schultz, Tannebaum, and Lauterborn 1993, 87). Similar to Gestalt theory, which examines the renowned phrase, "the whole is more than the sum of its parts," that lies in Aristotle's *Metaphysics,* integration allows ideas to come together in a unique way. In *A System of Logic: Ratiocinative and Inductive,* John Stuart Mill (2002) stated that gestalt assumes that parts have different qualities than the whole. The parts can stand alone, as the fields of public relations, marketing, and advertising can, but when assembled create something distinctive.

The marketing aspect is a combination of understanding human psychology and scientific analysis to develop a plan that must seek not only to identify and reach target audiences, but also to satisfy those audiences as well (Hoyle 2002, 147-48). Marketing relies on imagination and innovation as well as true market research, which shows that the most effective marketers are able to reach the consumer on a variety of levels through many different opportunities (Gupta 2003, 93; Kotler and Zaltman 1971, 4-5).

The last component of IMC, communication, allows for one clear, concise, and consistent message to be heard throughout the project, resulting in everyone understanding the same goals and objectives. Communication is essential in all aspects of life; however, understanding the importance of communication allows for reflection on what is said and how it is said, resulting in communication competence (Littlejohn and Foss 2010, 5-9). Appreciating the importance of an integrated marketing approach allows individuals to comprehend the big picture and see more than what is needed, but also why something is needed.

Even though practitioners might not call what they are doing IMC (Kliatchko and Schultz 2014, 380), in today's marketplace of constant communication, IMC is the main concept behind many client-based organizations and is not considered just another management fad (Kitchen, Kim, and Schultz 2008, 545). Moreover, there is a plethora of definitions associated with IMC that focus on effective two-way, interactive, strategic, and integrated forms of communication that emphasize establishing long-term relationships (Blakeman 2009, 159-60). In addition to an emphasis on forming relationships, some definitions also address the necessary role of planning. A definition that shares this theme of planning comes from Percy, who states:

> IMC is really all about *planning* in order to deliver a *consistent message.* Effective IMC should certainly encourage strong customer relationships, but it does that through effective planning in order to develop an integrated communication program that will optimize specific communication objectives that lead to a desired behavior on the part of a target audience. (2008, 8)

Through the planning process, one consistent strategic communicative message needs to reach the target audience. In event planning, individuals are constantly communicating with others to plan successful events; as a result, the message must be consistent so that the integration of ideas is understood by all parties involved. Planning out the details will provide clients with both communication clarity and consistency (Schultz, Tannebaum and Lauterborn 1993, 39).

Understanding the importance of communicative interactions lends itself to a greater comprehension of the client's wants and needs. Engaging others and listening to what they desire and require is imperative in all fields that deal with human interaction. As Blakeman (2009, 294) articulates, the goal of IMC is to create effective two-way interactive communication that builds long-term relationships. From an IMC perspective, every element of inter-organizational and intra-organizational interaction is part of the total IMC package, part of the larger organizational narrative or story that establishes organizational identity and integrity (Groom 2005, 2). Research in IMC focuses on how all the integrated functions of IMC work together to promote a brand and establish organizational recognition and identity. IMC cannot be done in a vacuum; the client has to lead the way and be committed to the process (Schultz and Kitchen 1997, 7-18). For example, in planning an event, a client has to have a vision that is implemented by the event planner. Without the client's vision, the event does not get branded in a way that is true to the client. One instance in which the organization's brand remained central through an integrated approach is the convention of the Eastern Communication Association (ECA).

APPLICATION: EASTERN COMMUNICATION ASSOCIATION ANNUAL CONVENTION

Established in 1910 as a non-profit organization, the ECA is one of the oldest professional communication associations in the United States, with a rich history of teaching, scholarship, and service. According to its constitution, the purpose of the ECA is to "promote the study, criticism, research, teaching, and application of the artistic, humanistic, and scientific principles of communication" (ecasite.org, 1). To accomplish this purpose, the organization hosts an annual convention in a selection of cities on the east coast promoting community engagement and collaboration among communication students, professionals and practitioners.

In 2010 and 2016, the convention was held in Baltimore, Maryland. The vice presidents, Janie Harden Fritz (2010) and Jason Wrench (2016), appointed second vice president Leeanne Bell McManus to be the point person for all local arrangements both years. A team from Stevenson University, including faculty members Chip Rouse and Stephanie Verni, along with students in the business communication major, was charged with creating an IMC plan to make these conventions a success. The convention planning team was accountable for assisting with many other tasks and responsibilities in preparation for the convention, including participating as professional communicators and relying on their integrated marketing skills, including public relations, advertising, promotions, writing, and design, to implement a strategic vision. In addition to the team's work, there were other goals; since one of the association's tenets is education, for instance, the planning teams saw it as essential to work with university undergraduate students to help them understand how event planning and integrated marketing communication partnered during the year preceding each convention.

Unfortunately, both of the Baltimore conventions coincidentally followed a time of turmoil and chaos in the city. Prior to 2010, the convention had not been held in Baltimore in over a decade because of a negative perception of the city. A previous convention held there in 1997 did not receive good reviews, and an incident of violence outside the hotel had produced cynicism and even fear about a return to Baltimore. The popular television drama *The Wire,* on HBO, examined the narcotics scene in Baltimore through the eyes of both drug dealers and law enforcement and continued to enhance the negative perception of the city. This attitude was compounded five years later by the Baltimore protests of 2015 that again produced an adverse association with the city. In 2016, the landscape of Baltimore was still recovering from a series of urban protests that had gained damaging national attention, and the city was trying to restore its image. As a convention was being planned, the negative perception of Baltimore needed to be addressed.

In his seminal work in psychology of interpersonal communication, Heider postulated that it is through perception that people come to understand the world around them, including that which brings the environment together: people, things, and events (1958, 20). Using Heider's theory as a guide, the planning team understood that prospective attendees would have various perceptions of the city; however, it was the team's job to create a positive view of Baltimore. This conflict, like most conflicts, was situated in various perceptions, goals, and values (Putnam and Poole 1987, 549), and involved heightened senses and emotions (Arnett, Bell McManus, and McKendree 2014, 124). Many members were skeptical of attending a convention in a location that they associated with violence. However, the convention planning team knew they needed to work hard to help ECA members understand the progressive changes the city had made. The local convention planning team knew that it would be important to balance the negative press Baltimore had received with a public relations effort prior to and during the convention that exceeded any work that had been done in the past. Changing perceptions was not an easy task, but showing all the positive features Baltimore had to offer gave some reassurance to those who were doubtful about attending.

Student teams began working with faculty members of Stevenson University a year before the convention began. One main goal was to develop a strong public relations team. Following the Public Relations Society of America's definition, the team's goal was to create "a strategic communication process that builds mutually beneficial relationships between organizations and their publics" (Public Relations Society of America 2015, para. 3). The public relations team visited and worked with the hotel staff in determining the kind of concierge services that would be available through the hotel and what kind of public relations efforts would be important for the student team to carry out. Once these duties were clearly understood, the student public relations team went to work, bringing in members of the university's communication club, '47 House, soliciting local restaurants for coupons, writing letters to Baltimore-area producers such as McCormick, Inc., Domino Sugar, and Goetze's Candy, to name a few, for donations and giveaways, and working with local merchants to find ways to involve them in the convention. The team also worked intimately with local merchants in the hotel vicinity to implement a "show your badge" program for which discounts would be available. Students scoured on foot the geographic area surrounding the hotel to add merchants, restauranteurs, and bars to the program. A list of the participating merchants was made available in a brochure handed out at the convention concierge desk as well as online; convention-goers could easily access the online version by submitting an email address. The program proved immensely popular, especially when the convention hotel itself offered the meal and beverage discount to those who showed their badge. Moreover, public relations efforts also extended into the political arena, where the public relations team solicited letters from the mayor and governor welcoming the convention into the city. In addition, the public relations team hoped to arrange for the mayor of Baltimore to actually visit the convention and greet those in attendance. The goal of every one of these efforts was to show the convention, the attendees, and the city of Baltimore in the best possible light.

Students gained a clear understanding of the role of the public relations professional by making a lasting, positive connection with the community. One student said it best: "Public relations is all about relationships. Our job is to build relationships between the city of Baltimore, the ECA, and every attendee. We just need to focus on what it takes to build those interactions." A student-faculty public relations team once again determined that the experience of every convention-goer should be memorable, comfortable, and stress-free. In order to make this happen, the team reached out to the convention hotel to see what was already in place to make guests feel content. Because the staff was busy responding to the needs of other groups in the hotel at the same time, a student team was designated to check every breakout room prior to each session to make sure the temperature was comfortable, the chairs were placed correctly, the available media was working, and the speakers and panelists had everything they needed. If something was amiss, the team could contact the hotel staff to take action, but the student team's responsiveness to the needs of everyone participating was seen as a priority. The team's work expanded the students' definition of public relations to include internal as well as external publics.

The responsiveness began with a team whose job it was to oversee welcoming, directions, and concierge services. Because many of the students who would be working the convention were not local to Baltimore, before the event began, faculty trained them in knowledge of the geography and history of Baltimore so that they had answers when asked. The public relations team scouted the hotel to discover key locations of entry and egress in order to set up welcome points where students would be stationed to greet visitors. If the job of the students was to help convention-goers adjust to the hotel and the city, the team knew they had to see the hotel and its location through new eyes. They had to recognize their audience and think like professors of communication, like families accompanying a convention presenter, or like discipline professionals who might want to get out of the hotel for some sightseeing. This shift in their approach to public relations was essential if they were to be able to respond to a wide variety of public needs. Ultimately, their diligence, creativity, and perspective gave them just what the convention needed: a well-rehearsed team of public relations advocates. They were able to troubleshoot during poster presentations, make restaurant reservations for out-of-town student groups, offer advice about local museums, shopping, and points of interest, and direct those who needed information about taxis versus Über service. In short, their preparation paid off a thousand-fold by helping to create a positive perception of the Baltimore convention.

An event that is designed to promote a special occasion, such as an annual convention, must develop a marketing plan. The marketing plan for the ECA convention was based on Hoyle's concept that one must seek to develop a plan that does not just identify and reach the target audiences, but satisfies them as well (2002, 147-148). Creating a plan that is thoughtful, holistic, and detailed, relying on imagination and innovation as well as true market research, was the goal. Additionally, understanding the rich history of ECA and the members was an integral component of the plan. As Cockrum (2011, 231) believes, knowing the story behind the client is vital to overall marketing success. Marketing the ECA convention in 2010 was a great deal less complicated than in 2016. In 2010, signage for every convention event adhered to the theme and used the same set of images, fonts, colors, and sizes. One particular event was held off-site, about a half-mile walk from the convention hotel, and in order to market the event, the student marketing team designed a plan in which they would station themselves at 50-foot intervals along the walk route so that no one would get lost along the way. In addition, they were able to market the city of Baltimore through donated giveaways they received in conjunction with the public relations team, always tagged with a short description of the company that had made the donation. The student marketing and public relations teams knew they had to work together to avoid redundancy and overlap, as within the world of IMC professionals must constantly consult about their responsibilities.

In 2016 the marketing team was facing a larger set of tasks, brought on by the growth of social media. As a result, another group of social media marketing undergraduates worked directly though remotely with the convention's directors of social media, learning the policies, procedures, ethics and etiquette of the use of social media prior to the start of the convention. The team realized that social media helps keep the conversation going and is a way to promote discussion before the event and even after the physical event has taken place (Fletcher 2011, 12).

Social media has a profound influence on promotion, visibility, and branding, and an added benefit of social media presence is that it is a relatively low-cost or free endeavor. The use of social media gave the 2016 convention the power to expand the potential reach to almost anyone interested in the field of communication. Today, social media users are connected in many different ways—not only to personal networks but also to unknown sources who share opinions, recommendations, and experiences (Ratchford, Talukdar and Lee 2001, 7). Social media opened up a plethora of opportunities to reach ECA members even if they were not attending the convention.

The social media group, also known as the "tech team," helped to set up, maintain, and contribute to Facebook and Twitter sites. The convention team also created the hashtag #ECA16, which conference attendees could use throughout the event to tweet about sessions, panels, and colleagues along with hot topics in communication. The social media platforms were used to engage and excite communication professionals and professors prior to the convention's start, and once the convention was underway, the student team's job was to interact with and engage those at the convention. They strategized early about what might interest those who would be attending the convention—and this group could include various target audiences such as undergraduates, graduate students, professors, and family members. They learned about how vital timing is in the execution of a plan, and discussed ways to time their work so that it would have the greatest impact. The tech team understood how social media is essential in event planning and how those in marketing also rely on it. They began to see their posts and tweets as one more piece of the puzzle that would help to make the convention eagerly anticipated and well-received. They took photos of the entire local undergraduate convention team wearing their specially designed and branded green ECA shirts and set up ECA accounts to create more buzz about the convention. From members of the public relations and marketing teams, they received prizes donated from some of the local merchants—a dinner voucher, movie tickets, and more—that would become giveaways via Twitter or Facebook engagement posts. They used video to capture the attention of the millennials, and they "live tweeted" through many breakout sessions. They made the convention personal. These marketing steps created a communal sense of engagement even before the event began and then lasted throughout the entire convention. In fact, their posts continued even after the convention ended, encouraging attendees to reflect on their experiences and anticipate the next year's event. In many ways, their pre-event posts served as advertising for the convention as well.

Advertising is seen as the "controlled" use of media that ensures the message is exactly the form the sender has intended (Bivins 2008, 5). For it to be effective, a clear and consistent message must be created (Marsh 2009, 116), and the best way to create this message is through conducting proper research. As the tech team learned, understanding the audience is necessary (Corbett 1996, 25). As a result, information was created that focused on students, faculty or professionals. For example, the advertising of inexpensive restaurants was targeted at students, whereas restaurants with a higher price tag and a quieter environment to promote discussion were advertised for faculty. The goal of their work was to evoke those fond memories of participating in the convention back in 2010 and create a desire to return to Baltimore.

In addition to thinking about the public relations, marketing, and advertising, all teams needed to think about the big picture of the convention, which encompasses many components. First, the event planners needed to forecast the possibilities for mishaps, and then devise a "just-in-case" plan for handling those occurrences. Students saw the necessity of troubleshooting ahead of time in order to control and contain the things they could control. In 2016, they learned from their mentors the kind of slip-ups to avoid, based on past experience, and they extended their "what-if?" scenarios to cover an even greater host of possibilities. A crisis situation can happen at any time during an event, but being prepared for various situations is one way to alleviate some of the stress associated with the chaos. Even though a crisis is difficult to address because it includes unexpected moments that cause stress, crises can be managed if individuals are knowledgeable about how to handle them (Ulmer, Sellnow and Seeger 2007, 90). More information will allow those who face a crisis to act with confidence. To gain as much information as possible, the students learned that asking questions of those in the situation would be crucial (Amen 1999, 297). For example, the student team needed to construct a "what if" plan if another protest in the city would occur during the convention. Even though these situations are never easy to deal with, discussing possible scenarios with the hotel staff helped the team see the big picture and consider options such as a lockdown or curfew if something were to occur.

Second, students learned how communication helps the big picture come to fruition. During both conventions, when minor slips occurred, it was generally because someone failed to apprise someone else of changes to an event or an activity. The event planning background of the student workers gave them the knowledge to make certain that competent and clear communication was priority one. For both conventions, they worked especially hard to repeat back directions so there were no misunderstandings, to keep every worker in the loop, and to ask questions if they were uncertain about how to execute a particular task. Communication is essential in almost every field, but it is especially important in planning large-scale conventions (Arcodia and Barker 2005, 4-6); as a result, clear communication was seen as a priority of all involved in the planning process.

Finally, the student teams learned that developing a successful event from start to finish takes creativity. As Jacobson states, "Hosting events in a creative way not only demonstrates an organization's appreciation for its attendees, but helps make the event or meeting a worthwhile investment for the company or organization" (2014, 12). Creativity is not just about developing new ideas; it also includes new combinations or regrouping and restructuring of ideas that have already been well thought out (Lewin 1935, 388-89; Vygotsky 1962, 193). The faculty and some students had attended previous conventions that allowed them to tweak and restructure old ideas for the following year's convention. For example, in 2010 students used UTZ crab chips and Domino sugar, two iconic items in Baltimore's culture, as welcome gifts for all participants. In 2016, students reimagined a welcome gift that included similar icons of Baltimore life, choosing crab mallets and Old Bay seasoning for participants. As students worked through their marketing plan, they realized that creativity is not just about playing with ideas; it has to include a clear focus and the ability to analyze suggestions to make informed judgments about what works best in a particular circumstance (Robinson 2011, 83). Creativity was a challenge for some students, yet they found that inspiration is contagious, and they realized they could build on the obvious strengths of others. Those who considered themselves less creative learned to rely on various resources including textbooks, their classmates, and the answers they received from the myriad of questions they asked. Faculty learned that students need help with organization and execution of creative ideas at the start, but that it is not long before team members can work under their own power to produce innovative ideas.

Overall, event planning and integrated marketing communication work together to construct a comprehensive plan that produces a seamless event. For the event to be successful and reach a variety of attendees, it must rely on an assortment of strategies and approaches. Social media is not the only answer, nor are public relations, marketing and advertising by themselves; while they are all possibilities for engagement, when combined, they are formidable forces. Along with strong interpersonal communication skills and even stronger planning abilities, event planners can benefit from studying the strategies of integrated marketing communication. For the students who had not previously participated in a professional convention, understanding the expectations of the convention-goers was a particularly harrowing task, but the students knew they had to develop that understanding. Because the convention is yearly and many professionals attend year after year for the whole of their professional careers, the student teams realized they had to make "their" convention stand out from the rest. Thus, they created a powerful integrated marketing communication plan with a holistic marketing strategy, attention to public relations, and social media that doubled as advertising, in order to execute an event that was one for the record books. The planners' "commitment to a customer-centric approach" (Fehrnstrom and Rich 2009, 37), one of the hallmarks of the integrated marketing communication methodology, gave them a solid grounding though which to consider convention attendees. With good pre-promotion, enticing giveaways, excellent representation, and clever positioning, both conferences ended up being extraordinarily successful.

The success of a convention is measured in many ways. One way is to examine the number of attendees: in 2016, the number was 605, the second-highest recorded number of ECA convention-goers ever, just behind the 2010 Baltimore convention, which included 816 attendees. To what can those outstanding numbers be attributed? There are many things that helped create these successful conferences; however, a comprehensive IMC plan was one of these key elements.

CONCLUSION

As Jim Collins and Jerry Porras write in their best-selling book, *Built to Last: Successful Habits of Visionary Companies*, there is absolutely no "cookbook recipe for success" (2004, 248). Event planners need to have a plan but be ready to change it when things no longer work. As the event planning industry continues to grow, the need for understanding IMC becomes imperative. Understanding not only the "how" but also the "why" allows a unique experience to develop. Event planners have always relied on a variety of strategies through which they execute successful events, but combining their knowledge of events with a systematic and integrated marketing communication approach can only strengthen their success. IMC does not seek to add layers and levels of strategies to the planning process, but rather works to assimilate these tactics into one cohesive plan. More is not necessarily better unless all of the pieces are actually unified for one purpose. As seen through the planning of the 2010 and 2016 Eastern Communication Association conventions, event planners can rely on the methods of IMC to produce a successful event.

REFERENCES

Allen, Judy. 2009. *Event Planning: The Ultimate Guide to Successful Meetings, Corporate Events, Fundraising Galas, Conferences, Conventions, Incentives and Other Special Events.* Hoboken, NJ: John Wiley & Sons.

Amen, Daniel G. 1999. *Change Your Brain, Change Your Life.* New York: Crown Publishing Group.
Arcodia, Charles and Tanuja Barker. 2005. "The Employability Prospects of Graduates in Event Management: Using Data From Job Advertisements." In *Impacts of Events: Proceeding of the International Events Research Conference,* edited by Judy Allen. 175-202. Sydney, Australia: University of Technology, Sydney.
Arnett, Ronald C., Leeanne M. Bell McManus, and Amanda G. McKendree. 2014. *Conflicts Between Persons: The Origins of Leadership.* Iowa: Kendall Hunt.
Bell McManus, Leeanne M., Chip Rouse and Stephanie Verni. 2016. *Event Planning: Communicating Theory and Practice.* Iowa: Kendall Hunt.
Bivins, Thomas. 2008. *Public Relations Writing: The Essentials of Style and Format.* New York: McGraw-Hill.
Bladen, Charles, James Kennell, Emma Abson, and Nick Wilde. 2012. *Events Management: An Introduction.* New York: Routledge.
Blakeman, Robyn. 2009. *The Barebones Introduction to Integrated Marketing Communication.* Lanham, Md.: Rowman & Littlefield.
Bureau of Labor Statistics, U.S. Department of Labor. "Meeting, Convention, and Event Planners." Occupational Outlook Handbook , 2016-17 http://www.bls.gov/ooh/business-and-financial/meeting-convention-and-event-planners.htm.
Cockrum, Jim. 2011. *Marketing: 101 Low and No-Cost Ways To Grow Your Business Online and Off.* Hoboken, NJ: John Wiley & Sons, Inc.
Collins, James and Jerry Porras. 2004. *Built to Last: Successful Habits of Visionary Companies.* New York: HarperCollins.
Corbett, Jenny. 1995. Bad Mouthing: The Language of Special Needs. London: Routledge.
Eastern Communication Association. "History." www.ecasite.org
Entrepreneur Media staff. 2015. *Event Planning Business: Entrepreneur's Step-by-Step Startup Guide.* 4th ed. Irvine, Ca: Entrepreneur Media, Inc.
Erozkan, Atilgan. 2013. "The Effect of Communication Skills and Interpersonal Problem Solving Skills on Social Self-Efficacy." *Educational Sciences: Theory & Practice, 13,* 739-745.
Fehrnstrom, Mary and David M. Rich. 2009. "Using Events To Drive an Integrated Marketing Model." *Journal of Integrated Marketing Communication,* 31-37.
Fitzpatrick, K. R. 2005. "The Legal Challenge of Integrated Marketing Communication (IMC):Integrating Commercial and Political Speech." *Journal of Advertising, 34,* 93-112.
Fletcher, Michael. 2011. "How To . . . Use Social Media and Keep the Event Alive." *Conference & Incentive Travel* 12.
Goldblatt, Joe. 2014. *Special Events: Creating and Sustaining a New World for Celebration.* 7th ed. Hoboken: New Jersey: John Wiley & Sons.
Grimaldi, Lisa A. 2015. "Third parties: Big, Small or None At All?" *Meetings and Conventions, 49,* Retrieved from http://www.meetings-conventions.com.
Groom, S. Alyssa. 2005. *Story-centered Marketing: A Communicative Turn.* Unpublished Ph.D. dissertation, Duquesne University, Pittsburgh, PA.
Gupta, Seema. 2003. "Event Marketing: Issues and Challenges." *UMB Management Review, 15,* 87-96.
Halinen, Aino. 2012. *Relationship Marketing in Professional Services: A Study of Agency-Client Dynamics in the Advertising Sector.* NY: Routledge.
Heider, Fritz. 1958. *The Psychology of Interpersonal Relations.* New York: John Wiley & Sons.
Hoyle, Leonard H. 2002. *Event Marketing: How to Successfully Promote Events, Festivals, Conventions, and Expositions.* New York: John Wiley & Sons.
Jain, Mitushi. 2012. "Business Communication and Its Strategy." *Journal of Social Welfare and Management, 4,* 109-112.
Kitchen, Philip J. 1993. Towards the Integration of Marketing and Public Relations. *Marketing Intelligence and Planning, 11,* 15-21.

Kitchen, Philip J., Ilchul Kim and Don E. Schultz. 2008. "Integrated Marketing Communications: Practice Leads Theory." *Journal of Advertising Research, 48,* 531-546.

Kliatchko, Jerry. 2005. "Towards a New Definition of Integrated Marketing Communications (IMC)." *International Journal of Advertising, 24,* 7-34.

Kliatchko, Jerry and Don Schultz, 2014. "Twenty Years of IMC." *International Journal of Advertising, 33,* 373-390.

Kotler, Philip and Gerald Zaltman. 1971. "Social Marketing: An Approach to Planned Social Change." *Journal of Marketing, 35,* 3-12.

Lewin, Kurt. 1935. *A Dynamic Theory of Personality.* New York: McGraw-Hill.

Littlejohn, Stephen and Karen A. Foss. 2010. *Theories of Human Communication.* 10th ed. Belmont, CA: Wadsworth.

Marsh, Charles, David Guth and Bonnie Short. 2009. *Strategic Writing: Multimedia Writing for Public Relations, Advertising, and More.* Boston: Pearson.

Mill, John Stuart. 2002. A System of Logic: Ratiocinative and Inductive. 8th ed. New York: Harper & Brothers Publishers, Franklin Square.

Pearce, Walter. 1994. *Interpersonal Communication: Making Social Worlds.* New York: Harper Collins

Percy, Larry. 2008. Strategies for Implementing Integrated Marketing Communications: Theory and Practice. Amsterdam: Butterworth-Heinemann.

Public Relations Society of America. 2015. "What Is Public Relations?" http://prdefinition.prsa.org

Putnam, Linda and Marshall Poole. 1987. Conflict and Negotiation. In *Handbook of Organizational Communication: An Interdisciplinary Perspective,* edited by Frederic Jablin, Linda Putnam, Karlene Roberts and Lyman Porter. 549–599. Newbury Park, CA: Sage.

Ratchford, Brian, Debabrata Talukdar and Myung-Soo Lee. 2001. A Model of Consumer Choice of the Internet as an Information Source. *International Journal of Electronic Commerce, 5,* 7-21.

Robinson, Ken. 2011. *Out of Our Minds: Learning to Be Creative.* West Sussex: United Kingdom: Capstone Publishing.

Schultz, Don E. and Philip Kitchen. 1997. "Integrated Marketing Communications in U.S. Advertising Agencies: An Exploratory Study." *Journal of Advertising Research* 7-18.

Schultz, Don E. and Philip Kitchen. 2000. *Communicating Globally: An Integrated Marketing Approach.* London: Macmillan Press.

Schultz, Don E., Stanley Tannebaum and Robert Lauterborn. 1993. *Integrated Marketing Communication.* Lincolnwood, IL: NTC Business Books.

Schultz, Don E., Stanley Tannebaum and Robert Lauterborn. 1994. *The New Marketing Paradigm: Integrated Marketing Communications.* Chicago: NTC Business Books.

Smart, Karl L. and Richard Featheringham. 2006. "Developing Effective Interpersonal Communication and Discussion Skills." *Business Communication Quarterly, 69,* 276-283.

Ulmer, Robert, Timothy Sellnow and Matthew Seeger. 2007. *Effective Crisis Communication: Moving from Crisis to Opportunity.* Thousand Oaks, CA: Sage.

Vygotsky, Lev. 1962. *Thought and Language.* Cambridge: MIT Press.

FOUR

Integrated Marketing Communications and Goods as Toys

Marketing Childhood to Adults

Paul A. Lucas

Marketing practices often attempt to make consumers feel a certain way; to introduce consumers to products and brands in an emotional effort designed to forge brand character. Schultz and Schultz (2003) explained that "the end user, customer, or consumer must be at the center" (50). Within integrated marketing communication (IMC), the goal is to "accelerate returns by aligning communication objectives with corporate goals" (Schultz and Schultz 2003, 3). By crafting a consumer-focused approach with consistent messaging, a brand can hope to attain a specific and clear identity.

Subaru, a well-known and popular car brand, targets consumers by making them believe as though they are once again children, uniting the brand with positive and carefree feelings. In order to reinforce the childhood identity, Subaru utilizes a number of persuasive commercials that demonstrate various features of childhood. Barber's (2007) work on marketing linked with child psychology provides evidence for making such an assessment, and demonstrates the way in which Subaru places emphasis on the consumer, linking feeling to the brand, and, ultimately, the product.

CONSUMER-CHILD CENTERED APPROACH

The consumer-child centered approach is meant to create a positive feeling. For example, a commercial for AT&T that plays the song "Pure Imagination" progresses by showing kids' drawings amidst a city backdrop. The atmosphere it portrays is one of wonder, simply because of the song and the drawing that remind viewers of childhood. At the end of the commercial, a man is shown. The narrator says, "Remember when you were five, and anything was possible? Happy fifth birthday again." As these words are said, the man picks up an electronic device, looks at it, and smiles.

The older people get, the less likely they can be to get excited about their consumer goods. For example, getting a gift for a holiday or a birthday is great for a kid. The anticipation and the delight that come with having something you want, or at least that you could perhaps not get on your own, is great. As people become older, though, they can afford more things on their own, they can make purchase decisions on their own; the anticipation can still be present to an extent, but it never feels quite the same way—such as when you were five.

The AT&T commercial is obvious in its goal. The commercial attempts to remind viewers of how great and wonderful childhood was, complete with pictures and narration that are designed to directly represent what it is like to be a kid. At the same time, the commercial links devices and products offered from AT&T as being able to instill the same feeling of being five, and having gifts for holidays and birthdays at the present age, even though consumers are now adults. The persuasion embodies a very specific strategy that tries to create a sense of youth and childhood comparable to a purchase decision in adulthood.

There are a variety of different indicators in our society meant to signify becoming an adult: getting a job, obtaining a driver's license, paying bills and taxes, and so on. As people age, their consumer perspectives and needs can change according to life-stage. Marketing practitioners should be aware that "products can serve different purposes throughout a person's lifetime," and "numerous brands . . . correspond to these varying needs" (Braun-LaTour, LaTour and Zinkhan 2007, 57). Of course, products can meet different ends during a person's life, but some products are meant to actually correspond directly to life-stage.

Getting a driver's license, for example, can be a monumental moment in a person's life, signifying an important step to a more independent lifestyle. As a result, cars become an important cultural indicator of life progression. A work specifically about cars by Campos, Suarez, Nascimento, and Molica (2015) explained that the consumption of goods can be part of "negotiating . . . trajectories of life" (327). The passage to adulthood includes specific consumer decisions and products, and marketing practitioners are well aware of such touch points.

LIKE A KID AGAIN

Any adult knows that adulthood is much more complicated than just gaining independence and having fun. Though some indicators of adulthood include gaining independence, other indicators are not necessarily the most pleasant to deal with. As mentioned above, being accountable for bills and taxes are great examples. Being thrust into an adult mindset means more responsibility and a loss of the innocence and wonderment of being a child. Feeling young is in many ways a pleasant feeling; even though there are a variety of cultural markers designated as part of the path to adulthood, longing for certain feelings of being a kid and recapturing the wonderful feeling of gifts, birthdays, and holidays while having a seemingly less complicated life are commonplace.

Understandably, there are people who would like to recapture the lost feelings of being a kid again, especially since, as people grow older, they oftentimes become more ingrained in and disillusioned with the world. The process of getting older involves coming to terms with everything it means to be an adult, not only the positives that children might assume are associated with growing up. Even the positive sentiments related to gaining independence can fade when considered against how life felt as a kid.

The characteristics of "fantasy and play" are at their most pronounced in contemporary advertising and marketing," and are indicative of a kind of "regression to childhood" (Hayward 2013, 531). Linked to fantasy and play, the childhood regression is often meant to invoke positive feelings for the consumer, where those feelings are then connected to the brand and its marketing strategies. Accordingly, childhood may include fond memories; it may help recall a better, simpler time in life. Playing its role in culture and in our lives, "childhood is not a biological necessity but a social construction" (Postman 1999, 116). The persuasion offered by marketing practitioners directly feeds into these kinds of constructions, not relying on anything dealing with biological or physiological components; rather, the persuasion has more to do with attitude, feeling, and memory. It should come as no surprise, then, that persuasion can be effectively geared toward providing a socially constructed childhood of sorts. Fantasy and play can be then tailored to fit the attitude toward the consumption process, as well.

The fantastical and play elements are present both in storylines and purchase decision framing in advertising. It is important to differentiate the attitudinal strategies from those that value the physical appearance of youth. Youth appeals are undeniably often central to marketing practices, given that consumerism and advertising have long focused on products designed to give "youth" and a kind of "eternal life" (Gossage 1967, 367) to consumers.

FEELINGS OF YOUTH

A common practice for marketing practitioners is to attempt to show consumers the value of a youthful appearance, stressing physical looks and characteristics that are generally attributed to younger people. Culturally, the physical appearance of eternal life is thought to be desirable. The kinds of products that help to superficially fight aging are abundant in the marketplace. Makeup and hair dye are products that typically embody these kinds of strategies.

If products can really grant feelings of youth, whether realistically or in the minds of consumers only, to many consumers it might be "worth taking the chance" (Gossage 1967, 367). With "promise-centric rather than product-centric" (Travis 2000, 190) approaches to marketing, products that promise youthful appearance to consumers may or may not deliver, but a try may be worthwhile just in case the product works. This is because consumers often view exchanges as a "balance between sacrifice and gain" (Simmel trans. 1978, 81), and putting out a bit of money for something that may potentially make good on a promise is something that consumers may be willing to do.

The trouble is when people start to base their worth on the products; because the "impact of inanimate objects in [the] self-awareness process" (Csikszentmihalyi and Rochberg-Halton 1981, 91) is so vital to human development, scholars have unsurprisingly criticized marketing practitioners for their focus on trying to make consumers feel young for years. Despite the inclination to value physical attributes of youth, though, both culturally and as a result of persuasion in the marketplace, there is more to embracing youth culture than only those characteristics linked to appearance.

THE CHILD MENTALITY

Rather than look at marketing practices designed to fight aging by way signs of physical signs of aging, this work will evaluate persuasion intended to make consumers psychologically feel like kids again; in effect, to retreat back to a childlike state. Again, while physical appearance can be part of youth, there are other ways for marketing practitioners to use persuasion to enact youthful feelings. Specifically, this work will focus on the desire consumers have to be driven by the wants and wishes connected to childhood, primarily stemming from "glory of work" being driven by "rewards of play" (Barber 2007, 114). The base recognition is that working is an indicator of what it means to be an adult. Brands and products, then, become the reward—they are the play, the good feeling at the end that a consumer can have once they put in the necessary work to achieve the product.

Having the goal of great play helps to build a foundation for marketing practitioners to persuade consumers to want and value certain products, products that can be achieved or bought through putting in time at work. Once the marketing practitioners form the association of understanding particular brands and products as like play to a child, those particular brands and products gain an identity that is considered as part of life and life-stage. In order to grasp this marketing strategy and in order to identify how consumer bases of adults might respond to being targeted as children, this work will draw from some of Barber's (2007) comparison ideas on how marketing pushes adults into a childlike psychology of decision making, notably rooted in the following:

> Impulse over Deliberation; Feeling over Reason; Certainty over Uncertainty; Dogmatism over Doubt; Play over Work; Pictures over Words; Images over Ideas; Pleasure over Happiness; Entitlement over Obligation; Timeless Present over Temporality; Individualism over Community. (Barber 2007, 83)

Though these psychological characteristics could be evaluated negatively, especially since they are simplifying brand identities and consumer choices, this work will draw on specific examples of advertisements and argue that children and adults can be treated similarly through marketing practices. Consequently, adults can come to value their goods in much the same way that children can value toys. As in the AT&T commercial, the product becomes a desirable thing that mimics what a desired toy would have once been to a child. Additionally, the product can be shaped into a kind of focal point for parents and their concerns and feelings for their children, as well.

PERSUASIVE APPEAL TO CONSUMERS

Generating these kinds of persuasive tactics can lead consumers to feel like kids again, allowing the consumers a temporary escape where they can appreciate and get excited about purchase decisions once more. The prescriptive element to marketing that utilizes childhood-based appeals in a different way hinges on how messages are targeted. Since children comprise a specific demographic and sought-after target market, it makes sense that ads are at times built to appeal to them; however, a look at ads will bring to light that ads targeting adults do so by targeting them as children, perhaps suggesting treating adults as children is more effective than trying to give children a positive outlook on what being an adult would be.

Within an IMC framework, the specific recommendation is for branding practices to show consumers that they can look to their brands as socially constructed reminders of childhood. Since brands are about creating a "seamless whole" (Travis 2000, 188) for consumers, the entire brand can forge an identity using the above named psychological characteristics. Unmistakably, "by identifying the development of the consumer self in relation to a specific product or brand, marketers can uncover a powerful, emotional means of connecting—or reconnecting—their brand to consumers" (Braun-LaTour, LaTour, and Zinkhan 2007, 45). Linking childhood to the brand is a way to construct a connection to the brand in a way that is reminiscent of childhood. After all, goods have the capacity to "carry social meanings" (Douglas and Isherwood 1996, 38), meaning the commercials can feed into a social construction of childhood.

With advertising efforts rooted in "fantasy" (Ewen 2001, 210), messages idealizing feelings of childhood can be fantastical while still managing to be persuasive. In addition, persuasive efforts can become centralized among target audiences, especially since culture is missing certain elements that marketing efforts can fill in.

Douglas and Isherwood (1996) claimed that "without some conventional ways of selecting and fixing agreed meanings, the minimum consensual basis of society is missing" (43). Advertising efforts are a way to have some consistent meaning present with culture, given that mass messages can create somewhat uniform impressions. Message exposure to the persuasive messages will take particular hold when the persuasion is appealing and effective. With marketing trends the way they are now, "what the advertiser needs to know is not what is right about the product but what is wrong about the buyer" (Postman 1992, 170). In a sense, marketing practitioners understand how to tap into certain characteristics that consumers hold as valuable. As consumers long for childhood, marketing practitioners can tap into that longing for the purposes of their brand messages.

Marketing persuasion can blur the line between adulthood and childhood, doing so with one important feature. On one hand, "children prefer the easy way to do things" (Barber 2007, 84). On the other, adults utilize "the seeming ease that comes with extensive learning, effort, and discipline" (2007, 84). In other words, marketing practitioners are able to blur the line because it is easy to do so; "the premature ageing of children and increasing immaturity of adults" (Hayward 2013, 533) allow for conditions that make the specific persuasive efforts effective. For both children and adults, deciding to make a purchase is a choice. The way that ease is in those choices is characterized as distinct.

For the child, the choice is easy because the thought process involved is not as complex or experienced as it is for an adult. For example, children might choose to buy and eat candy bars because they are hungry, or because they desire something sweet. Adults might choose to buy and eat candy bars, too, but they may entertain thoughts, such as the amount of calories and sugar in the candy bar in comparison with the amount of calories and sugar the person has already eaten in the day. With the base foundation of how people make choices in mind, marketing practitioners have the basis to take the more elaborate decision-making process of an adult and turn it into something more comparable to a child's, where the ease of making a decision has less depth. Again, the best insight into these kinds of strategies comes from a sample of Barber's (2007) ideas on child psychology as part of the decision-making process, notably based in the child world versus the adult world:

> Impulse over Deliberation [quick, reactionary decisions]; Feeling over Reason [emotions rather than logic]; Certainty over Uncertainty [clear concrete decisions]; Play over Work [enjoying oneself and having fun]; Pictures over Words [responding more to visuals]; Pleasure over Happiness [sensory; feeling good in the moment rather than establishing feeling good long term]; Entitlement over Obligation [feeling things are deserved rather than achieved]; Timeless Present over Temporality [decisions are made in the moment, a timeless present, as opposed to considering the past and having concern for the future]; Individualism over Community [prioritizing self over others]. (Barber 2007, 83)

In the following section, commercial advertisements from the Subaru "Love" campaign will be analyzed using these criteria in order to argue that adults can be targeted as children, within a child frame of mind, and that adults can come to value their goods in much the same way that children can value toys.

SUBARU'S APPROACH TO CHILD PSYCHOLOGY

The Subaru "Love" campaign shows adults how to think about responsibility and safety with their Subaru vehicles, while also having fun and remembering childhood at the same time. This way the product function and the childhood emotions are both part of the persuasive messages. The campaign also promotes the longevity of the Subaru vehicles, presenting parents with the idea that their Subaru vehicles can one day actually be given to their children—children who will value the same traits in the Subaru. There are six main commercials that will be used for analysis: the Subaru Crosstrek "Fountain" commercial, the Subaru Legacy "Jr. Driver" commercial, the "Father-Daughter" Subaru commercial, the "First Day of School," the "Memory Lane" commercial, and "Grew Up in the Backseat."

In the Subaru Crosstrek "Fountain" commercial, a couple takes a trip in their Subaru Crosstrek. They go swimming, and imagine themselves being kids again. The day they spend together is fun and carefree, reminding them of how they felt as children. The commercial includes the tagline, "You're only young once, unless you have a Subaru." Not only is the fun linked to childhood, but the ownership of a Subaru is linked to childhood, as well. The couple use the Subaru to go out for the day, so, within the commercial's content, there is no question the assumption is that feeling like a kid is positive. The marketing practitioners want a clear association between that feeling and the brand.

The Subaru Legacy "Jr. Driver" commercial shows a boy taking on the role of his father, envisioning himself being able to drive his father's Subaru. Though the boy desires the independence of adulthood, looking forward to coming of age and being able to drive, he also comes to terms with the responsibilities and obligations that come with driving. For example, in the commercial the boy pays highway tolls and tries to avoid parking tickets. In both cases, the boy expresses frustration.

The boy starts the commercial by claiming he is ready to be an adult, but, ultimately, he decides he would rather not grow up too fast, settling for his current status as a child in the world. In fact, at one point in the commercial, the boy's father says, "Life can be hard, buddy," making sure the boy understands that being an adult is not all fun and games. The commercial is clearly designed to have a lighthearted and comical feel, reminding audiences of how great and carefree childhood was, absent of so much worry and concern; however, the commercial points out that being an adult is not necessarily as glamorous as children might imagine it to be. Since you do have to be a certain age to drive, the commercial's message is obviously intended more for adults than for children.

The "Father-Daughter" Subaru commercial is a little different. In this commercial, the father is advising his daughter about different safety tips as she is getting ready to go out driving on her own. He pictures his daughter as very young, until the end of the commercial when it is revealed she is actually a teenager. Near the end of the commercial the line, "We knew this day was coming" is used. The setup points to the idea that this will be the daughter's first time driving by herself. The commercial's message also stresses the importance of having a Subaru, which is a nod to the safety ratings that Subaru vehicles are known for. Here, the focus is still on the simplicity and ease of childhood, but this time it is for the father attempting to deal with his child getting older and being on track toward becoming an adult. The father recognizes that his daughter is gaining a certain level of independence, and that he has to accept the additional complexity that will come with her life transition. Despite the difference in commercial content, the message is still geared toward childhood being simpler.

The "First Day of School" commercial is also about a kind of life transition for a father and daughter. The commercial depicts a father getting his daughter on the bus so she can get to her first day of school. The father asks his daughter if she is excited for her first day; she replies, "Yes," though it is evident she is nervous. A bit later in the commercial, the father drives alongside the bus in his Subaru. He narrates that he is overprotective, which is why he got a Subaru. As in the "Father-Daughter" commercial, the message is in reference to the safety ratings of Subaru vehicles. While the life transition in this commercial is not directed toward adulthood the way driving might be, there is a life transition displayed nonetheless. The excitement of the first day of school coupled with the comfort and security the father feels when observing his daughter laughing with a new friend on the bus are emotional appeals designed to take hold of and influence a consumer's thought process.

The "Memory Lane" commercial is quite literally a commercial about a trip down memory lane. A mother and father take their young daughter to see a tree under which her grandparents met—the girl's grandmother accompanies them on the trip, as well. This commercial for the Subaru Outback displays how inquisitive the young girl is about her grandmother and her life; in fact, the girl hugs the tree when they finally get to it, demonstrating a certain willingness to accept the grandmother's words about the family's history. The commercial's tagline, "Some things are worth holding onto" is a reference to the tree and the longevity of the Subaru, though the tagline also demonstrates how a child might process information. The influence of the message is found in how a persuasive act can cause a child—or consumer—to accept an idea at face value. A Subaru is worth holding onto because it will last. A consumer can hold onto a Subaru because Subaru vehicles last. It is worth noting that the parents also eventually hug the tree, and, at the end of the commercial, the grandmother guesses that a different tree might actually be the one they are looking for.

The "Grew Up in the Backseat" Subaru Forester commercial focuses on a mother and a daughter. The mother narrates that she bought the Subaru when her daughter was born. From there, through a visual timeline, she talks about different life events her daughter experienced while in the Subaru—including saying her first word, seeing school on her first school day, and making a new best friend. At the end of the commercial, the mother states that her daughter actually grew up in the Subaru; while saying this, she stares at her daughter.

The tagline is that Subaru is "designed for your most precious cargo," which is again a mention of the safety ratings behind Subaru. The tagline also points toward the difference between an adult and a child. The child is to ride in the Subaru, while the adult should purchase a Subaru due to how safe they are. Furthermore, the adult should recognize that Subaru vehicles are so safe a child can grow up in one. When the commercial concludes, the daughter sees her mother staring at her. She asks her mother "What?" twice, getting no response from her mother.

THE SUBARU ANALYSIS

Before getting into the specifics from Barber (2007), it is important to establish the way in which these commercials have specific audiences in mind. Brand meaning can be generated by "experience" coupled with "imagination" (Travis 2000, 78), so a commercial that is realistic while indulging a childlike sentiment is ideal. Both characteristics can be accomplished. Experience in the commercials has to do with showcasing product functionality, such as with the emphasis on safety. The feelings of childhood are imaginative, allowing the viewer to grasp what it was like being a child in the past.

For example, nostalgia is a key part of the childhood-based appeal, and also narrows the intended audience. A study by Muehling, Sprott, & Sultan (2014) demonstrated "that brand attitudes and purchase intentions would be most favorable and strongest for those viewing a nostalgic ad and for whom some type of meaningful in-home exposure or personal attachment to the advertised brand had existed during childhood" (79). While no audience is excluded by design, the audience that will be the most impacted is the one that has some existing relationship with the brand. So when childhood-based appeals are used, their effectiveness can be determined at least in part by what the brand already means for the consumer.

Muehling, Sprott, and Sultan (2014) concluded that a nostalgic approach to marketing would likely "not yield universally beneficial results" (80), in the sense that it would not appeal to every audience equally. A nostalgic approach would, though, provide a foundation for understanding the strength of Subaru positioning itself toward particular audiences as a brand passed down through generations of family members. Generally, connections in the commercials are made by portraying the wonderment of childhood experienced through Subaru ownership, while also showing that a child should expect to have the same exact Subaru at some point in the future. In either case, there is a joy derived from having the Subaru. Connections are also made in the commercials by stressing safety, which translates to the parents feeling better about their children riding as passengers or eventually getting the Subaru one day. Each one of the commerciala gives a unique take, as well.

First, the Crosstrek "Fountain" commercial serves as a reminder of what having fun can be like as a child. The adults in the commercial go out in their Subaru and have fun, but the fun they have transforms them back into being kids again. In this case, "play over work" (Barber 2007, 83) is fundamental. The benefit of work is having and making use of the Crosstrek, but as kids all they do is play. There is no emphasis on having to work at all. A Crosstrek is an expense for anyone, and buying a vehicle is a big decision. The commercial shows kids having fun, getting a chance to be young, simply because they are in possession of the Crosstrek. As mentioned previously, the Crosstrek becomes a kind of reward, and the feeling of being young is only achieved through having it.

A child could look at the commercial and understand that the vehicle is something rooted in play; that it is purchased for the function of having a good time. An adult would be able to understand that, too, but an adult would also think about vehicle ownership in terms of cost, reliability, use in city/on highway, use in snow, and so on. By showing the Subaru as something linked to play, the commercial reduces the thought process down to a child's. The message only asks the consumer to understand the Crosstrek as something used to have fun, which takes the content out of an informed buying decision and into a fantastical state.

In that regard, the commercial also embodies "certainty over uncertainty" and "pleasure over happiness" (Barber 2007, 83). The idea that people are only young once unless they have a Subaru cements a clear and concrete choice, rather than entertaining doubt. Simply, to feel like a kid, you need the Subaru. There should be no skepticism, no doubt, no second guesses. To a child, a decision is less complicated, and the commercial does everything possible to uncomplicate what an adult knows should be an informed and educated decision. Because the Crosstrek is linked to being young and having fun, a childlike mindset would understand that fun and play are important and good, so the decision to buy the Crosstrek is essentially a no-brainer because it is how you get there.

The childlike feeling of play without worry or concern is more in line with pleasure than any kind of long-term happiness. There is an immediate gratification to having a carefree day of play, though it would not necessarily yield any kind of long-term results. The consumer is told a feeling will emerge from the Subaru ownership, so the feeling will be granted with the Crosstrek. Feeling good in the long term, which is part of the adult mentality, however, would not be a concern here. Realistically, a vehicle likely cannot grant the childlike feeling, so such an expenditure may affect long-term happiness. If a consumer buys something as expensive as a vehicle, understanding the purchase decision only within the framework of fun the vehicle would provide, there would likely be a certain level of disappointment to it. In addition, devoting a day to play can affect work and deadlines, if done at the expense of other obligations. The commercial strives to point consumers away from that mode of thinking in hopes that the brand has the simplistic, fun, carefree identity.

Second, the Subaru "Legacy "Jr. Driver" commercial also reminds the audience of how great childhood can be, but it does so by showing how tough adult life and responsibility can be. In the Crosstrek commercial, the persuasive goal is more in line with showing how great it can be to have fun as a kid. In this commercial, however, the goal is to show that one should not be eager to grow up too fast, as being an adult brings more troubles, responsibilities, and concerns than what a kid will have. In a way, the "Jr. Driver" commercial takes an opposite approach. Significantly, from Barber (2007) concepts, "feeling over reason" and "entitlement over obligation" (83) are on display because of the way the boy envisions independence and adulthood; by commercial's end, the boy comes to terms with what adulthood really is like. The vantage point of the boy in the commercial gives the viewer these impressions by showing his exasperation with needing to be held accountable for things.

The boy in the commercial believes he is ready for adult life and all that comes with it. He expresses how happy he is to finally have a car and the capability and allowance to drive. When the boy's father lets him have the Subaru to drive, the boy is extremely excited to get started on driving. Shortly thereafter, though, the boy realizes the challenges and expectations thrust upon him due to the life progression. Giving his father a ride, for example, is something the boy is displeased in needing to do. The boy's emotional state, his feeling in the commercial, is that he should be allowed the independence of adulthood, including being able to drive. That much he can process, though it is clear he views adulthood as also being as much fun as being a kid. When reason kicks in, and the boy must apply logic to what he needs to do as an adult, he sees that being an adult includes additional responsibilities that are not so desirable. Certainly, within his frame of mind, he realizes that being a kid is better, and that he should put off adulthood for the normal duration of his life.

So really, the boy feels entitled in the sense that he would like to have all the perks of adulthood, not understanding the added responsibility that comes with it. He sees adulthood as this wonderful, marvelous construct, yet that is primarily because he wants the good that comes with it and not the bad. When the boy's father requests to be picked up later, the boy reacts negatively. For audiences, feeling entitled would be much more fun and desirable than feeling obligated, so the childlike state is again depicted as positive when compared with what is expected of an adult.

The "Jr. Driver "commercial also includes "play over work" (Barber 2007, 83), since the boy reasons at the commercial's end that he would much rather stay a child. Throughout the commercial, the boy integrates his newfound understanding of work into the play elements he initially perceived, and in doing so alters his take. He ultimately sees work as at least a part of the role of being an adult, and he rejects that aspect of it. In the end, the boy would rather just stay a child, and that mentality is directly conveyed to the consumer through his decision. Just like in the previous commercial, childhood is depicted as much more desirable. Being an adult is not as great as one might think it is as a child.

Third, the "Father-Daughter" commercial has a parent expressing safety concerns, as articulated through his recommendations about driving, to his daughter who is about to drive on her own. Given the approach of this particular commercial using the father's standpoint, the child psychology characteristics are less apparent. Still, though, the childhood construction is shown in relation to adulthood. In this particular case, the "timeless present over temporality" (Barber 2007, 83) concept is clear, despite the fact it is conveyed to the audience through the father and not the daughter.

The father in the commercial makes the decision to advise his daughter about a whole number of rules and laws she should follow while driving. His daughter reacts by voicing a kind of reassurance to her father, suggesting she is well aware of everything he tells her; the audience can at least assume she knows to be safe while behind the wheel. Because the father pictures his daughter as much younger than she is revealed to actually be, he is rooting his decision to advise her in a timeless present because he sees her as a little girl who has not yet grown up. She is in a way stuck in that timeframe.

Temporality, as part of being an adult, is not applied in this commercial. Though the father is considering the past by seeing his daughter as a little girl, he is not considering the past as a basis for his decision to provide advice. Since his daughter is about to drive on her own, she must have accomplished enough to be able to do so—permit, license, and so on. Foundationally, she is likely capable of driving on her own and is already considering everything that he suggests.

The audience also knows the father is rejecting the future, because he cannot bring himself to accept his daughter as the age she really is, let alone think about her aging further. He is trapping her in a past state, and has a difficult time believing she is, in fact, growing up. In a way, it is nice for the audience to look upon a child as not ever growing up or needing to grow up, which also reverts to child psychology. Time is affected, time is frozen, and being a child forever is again viewed as desirable.

Fourth, the "First Day of School" commercial stresses a father and daughter relationship, as well. The "play over work" (Barber 2007, 83) aspect is certainly displayed here, as the daughter in the commercial worries about the first day of school. The father in the commercial is relieved—and the audience can assume the daughter is, too—when he sees his daughter laughing with a new friend. For the audience, this act can cue a feeling of the social feature of school, even though work involved with school could also be a source of anxiety on the first day. The focus is on whether school will prove to be fun and enjoyable, as opposed to challenging and demanding. Play is assimilated into the commercial's message while work is not, and it is certainly a nice feeling to see how happy both the father and the daughter are as a result.

Likewise, "pleasure over happiness" (Barber 2007, 83) is all the audience can really derive from the message, since the long-term effects of dealing with school are left unknown. The audience is given enough information to know that, in the moment at least, the daughter is happy. Since the commercial ends the story there, though, any long-term feelings of happiness associated with going to school are left unknown. To be fair, that particular interpretation is symptomatic of commercial length, but all the audience can really know is in the short-term.

Fifth, the "Memory Lane" commercial shows a family and their experience with the past; the grandmother in the commercial dispenses information. Given the young granddaughter's willingness to absorb and accept her grandmother's words, "impulse over deliberation" (Barber 2007, 83) is clearly used. The granddaughter does not need an especially sophisticated thought process, given that she believes in her grandmother's words absolutely.

Deliberation and reflection are much more complex thought processes, in which the granddaughter does not engage. The best example is near the end of the commercial when the granddaughter hugs the tree. The granddaughter decides to hug the tree almost immediately because of the story her grandmother tells her. Of course, her grandmother does not appear to have a good sense of whether the specific tree she names is the actual one in question, so the audience is led to understand that the granddaughter just reacted, while the grandmother may well have been wrong about what she said. At face value, the granddaughter hugging the tree is not a huge deal, but it is the commercial's content that connects the action to a specific concept within child psychology.

The tagline of the commercial is telling in this way, "Some things are worth holding onto." Hugging a tree is very different from buying a Subaru, but the marketing practitioners are hoping to associate that simplistic level of thought with the purchase decision. Hold onto a tree, hold onto family, and hold onto the Subaru. The Subaru will last, so it needs the same level of affection, care, and attention as the family and the family's stories and lineage. If the Subaru can be relied on, in a similar fashion to how the grandmother can, then it would make sense to give the Subaru the same feeling.

Of course, "certainty over uncertainty" (Barber 2007, 83) would point to the granddaughter's decisions. Because of how willing she is to accept her grandmother's words, there is no doubt or skepticism in her mind. This sentiment can also be linked to the Subaru; if the Subaru is indeed worth holding onto, then it should be an obvious decision for the consumer to get one. Hopefully, the decisions of the consumers, guided by the decisions of the granddaughter, are concrete and without question.

Sixth and finally, the "Grew Up in the Backseat" commercial presents the daughter's life transition. This commercial also stresses the safety of the Subaru, and the "pictures over words" (Barber 2007, 83) characteristic is crucial. Advertisements are generally based in visuals, but for this commercial the visuals play out as a timeline progression of the daughter's life as it is applied to happening in the vehicle.

The "pictures over words" (Barber 2007, 83) idea stresses the way that children are thought to respond more to visuals, and the visuals here are provided to show the audience the daughter's life. The audience sees the daughter with a friend, sees the daughter's school, and sees the family dog, among other visuals provided. By matching the moving visuals to the daughter's life, the audience gets a sort of cinematic event that plays out in the commercial, and the emotional impact of the daughter's life is heightened in a way that words would not provide on their own.

Given that the daughter is still very young even by the end of the commercial, the connection to childhood is all the more apparent. In other words, even though the daughter's life progression is given through the words and visuals, the daughter still has much growing up to do even by the end. The audience is not made to disconnect from the daughter being a child. The daughter reacting to her mother's stare also demonstrates a child being more prone to respond to a visual cue. She sees her mother giving a nonverbal cue, which prompts her to question what exactly her mother is doing.

GOODS AS TOYS

The attempt to work with childlike, psychological states of being is strongly communicated through these commercials. The reward of work through idea is the primary goal, demonstrating how the vehicles can be linked to family activities, fun, and childhood. An adult processes the way that work can lead to play, and in these commercials the Subaru vehicles are shown to allow for play to take place.

The AT&T commercial discussed at the beginning of the chapter allows for the consumer to think of the consumer good as having all the excitement of a toy, and using child psychology in the Subaru commercials does the same. A child could get excited about a new toy because the toy is going to provide a level of fun and enjoyment. The Subaru vehicles can be like toys because they provide fun and enjoyment, too, but they can only really have that identity for a consumer if they manage to become ascribed to the wonderment associated with childhood. In each case, a reminiscent good feeling attributed to childhood is given with the expectation that the Subaru vehicles will do just that.

The attempt at nostalgia is communicated throughout the commercials, as well, since generational and youthful portrayals are also given. The target audience is revealed by trying to rationalize the decision to buy a Subaru. For those looking to have a reliable vehicle that provides safety to the family, the decision is an obvious one—so obvious, in fact, a child's mentality could be applied. The complexity of an adult's thought process is completely unnecessary. For those who already have a Subaru, and thus a nostalgic feeling, they may recall their parents having a Subaru or the pride they have in making what was such an obvious consumer choice in brand of vehicle.

The additionally named characteristic of "individualism over community" (Barber 2007, 83) is stressed in each commercial. Given that children are thought to prioritize their wants, desires, and needs over those of others, the commercials focus on caring for oneself. The state of play and the lack of obligation and responsibility and reflection connected to adulthood allow consumers to identify Subaru with a kind of wish fulfillment, where they can look forward to immediate gratification.

Granted, in some cases in the commercials, family is put over the individual, but in those cases it is the parent who is doing so—not the child. Arguably, the safety features of the vehicles are also rooted in individualism, considering that the parents get the benefit of safety, too. Children in the commercials also recognize their parents as authority figures and providers, so their individualism centers on the parents knowing how to take care of them and provide them with resources and information; the children do not have to concern themselves with worrying about such things on their own.

Moves toward gratification, pleasure, and play allow for very individualistic ways of thinking, since there is a "me" kind of focus and mentality to getting what one wants and denying responsibility and obligation. Children can be in a never-ending state of present if they do not use the past to inform their decisions and if they do not consider future consequences. With the Subaru vehicles playing on this idea for the purpose of a purchase, similar to how a child might decide to purchase a toy, there is almost no thought happening whatsoever.

Subaru vehicles being represented as a reward of work through play allows for consumers to see them as fun. Adults are encouraged to justify through the commercials that Subaru vehicles are fun purchase choices, again, like toys are, but that is a present-oriented mindset. Past experiences should inform an adult to consider other brands of vehicles and to think about future consequences of such an expenditure.

As mentioned early in the chapter, children can make more simplistic decisions, but adults make decisions that only appear simple. An adult would typically engage knowledge, wisdom, and experience in order to come to a concrete decision about something, especially if it is a consumer decision for something as expensive and as important as a vehicle. Understanding that consumers consider risks worthwhile if they are losing money is important, but a vehicle is a substantial purchase with a number of features and options to consider.

Once child psychology elements are fused into a brand's messages, the brand can become an extension of the great feelings associated with what it was like being young. The AT&T commercial hopes that audiences will recall their fifth birthday, including the excitement of having a new toy. The recognition is that, eventually, purchases and ownership will not carry the same level of enthusiasm they once did. For an adult, the anticipation and excitement and surprise of having something fades, especially given the ways an adult might make choices.

For example, the Subaru commercials might instead choose to focus on psychology thought more prevalent for adults. Deliberation and obligation could, in theory, be given precedent. In that case, the commercials would likely not grip consumers and their imaginative sense the way commercials suggestive of childhood would. The safety messages are one way to comprehend this approach.

The commercials could do away with the emotional appeals, hoping to let the adults come to a logical decision based around features of the car. All-wheel drive, airbags, and crash test ratings could be given. While some critics might see that as a positive move, it would likely not work for mass audiences the way a fictitious, encapsulated story would. The marketing practitioners have made a conscious judgment to allow the commercials to loosely touch upon important features such as reliability and safety, but they do so by showing a narrative that plays out to show how much fun Subaru vehicles can be. Once the narrative is given, and imaginations are hopefully sparked, the commercial's content is linked to some feature the car has with the intention of making the Subaru like a toy to be possessed with a child's mentality backing the decision.

Buying into Subaru becomes something akin to buying a toy, and childhood memory becomes part of Subaru, as well. The feeling of getting a toy as a child can be lost in adulthood, but regained through the persuasion demonstrated by the Subaru brand. A socially constructed childhood can be obtained through using a Subaru to make a simple decision and have fun.

As stated earlier, buying a vehicle as an adult should require much more consideration than buying a toy as a child, or making the choice to have someone else buy the toy for a child for that matter. A goal with this kind of marketing strategy is to link the two together, or at least to take the purchase decision and boil it down to the same level of impulsive thought used when buying the toy. Ultimately, the toy is the Subaru, and the feeling of being young is described as being accessible through Subaru ownership.

CONCLUSION

In an integrated framework, the focus is "not just [on] the sending but also the reception of the communication" (Torp 2009, 191). In order to achieve a focus on reception of persuasive messages, advertising should consider the consumer. In the case of the Subaru ads, Subaru was able to create and reinforce a link to childhood sentiment that was then applied to their brand and its products. The child psychology involved allows a consumer to think of a purchase as fun, a good as a toy, in such a way that the consumption process becomes reminiscent of childhood. Ease of choice is sparked by the wonderment of a variety of childhood-based activities, which generates a powerful and effective means by which to sway the consumer.

REFERENCES

Barber, Benjamin. 2007. *Consumed: How Markets Corrupt Children, Infantalize Adults, and Swallow Citizens Whole.* New York: W. W. Norton & Company, Inc.

Braun-LaTour, Kathryn A., LaTour, Michael S., and George M. Zinkhan. 2007. "Using Childhood Memories to Gain Insight into Brand Meaning." *Journal of Marketing* 71: 45-60.

Campos, Roberta, Suarez, Maribel, Nascimento, Thaysa do, and Fabricio Molica. 2015. "I am Dreaming of a Car: Longitudinal Rites of Passage and Car Consumption." *Advances in Consumer Research* 43: 324-328.

Csikszentmihalyi, Mihaly, and Eugene Rochberg-Halton. 1981. *The Meaning of Things: Domestic Symbols and the Self.* New York: Cambridge University Press.

Douglas, Mary and Baron Isherwood. 1996. *The World of Goods: Towards an Anthropology of Consumption.* New York: Routledge.

Ewen, Stuart. 2001. *Captains of Consciousness: Advertising and the Social Roots of Consumer Culture.* New York: Basic Books.

Gossage, Howard Luck. 1967. "The Guilded Bough: Magic and Advertising." *In The Human Dialogue: Perspectives on Communication,* edited by Floyd W. Matson and Ashley Montagu. 363-370. New York: The Free Press.

Hayward, Keith. 2013. "'Life Stage Dissolution' in Anglo-American Advertising and Popular Culture: Kidults, Lil' Britneys and Middle Youths." *The Sociological Review* 61: 525-548.

Muehling, Darrel, D., Sprott, David E., and Abdullah J. Sultan. 2014."Exploring the Boundaries of Nostalgic Advertising Effects: A Consideration of Childhood Brand Exposure and Attachment on Consumers' Reponses to Nostalgia-Themed Advertisements." *Journal of Advertising* 43(1): 73-84.

Postman, Neil. 1992. *Technopoly: The Surrender of Culture to Technology.* New York: Vintage Books.

Postman, Neil. 1999. *Building a Bridge to the 18 th Century: How the Past can Improve our Future.* New York: Vintage Books.

Schultz, Don E., and Heidi Schultz. 2003. *IMC, the Next Generation: Five Steps for Delivering Value and Measuring Returns Using Marketing Communication.* New York: The McGraw-Hill Companies.

Simmel, Goerg, trans. 1978. *The Philosophy of Money.* Translated by Tom Bottomore and David Frisby. London: Routledge & Kegan Paul.

Torp, Simon. 2009. "Integrated Communications: From One Look to Normative Consistency." *Corporate Communications: An International Journal* 14(2): 190-206.

Travis, Daryl. 2000. *Emotional Branding: How Successful Brands Gain the Irrational Edge.* Roseville, CA: Prima Venture.

FIVE

Integrated Marketing Communication and Public Relations

Epideictic Rhetoric, Kairos, and Ireland's Vote Yes Campaign

Jeanne M. Persuit

In public relations, audiences are often referred to as *publics*, with whom an organization must engage to produce short- and long-term success. The orientation of public relations is often to generate awareness, but public relations with an integrated marketing communication (IMC) orientation aims to effect behavioral change, not just attitudinal change. In the chapter, I will explore how PR with an IMC orientation is a form of rhetoric and can be informed by two ideas from ancient rhetorical theory: epideictic rhetoric and kairos, and that this theoretical ground offers a productive direction for an ethical and effective approach to IMC.

PUBLIC RELATIONS AND IMC

Torp (2009) refers to the expanded scope of IMC, which as he states "has been broadened to include virtually everything an organization says and does and everyone who is affected by the organization's existence and activities" (191). Kitchen and De Pelsmacker (2004) explain the aims of IMC: "To persuade by all means of communication, to affect behavior, not just attitudes, and to start with customers or prospects and then work backwards to develop effective communication" (7). This emphasis on changing behavior, not just attitudes, presents an avenue for IMC that connects not only with products or services and consumers but with voters and issues, donors and causes, and volunteers and organizations. While a positive or negative attitude toward an issue or brand can help predict behavior with some reliability, it is the behavior itself (votes, money raised, sales) that can measure the effects of an organization's IMC.

Public relations as part of an IMC approach is necessary to foster these relationships that lead to behavioral change. By creating and maintaining long-term relationships with audiences, organizations can build trust with its publics and vice versa. The reciprocal nature of public relations is often forgotten in the negative connotations of spin and hype that PR often engenders. An IMC framework reminds us that every communication between an organization and its audiences carries meaning and the opportunity for understanding or misunderstanding.

IMC AS RHETORIC

In order to utilize a rhetorical framework for IMC, we must consider integrated marketing communication, public relations, advertising, and so on as forms of rhetoric. We not only can analyze artifacts such as specific ads, PR campaigns, and promotional events through rhetorical analysis, but these artifacts only function because "through rhetoric, we interpret and share the meaning of messages" (Persuit 2013, 38). Botan and Soto (1998) identify the limitations of how "publics" are constructed and communicated with, and hope that their efforts lead to not only more effecting marketing communication but also "in the hope that understanding publics as something more than reactive bodies will ultimately advance our purpose of more socially responsible strategic communication campaigns, including those conducted by activist organizations, government bodies, and the like (22)." Botan and Soto's sophisticated analysis, relying on the theories of Charles Sanders Peirce and Umberto Eco, is not necessarily simple to explain, but they do note that the key to the construction of publics is in a semiotic conception of rhetoric—where rhetoric is "an endless process by which signs give birth to other signs." When this process stops because the sign stops producing other signs, it is considered "extinct." The purpose of an organization or a public is, according to Botan and Soto, to keep its sign producing other signs. What this ultimately means is that a public itself is an "*ongoing process of agreement upon an interpretation*" (1998, 38). The constitution of publics is itself a rhetorical effort, and in the case I examine in this chapter, the "Vote Yes" campaign for marriage equality, the publics that form through this process effect significant behavioral change, ultimately resulting in the legalization of same-sex marriage in Ireland.

Examining IMC through a rhetorical approach relies on language as carrying meaning. Meaning, according to Aakhus (citing Jacobs 2004), is one of the "puzzling aspects" of communication, along with action and coherence (2007, 113). Twitchell claims branding is a "commercial narrative," and that "commercial narrative, like any kind of storytelling, depends as much on the listener as on the storyteller. The audience is always negotiating meaning, affirming and subverting" (2004, 297). IMC's close relationship to branding also relies on rhetorical action, since "the theory and practice of branding, a component of integrated marketing communication, requires interpretation of signs as a shared endeavor" (Persuit 2013). Finally, Persuit (2013, 36-7) describes the challenges in IMC in this historical moment of postmodernity marked by uncertainty; IMC must be responsive to multiple audiences and does not provide one good answer but perhaps multiple good answers, or sometimes no answer at all: "This understanding of IMC fits into the rhetorical tradition, which works in response to contingency, particularity, temporality, and locality, based on available knowledge, to determine a sound course of action."

With publics understood as rhetorically constructed, and IMC as rhetorical communication, we can then turn our attention to the two areas of the study of rhetoric that might help us engage publics through co-creation of meaning: epideictic and kairos.

IMC AND EPIDEICTIC RHETORIC

In his overview of the study of epideictic rhetoric, Lauer (2015) traces its development from ancient Greece and Aristotle's understanding of the role and nature of epideictic in *The Rhetoric:* "Aristotle's identification of the topic (praise/blame), temporal nature (present), and audience (observers) of an epideictic speech constitute the fundamental *topoi* for the genre" (5). The classic example of epideictic, a funeral oration, presented an opportunity in Ancient Greece to connect democracy with the conservative virtues of the society: "The Athenian funeral oration elided any topical tension between a contemporary discourse of democracy and aristocratic traditionalism by praising bellicose ambition as a virtue of yesteryear. By successfully invoking the citizenry as a collective body, the funeral orator consolidated support for Athenian policy" (5). Lauer then considers the expansion of epideictic during the Roman era from Cicero to Antonius, explaining, "Roman epideictic could become a flexible rhetorical form, capable of reorienting the basis of Roman values and supplying a new watermark to preserve the integrity of subsequent rhetorical transactions" (6). Rhetoric in antiquity allowed for the study of epideictic as it connects to the preservation and promulgation of culture. These core characteristics of epideictic continue to contemporary scholarship, and Lauer describes the efforts in the past fifty years to identify new theoretical ground for epideictic rhetoric, including its educative function (Perelman); its audience emphasis (Oravec); its potential for shared meaning and production of new knowledge (Rosenfield); and the functional pairs of rhetoric which provide a helpful heuristic for analysis of artifacts (Condit) (Lauer 2015, 9).

In their study of Michelle Obama's epideictic rhetoric that constructs her First Lady brand, Persuit and Brunson (2015, 41-2) argue that the First Lady's rhetoric served multiple epideictic functions and that these work together to construct the brand of First Lady: "communicating what is virtuous or problematic in a culture; inculcating and educating on virtues necessary for a civil society, cultivating adherence to these shared virtues (Perelman and Olbrechts-Tyteca), and uncovering or 'showing forth' a brand as it is co-constructed with audiences . . . epideictic rhetoric can serve to construct a brand through reinforcing of virtues that are publicly agreed-upon by a fragmented audience while serving to uncover new meanings and relationships between the brand and this audience." For the purposes of the case studied in this chapter, I rely on Condit's (1985) three functional pairs of epideictic discourse: definition/understanding, display/entertainment, and shaping/sharing community. While not every example of epideictic discourse contains all three pairs, most serve at least one of these functions. According to Condit, "the first term in each pair indicates the function the speech serves for the speaker. The second term indicates the corresponding function served for the audience" (1985, 288). The first pair, definition/understanding, has explanatory characteristics. The speaker has the power to define the situation that, in Condit's words, is "troubling" or "confusing" to the audience in order to provide understanding and and comfort.

Display/entertainment, the second functional pair, seems to reinforce epideictic rhetoric's reputation as merely ornamental. Since epideictic does not mete out justice (like judicial rhetoric) or formulate a future course of action (like deliberative rhetoric); it often receives the title "ceremonial" and refers to feats of oratorical prowess only applicable in the academy. However, Condit reminds us that a characteristic of display/entertainment speech is eloquence: "the combination of truth, beauty and power in human speech, and is a unique capacity of humanity." Therefore, she states, "The epideictic experience offers speakers the opportunity for creativity by releasing them from concern with specific issues and charging them to take on broader vistas" (1985, 290).

The third pair, shaping/sharing community, is most connected to the co-creation of meaning that rhetoric and language encourages; sharing community begins with the definitional/understanding pair: "Interlaced with the definitional/understanding function is the need to share community. Because human beings are symbol-creators, they need forms of symbolic sharing. A sense of community is developed and maintained in a large part through public speaking and hearing of the community heritage and identity (Condit 1985, 289)." She warns, however, that community is not always an idyllic construction; some communities form around problematic symbols or exclude those who should be rightly included. These three pairs will serve as the heuristic to analyze the "Vote Yes!" marriage equality campaign in Ireland later in this chapter.

Lauer (2015, 15) explains the flexibility of epideictic as a means of inquiry that can be used to interrogate a variety of occasions and artifacts, including advertising: "Epideictic analysis of advertising themes demonstrate how praise for accepted cultural values can subtly endorse products." At the same time, Lauer claims, epideictic creates space for building community and potentially for "the emancipatory potential of a revolutionary epideictic." This flexibility allows for an interpretive frame that can accommodate the spectrum of epideictic rhetoric from ceremonial speeches to Twitter hashtags.

Lauer (2015) mines the study of epideictic rhetoric for its potential as a heuristic and for the extension of the types of fields and objects the study of epideictic could include. One of these, reflective epideictic, espoused by Garrison (2003) that "is an intelligent and moral discourse emerging from the particular values of individual celebrants and arising from the open questioning and revising of moral determinations" which "offers an alternative to epideictic which rigidly imposes moral themes upon its audience and subjects them to . . . a highly limiting narrative of action" and incorporates the ancient idea of kairos in rhetoric.

KAIROS AND IMC

In the last season of Mad Men, the AMC television show that focused on the archetypical ad man Don Draper, the sun sets on the 1960s, which served as the temporal setting for Mad Men. Don has divested himself of the belongings that he made a living promoting to others and traveled across the U.S. to a mountain retreat in California. The last scene shows Don, sitting in the lotus position and chanting "ohm" with a group, and slowly a smile steals across his face. In that moment, we think "At last, Don is at peace with himself." Then the scene cuts to the iconic "I'd like to buy the world a Coke" commercial, at which point we realize that Don took the sights, sounds, and atmosphere he found on that mountain and turned it into one of the most famous ads in American history. The moment of Don smiling is what is the most compelling; what we're seeing, in essence, is Don experiencing a kairotic moment. In that moment, he sees the right fitting, right time for this counterculture wave to be captured to serve an epideictic rhetorical function: to communicate Coke's brand to America.

Kairos, according to Sipiora (2002, 8), has a long and rich etymology in the Greek rhetorical tradition. The two sides of the coin of time are chronos, cosmic timetelling, and kairos, which is timing. There can be the right time (eukairos) or the wrong time (kakakairos) but kairos refers to how the opportune time presents itself. Sipiora claims that the true magnitude of the Greeks' understanding of kairos did not occur until Isocrates: "One of Isocrates' important contributions to rhetorical history is the conjoining of phronesis, or practical wisdom, and pragmatic ethics within the situation and time of discourse, an emphasis upon contexts that give primacy to the kairic dimensions of any rhetorical act."

Isocrates, considered to be the father of the humanities, really brought the study of rhetoric into the realm of cultivating civic virtue, and his understanding of a rhetorical education included this attention to kairos. One of his critiques of the Sophists, according to Sipiora, is that they were unable to "recognize the kairic exigencies of particular discourses. They failed to consider the *right time* or make the *appropriate* adjustments in any given rhetorical situation."

Isocrates, therefore, espouses in his paideia a life lived with kairos, according to Sipiora: "This pragmatic, personal, and socially conscious recapitulation of what it means to be 'educated' encapsulates the principle of kairos in all its nuances: the importance of living by phronesis or practical wisdom (which is in itself based on an epistemology of probability) with, always, an intense awareness of occasion, audience, and situation context. Such a life is based on kairos."

In IMC, attention to kairos can at the very least be an approach that avoids crisis. What Coombs and Holliday (2012) call "paracrisis—events that mimic crises, usually on the Internet, and cause reputational but not physical harm" can possibly be avoided by an attention to kairos. For example, commemorating the solemnity of 9/11 with a branded tweet is epideictic rhetoric that ignores kairos, trying to form community around shared virtues, but doing so at an inopportune time. An ethical practice of IMC depends on an "intense awareness of occasion, audience, and situation context" by practitioners and organizations. IMC understood as epideictic rhetoric with attentiveness to kairos results in behavioral change that moves beyond the creation of relationships between an organization and its publics—it creates new meaning and knowledge with transformative power. In addition, as mentioned earlier, publics are constituted by the constant and ongoing process of interpretation of signs (Botan and Soto 1998). As the kairotic moment changes, so does the process of interpreting signs, leading to newly constituted publics who may have not participated in this process in the past. The case of the Republic of Ireland's same-sex marriage referendum of 2015, when for the first time the right to same-sex marriage was legalized through a popular vote, is an example of IMC as epideictic rhetoric in a kairotic moment.

THE IRELAND SAME-SEX MARRIAGE REFERENDUM OF 2015

In 2011, the discussion of a referendum on same-sex marriage in the Republic of Ireland began to take shape, with the Labour Party preferring a referendum. As part of a compromise with Fine Gael (the other ruling party of Ireland), "the compromise was to send the issue to the constitutional convention, a deliberative forum comprising 33 politicians and 66 members of the public, on the understanding that if it recommended a referendum the Government would hold one" (Mac Cormaic 2015). Since 79 percent of this body recommended the referendum, it was added to the ballot in 2013 with the election to be held in May 2015. A "yes" vote for the referendum changed the Irish Constitution to allow for civil marriage regardless of the sex of the partners and the same constitutional protection of marriage as that between two different sexes (Mac Cormaic 2015). The referendum's success takes on even more significance when considering the history of Ireland and its relationship to the Roman Catholic Church, which prohibits same-sex marriages. How did this referendum succeed via popular vote in Ireland, especially considering that homosexuality was decriminalized in Ireland in 1993, a mere 22 years before (Schiavenza 2015)? The historical moment in which the referendum was introduced demonstrates the connection to kairos.

The role of the Church in Ireland's civic and religious life in the nineteenth and twentieth centuries was driven by the necessity of unifying Ireland against the ruling British in the wake of a declining Gaelic Irish culture (White 2007). Because the Church served to unite Ireland, it became inextricably linked to Ireland's national identify, and identifying as Irish meant equally identifying as Catholic. "In addition, Catholicism was successfully conjoined with Irish nationalism by its identity as a persecuted church, by the faithfulness of its followers, by the ability of the church to organize and meet social circumstances, and by the need for nationalism to have some widely accepted source of identity in society" (White 2007). Because of the importance of the Church to national identity and to local, everyday lives, the Church also influenced political life; local schools were run by the Church as well, so the maintenance of a Catholic identity for the Irish passed from generation to generation. This connection continued after the Irish gained independence; according to White (2007), "The Church's strength as a social institution meant that it could complacently oversee Irish politics without worrying that state policy would deviate from its teachings."

However, the Church's influence appeared to wane in the late twentieth century due to modernization, secularization, and the decline of church attendance. "The Irish public has lost confidence in the Church as an organization, increasingly believing that the Church has too much power in society and increasingly disapproving of the Church trying to influence voting or the government" (Greeley and Ward 2001, in White

2007). White argues "the changing role and character of Irish Catholicism may yet transform Irish nationalism into a more tolerant and accepting ideology, ready to accept the diversity of all who live in Ireland" (2007).[1] With the move away from the Celtic-Catholic national identity came efforts to change the Republic's constitutional ban against divorce; the initial 1986 referendum to legalize divorce was defeated by a 27 percent margin. According to Christopher (1997), that the second attempt in 1995 succeeded by a narrow (0.5 percent) margin "is a measure . . . of not only the change in Irish attitudes but also of the persistence of deep-seated traditional values regarding the place of the family in society and the strictures of the Catholic Church." The initial attempt in 1986 was defeated, according to Christopher, by "a concerted campaign waged against the government of the day by a series of pressure groups, which had the support of the Catholic hierarchy." This shift over 10 years demonstrates, even with the narrow margin of votes, the shift away from the Catholic Church as the primary identity-marker of Ireland. In addition, according to Christopher, "Urban voters in general, not just in the wealthier suburbs, became more amenable to change" (1997, 80).

While these events indicate the Vote Yes campaign may have found the kairotic moment for Ireland to pass the same-sex marriage referendum, an additional factor pertaining to marriage equality referenda would also contribute to the kairos moment that enabled this effort to succeed. In California in 2008, voters considered Proposition 8, which would amend the California state constitution to define marriage as between one man and one woman. Since the Cailfornia Supreme Court had already ruled that same-sex marriage was legal, this would reverse that decision. California voters passed the amendment by a 4 percent margin, and in their examination of the rhetoric following Proposition 8's passage, Hanson and Dionisopoulos (2012, 34) describe the lessons learned from efforts of "No to Prop 8," including the fallacy of depending on one organization (No on 8) to organize the campaign against the amendment; the well-organized, well-funded movement to pass Proposition 8; the lack of a grassroots campaign to support the No vote; the absence of actual gay and lesbian couples in advertising from No on 8; and the sense of complacency that resulted from the assumption that Proposition 8 would be defeated, which surprised many of the high-profile supporters of the No to Prop 8 campaign. What emerged was the realization that a grassroots effort was required and that the passage of Proposition 8 needed to be framed as the fuel to continue the fight for gay rights and marriage equality. In post-election discussion, LGBT press called for more inclusive, grassroots efforts that focused on interpersonal communication with individual voters and compassion, not vengeance: "Problem-focused guidance within this dialogue offered a way to make sense of defeat and manage postelection grief by keeping alive the community's relationship with what was lost. Instead of letting go of the past, the community was encouraged toward new efforts on behalf of gay rights" (2012, 37). Upon reflection, the LGBT and ally community worked to engage voters with dialogue and compassion, ultimately resulting in the U.S. Supreme Court's 2015 decision to legalize gay marriage in *Obergefell v. Hodges*, one month before Ireland's successful campaign. The kairotic moment for the popular vote on the marriage referendum could not have arrived without the shift in Ireland's national identity and the phronesis (practical wisdom) gained through previous marriage equality campaigns.

ENGAGEMENT AND EPIDEICTIC IN VOTE YES!

The No on Prop 8 movement in California differed from Ireland's marriage referendum in some significant ways: instead of being asked to vote *for* marriage equality, voters were being asked to vote *against* Proposition 8, and the diverse population of California does not resemble the relatively homogenous racial and ethnic population of Ireland. Finally, Irish law allows expatriates who have lived outside of Ireland for less than 18 months to participate in elections, provided they come back to their polling place in Ireland to cast their vote. Therefore, voter engagement in Ireland involved different IMC strategies and tactics. In this section, I will examine some of the main strategies of the Vote Yes! Campaign through Condit's epideictic functional pairs.

SINEAD'S HAND

Marriage Equality is a non-profit grassroots organization in Ireland working toward the legalization of same-sex marriage, founded in 2008. This group produced a long-form advertisement called "Sinead's Hand," which showed an earnest young man knocking on doors to ask if he can marry Sinead (a common female name in Ireland). At the beginning of the ad, the viewer is led to believe that this young man is asking Sinead's parents if he can marry their daughter; however, the ad goes on to show the young man in different areas of Ireland asking many people if he can marry Sinead, each time being met with a confused "yes." The man asks in both Irish and English, and with each question demonstrates the ludicrousness of having to ask every citizen of Ireland if he can marry the woman he wants to marry.

The video, produced in 2009, demonstrates Condit's epideictic functional pair of definition/understanding. Because defining the problem is essential for the audience, this video is associating the tradition of a young man asking for his beloved's hand in marriage from her parents with the notion that marriage equality in Ireland will come down to this – asking everyone in Ireland if they would consent for even one same-sex couple to be married. The ad utilizes the rhetorical figure of synecdoche, the part for the whole, where the young man is standing in for all of the LGBT community and the people he asks for permission represents all of Ireland. Using figures of speech such as synecdoche is common in both oratory and epideictic but also in advertising, according to Berger (2015). By defining the issue of marriage equality as an extension of a traditional approach to marriage, and by asking the voting public to see the various residents responding "yes" as extensions of themselves, this video provides understanding, through which "the troubled event will be made less confusing and threatening, providing a sense of comfort for the audience" (Condit 1985, 288). This video also contributes to setting the kairotic moment; the video, produced in 2009, helped to define the issue at stake for a marriage referendum in Ireland that would depend on a popular vote for success.

#HOMETOVOTE

One of the hallmarks of this election is the Irish law that allows emigrants abroad who have had residency in Ireland in the past 18 months to vote in national elections if they return home to their polling place to cast their votes (www.emigrantmanifesto.irish). Unlike the 123 other countries who allow citizens abroad to cast their votes, Ireland only allows for in-person voting and only in the previous 18 months of residency; even with Irish citizenship, emigrants cannot vote in Irish elections after 18 months abroad. According to the Emigrant Manifesto website, "Since the last election, according to the latest available CSO figures, the net exodus of Irish stands at 130,000 people, a minimum of up to 1,000 voters lost every fortnight. That's like telling the population of Mayo it cannot vote next year" (2015). Therefore, one of the challenges of the marriage referendum Vote Yes! campaign is to get eligible Irish voters abroad physically home to vote. In the weeks leading up to the vote, organizations like Get the Boat to Vote coordinated efforts to bring voters home to Ireland to vote. The Get the Boat to Vote referred to the Holyhead, Wales to Dublin ferry that has served as a main conduit of Irish to the UK and vice versa. Irish citizens living in London, Manchester, Liverpool, could use http://gettheboat2vote.com/ to find ferry schedules and prices and to coordinate travel with other Irish expatriates who would also be taking the train from London's Euston Station to Holyhead, Wales to catch the ferry to Dublin. As the website states, "We're calling on vote-eligible ex-pats to join us in making the journey home to vote yes and play our part in what we hope will be a massive step forward for equality in Ireland. . . . We're going to make the trip home and figure we might as well make an occasion of it" (2015). The website also has information on voter eligibility and pro-marriage referendum rhetoric.

The hashtag #hometovote emerged from the efforts of Irish abroad to return to Ireland to vote. People on their way back to Ireland tweeted photos of their transportation and the efforts they took to get #hometovote. The hashtag trended on Twitter the day of the referendum and became a news story itself; the photos of Irish men and women in front of a plane in Abu Dhabi, in a Bangkok hotel bar, on the Holyhead ferry, leaving the house in Berlin, collected around the hashtag, which was then reported on by traditional media outlets like *The Irish Times* and *The Guardian*. Many of the photos showed people wearing "Vote Yes!" stickers and carrying rainbow flags. Twitter user Kevin Beirne (@kevbeirne) took a photo of his room, decorated with rainbow flags and tie-dye sheets, tweeting "Came #hometovote all the way from London and found my mum had made some subtle changes to my room for me #VoteYes" (Kenny 2015). Another Twitter user, Ian McCafferty (@communalspoon) tweeted, "I'm coming back to @Ireland to vote in #MarRef. I'm coming back to help make history. I'm coming back for the future." (Kenny 2015).

This hashtag of #hometovote, organizing the responses of thousands of voters returning to Ireland to vote for the marriage referendum, performed the epideictic function of shaping/sharing community. According to Condit (1985), "Because humans are symbol-creators, they need forms of symbolic sharing. A sense of community is developed and maintained in large part through public speaking and hearing of the community heritage and identity." In this case, the shaping of the community comes from two overlapping sources: Irish expatriates who still love their home and want to participate in Ireland's future, and those to whom the issue of marriage equality is significant enough to warrant a time-consuming and expensive trip home to vote yes. In my review of the coverage of the vote, I did not see a single #hometovote No; the hashtag belonged to those who were supportive of the marriage referendum and who were prepared to demonstrate their support by going #hometovote.

Looking at the hashtagged tweets and the resulting coverage, one might think this was a well-oiled machine executing the plan to get voters home. However, the groundswell of tweets emerged as people realized others like them were returning to Ireland just to vote in the referendum. Although the deliberative discourse of the marriage referendum encouraged voters to vote yes, the epideictic rhetoric of the Get the Boat to Vote campaign and the hashtag #hometovote identified and created a community. This community was then reinforced through interpersonal relationships and communication—sharing a beer in an airport bar or taking the London train to Holyhead—but also virtually, where community could check Twitter and find common ground with others who may not be living in the same place but who shared, as Condit describes, common heritage and identity. In addition, this effort may not have worked in other countries; because of the significant amount of Irish living and working abroad and the relatively homogenous ethnic and religious makeup of Ireland, the common heritage and identity is even more pronounced; to replicate this moment in other countries would not recognize the kairos of this situation. Finally, those who were not eligible to vote or those who are descendants of 200 years of Irish immigration could also find common heritage and identity in seeing their ancestral home become a locus of social change and evolution. The shaping/sharing of community is an important function of epideictic rhetoric, as Condit describes: "The community renews its conception of itself and what is good by explaining what it has previously held to be good and by working through the relationships of those past values and beliefs to new situations . . . whenever change intrudes into the community's life, the epideictic speaker will be called forth by the community to help discover what the event means to the community, and what the community will come to be in the face of the new event" (1985, 289). In the case of #hometovote, the community determined that its conception of itself and what is good—Ireland as home—could change to officially reflect the more tolerant and inclusive society it has evolved into being.

POST-VOTE EFFORTS

As votes continued to roll in throughout the day, both sides held events to watch vote counting and hear results as they came in from every county. A video posted to YouTube by the GAZE LGBT International Film Festival Dublin shows a montage of the day following the vote, as 2000 people watched the vote results come in at Dublin Castle; with speeches, balloons, rainbow flags, the atmosphere resembled a party for the Yes side. One of the speakers at the event, featured early in the video, reminds the incoming crown at Dublin Castle that "you will be the face to the world of what's happening . . . there will be people all over the world here, and there will be people who don't agree with us here. We have to remember the respect and dignity we brought to this campaign, and we will make sure on the last day of this campaign, that this respect and dignity will be as real in this room as we made it in every single corner of our capital city" (Rodgers 2015). This speech and video illustrate the display/entertainment functions of epideictic rhetoric because of the eloquence of the speaker and also the creativity of the production. The inspiring background music of the video, the images of audience members crying, hugging, cheering, and the voiceovers of newscasters giving official vote tallies and announcing the marriage referendum has been passed add to the display of this video, entertaining the audience. However, Condit reminds us that functional pair is not just cheap entertainment: "The audience is 'entertained' by such speech in a most humane manner. They are allowed to stretch their daily experience into meanings more grand, sweet, noble, or delightful . . . the audience judges the fullness of the speaker's eloquence, because audiences rightfully take eloquence as a sign of leadership" (1985, 290-1). This video shows the possibilities of a future that was created by the audience who is watching and participating. It also shows the leadership of the Vote Yes side, who remind the audience that if a campaign for marriage equality is about dignity and respect, then that dignity and respect must be seen in winning and in losing, and will contribute to reforming the community around new possibilities for dignity and respect.

As for the Vote No side, they in turn responded with a dignity and respect. David Quinn, the leader of the Iona Institute, which organized much of the Vote No campaign, tweeted his concession after the vote: "Congratulations to the Yes side. Well done. #MarRef." Although a short tweet does not appear to have much power, the epideictic nature of this tweet was to reform community around a graceful loss and acknowledge a well-run campaign (Schiavenza 2015).

CONCLUSION

The Vote Yes campaign demonstrates the function of IMC as epideictic rhetoric and the importance of kairos to successful IMC efforts. The desired behavior of the Vote Yes campaign—voting in favor of the same-sex marriage referendum—was achieved through publics that participated in an ongoing interpretation of signs: what it means to be Irish, what it means to call Ireland "home," and what it means to participate in the future of their country. The timing and situation of the referendum relied on understanding the kairotic moment in both Ireland's history and learning from previous marriage equality efforts. In addition, the IMC employed in the Vote Yes campaign, including advertisements, events, social media campaigns, websites, videos, and symbols such as the rainbow pride flag and the Vote Yes! badge, served epideictic rhetorical functions to define and understand; to display and entertain, and to shape and share community. The possibility of ethical and effective IMC efforts increases with our understanding of the rhetorical nature of IMC and the formation of publics.

NOTE

1. For a more robust discussion of the Catholic Church and Ireland's national identity, please see White, Timothy J. (2007). "Catholicism and Nationalism in Ireland: From Fusion in the 19th Century to Separation in the 21st Century." *Westminster Papers in Communication and Culture*, Vol. 4(1):47-64.

REFERENCES

Aakhus, Mark. 2007. "Communication as Design." *Communication Monographs*. 74(12): 112-117.

Berger, Arthur Asa. 2015. *Ads, Fads, and Consumer Culture*. 5th ed. Lanham, MD: Rowman & Littlefield.

Botan, Carl H. and Francisco Soto. 1998. "A Semiotic Approach to the Internal Functioning of Publics: Implications for Strategic Communication and Public Relations." *Public Relations Review* 24(1): 21-44.

Christopher, A. J. 1997. "The Irish Divorce Referendum of 1995." *Geography, 82*, 79-81. http://search.proquest.com.liblink.uncw.edu/docview/194749410?accountid=14606

Condit, Celeste Michelle. 1985. "The Functions of Epideictic: the Boston Massacre Orations as Exemplar," *Communication Quarterly* 33(4): 284-298.

Coombs, W. Timothy and Sherry Holladay. 2012. "The Paracrisis: The Challenges Created by Publicly Managing Crisis Prevention." *Public Relations Review* 38: 408-15.

Cresci, Elena. 2015. "#hometovote: Irish abroad return to vote in gay marriage referendum."*The Guardian*. May 22, 2015. http://www.theguardian.com/world/2015/may/22/hometovote-irish-abroad-return-vote-twitter-gay-marriage-referendum

Emigrant Manifesto: A Voice for Irish Abroad. 2015. http://emigrantmanifesto.irish/. Accessed May 16, 2016.

Garrison, Jim. 2003. "Prophetic Epideictic Rhetoric: Poetic Education beyond Good and Evil." Educational Theory. 53(2): 221-241.

Get the Boat to Vote Website (2015). http://gettheboat2vote.com/ Accessed May 16, 2016.

Hanson, Wesley D. and George N. Dionisopoulos. 2012. "Eulogy Rhetoric as a Political Coping Mechanism: The Aftermath of Proposition 8." *Western Journal of Communication*. 76(1): 24-43.

Hogan, Fergus. 2010. "In Search of Forgiveness: Men and Abortion in Post-Catholic Ireland." *At The Interface / Probing The Boundaries* 66: 139-157. *Communication & Mass Media Complete*, EBSCO*host* (accessed May 18, 2016).

Kenny, Ciara. 2015. "The Journey #HometoVote: Selection of the Best Tweets." *The Irish Times*. May 25. 2015. http://www.irishtimes.com/life-and-style/generation-emigration/the-journey-hometovote-selection-of-the-best-tweets-1.2222250

Kitchen, Philip J. and De Pelsmacker, Patrick. 2004. *Integrated Marketing Communication: A Primer*. London: Routledge.

Mac Cormaic, Ruadhán. 2015."All you need to know about the marriage referendum" http://www.irishtimes.com/news/politics/marriage-referendum/all-you-need-to-know-about-the-marriage-referendum-1.2220103 May 21, 2015.

Marriage Equality. 2010. "Sinead's Hand Shortlisted in Better Together Awards." November 23, 2010. http://www.marriagequality.ie/news/2010/11/23/sineads-hand-shortlisted-in-better-together-awards/.

Oravec, Christine, "'Observation' in Aristotle's Theory of Epideictic," *Philosophy and Rhetoric* 9. no. 3(1976): 172.

Persuit, Jeanne M. 2013. *Social Media and Integrated Marketing Communication: A Rhetorical Approach*. Lanham, MD: Lexington Books.

——— and Deborah A. Brunson. 2015. "First Lady Brand the Epideictic Rhetoric of Michelle Obama." In *Michelle Obama: First Lady, American Rhetor*. Elizabeth J. Natalle and Jenni M. Simon, eds. Lanham, MD: Lexington Books.

Rodgers, Anna. 2015. "Making History – GAZE celebrates marriage equality vote in Ireland." YouTube video, 3:42, posted by GAZE International LGBT Film Festival Dublin, May 27, 2015, https://www.youtube.com/watch?v=9X_Xl6kCUUI.

Schiavenza, Matt. 2015. "'Well Done': The Legalization of Gay Marriage in Ireland." *The Atlantic*, May 23. http://www.theatlantic.com/international/archive/2015/05/ireland-gay-marriage/394052/

Sipiora, Phillip. 2002. "Introduction: the Ancient Concept of kairos." In *Rhetoric and kairos: Essays in History, Theory, and Praxis*. Phillip Sipiora and James S. Baumlin, Eds. Albany, NY: SUNY Press.

Torp, Simon. 2009. "Integrated communications: from one look to normative consistency." *Corporate Communications: An International Journal*. 14 (2), 190 – 206.

Twitchell, James B. 2004. Branded Nation: The Marketing of Megachurch, College Inc. and Museumworld. New York: Simon and Schuster.

White, Timothy J. 2007. "Catholicism and Nationalism in Ireland: From Fusion in the 19th Century to Separation in the 21st Century." *Westminster Papers in Communication and Culture*, Vol. 4(1):47-64.

SIX

Integrated Marketing Communication and Social Media

"Coordinated Management of Meaning" and Entrepreneurship

Cassandra Vinhateiro and Vernon E. Cronen

This chapter presents a study of a young entrepreneur who created a new business using integrated marketing communication (IMC) principles without any formal training in IMC. The study is based on the communication theory, Coordinated Management of Meaning (CMM). That theory, as extended here, can be used to show the interdependence of aesthetics, social media, and face–to–face talk within the umbrella of IMC principles. Included in this case study is a brief overview of CMM theory and its application in two specific episodes of communication. The study concludes with a discussion of how CMM can inform IMC and the ethical and personal implications of social media use for personal and professional branding.

This chapter is a case study of a young female entrepreneur, hereafter identified by the pseudonym "Raquel." She created a new business selling antiques and accessories at the site of a former flea market. Raquel was 22 years old at the time of this study. She worked consciously to produce a re-visioning and rebranding of the store, including new, different merchandise and new means of advertising. She stressed the use of social media and attention to the internal organization of the store. She was also attentive to creating a style of face-to-face communication that is consistent with other features of her marketing. She said that her youth obligated her to work hard at producing a professional image that is integrated with other aspects of her marketing efforts. Most IMC studies address larger scale businesses; this study presents a microcosm of IMC in action. Moreover, it illuminates the special problems and opportunities for a single entrepreneur of adhering to IMC principles in the age of social media. Her closely integrated sense of who she is and her now flourishing store is a continuing project. Raquel said it is inconceivable today to achieve the rebranding of self and store without the use of social media. We are particularly interested in Raquel's rebranding process because it requires close attention to social media use, aesthetic dimensions of communication, and face–to–face contact with customers. The store and Raquel's relationship to it are being created, as she said, by "her own artistic vision." This raises our curiosity about whether commitment to IMC has particular consequences for the single entrepreneur in the age of social media. This became an increasingly significant question as our work developed.

Some IMC studies are not theory-based (Torp, 2009). However, Persuit (2013) calls for exploration of how communication theory can inform IMC and for greater attention to social media in IMC research. Using CMM theory (Pearce & Cronen, 1980; Cronen & Pearce, 1981; Cronen & Chetro-Szivos, 2002; Cronen, Lang & Lang 2009) is consistent with IMC's focus on communication strategy, not attitudes (Schultz and Kitchens, 2000; Persuit, 2013; and Schultz et al. 1993). CMM is also appropriate because it focuses on multiple contexts including, as we will show, the salience of multiple contexts in a single encounter. By applying the theory to this case we also extend its application. CMM has most frequently been applied to situations of face–to–face communication. Here, it will be used to understand situations in which social media platforms play a crucial role. This extension is important because of the ubiquitous use of social media, especially by the Millennial generation. Of course, the use of social media is certainly not limited to any one age cohort. However, Raquel was very much aware that the use of particular platforms varies across generations. Raquel's emphasis on her "aesthetic vision" also required extension of CMM. Before introducing the main features of CMM theory, we need a short caveat to explain what we mean by "aesthetics." Interest in aesthetics has taken many directions, including efforts to define what is "beautiful," identify the faculty of "taste," explain the non-instrumental value of art, and many more (Schusterman, 2000). CMM takes none of these directions.

THE AESTHETIC DIMENSION OF COMMUNICATION: A SHORT CAVEAT

CMM is a theory in the tradition of American Philosophical Pragmatism. It follows Dewey's (1925, 1934) focus on the aesthetics of everyday life. All communication has both an instrumental and a consummatory [artistic] dimension. Experience comes from our human somatic experience of life in nature and within human community. The aesthetic dimension of experience refers to experience that has a unity of form, feeling, sound, and rhythm. Not all of these need to be unified at any one time for a consummatory moment. An aesthetic experience is a syndrome, not a fixed set of constituent parts.

Having a particular aesthetic experience is a learned ability to recognize a unity and the ability to respond to it. That means learning to have an aesthetic experience is also learning a set of skills. To appreciate a kind of music, for example, we must learn how to listen to it. Typically, we do not have language labels for kinds of aesthetic experiences as we do for labeling our emotions. That is the case with our young store owner. When asked if she had a word or phrase for the kind of feeling she wants her store to evoke, she said she could not think of a specific word or phrase. However, she said that when creating content, for example, she knew when the image she created fit the kind of image she wanted. She knew when a conversation had the kind of interactive feel that she highly valued. What has been said about aesthetics so far carries another implication. Objects and events have an aesthetic quality when they are experienced in public. Such experiences are social constructions, not strictly internal mental events. There can be no wholly private aesthetic, just as there cannot be an entirely private language. While all experience has an aesthetic dimension, not all experiences are particularly moving. These are situations in which elements of experience are not highly unified. Like all meaningful experiences, aesthetic experiences point into the future opening and closing possibilities. Suppose a group of civil engineers work together on a problem. Their discussions begin to take on a kind of sound and rhythm. There is growing enthusiasm and mutual respect. This makes continued team work desirable and the team may join together on other projects.

In his discussion of aesthetics, Dewey (1925; 1934) repeatedly uses the phrase "consummatory experience" and does so in in two ways. He sometimes used it for all aesthetic experience because all such experience has a unifying quality. He also used it for particularly powerful and clearly punctuated bits of experience that he calls having "an experience." In this restricted usage, a consummatory moment entails a powerful integration of hitherto discordant but important elements of experience. Because they integrate very important elements of experience, their consequentiality can be far reaching. In this study confusion will be avoided by reserving the phrase, "consummatory moment" for such powerful and discriminable events within the broader scope of aesthetic experience. In this study we stretch the idea of consummatory moments a little—applying the idea to situations that do not include highly discordant features of experience, but do bring harmony to elements that are fragile and require support.

In two prior CMM-based studies the aesthetic dimension has been a major focus of analysis. One was a study of a police department (Cronen & Chetro-Szivos, 2002). The second was a study of communication practices in the Acadian-American community (Chetro-Szivos, 2006). The first was limited to one kind of aesthetic experience, "consummatory moments." These moments are very important but they do not exhaust Dewey's position or fully comprehend the aesthetic dimension of everyday communication. The later study included the broad somatic feel of experience that permeates the Acadian experience of work, community, and religion, but it did not require analyzing the creation of "art objects." In neither of these studies, nor in others, do the special conditions of social media use play a significant role in the analysis. However, work in CMM has from its earliest years treated the technology of communication as inseparable from thought and content. In what follows the reader can observe and assess our effort to use CMM's basic model of communication to examine the unity of social media and aesthetics.

RESEARCH QUESTIONS

In this paper we address the following research questions:

RQ1: What does CMM offer to IMC?

- RQ1a: Can CMM illuminate the relationship of interpersonal communication and social media use for IMC practitioners?
- RQ 1b: Is CMM useful to explore the aesthetic dimension of communication for IMC practitioners?

RQ2: Does CMM identify unique problems for the single entrepreneur with an IMC perspective in the age of social media?

In the remainder of this chapter we first present a brief overview of the CMM heuristic model and the method of Circular Questions for gathering and organizing data. Next, we offer an account of the important emerging stories that the store owner, Raquel, brings to many of her conversations. These developing stories provide context for episodes of action. In the third section we present illustrative analyses of two episodes in which her stories are used, maintained, and developed. In the final section we return to the research questions and discuss further implications of the case study for IMC and for CMM theory.

THEORY AND METHOD

The theory Coordinated Management of Meaning has a view of meaning that comes from Dewey (1925), Wittgenstein (1953), and Bakhtin (1973). In CMM theory, the meaning of an utterance, behavior, or image is a co-construction. A person acts into an immediate physical situation including another person's prior act. The action one person takes sets conditions for making the next act coherent. Therefore, no action is entirely individual. The way we learn to think and feel is created in joint action. All experience is between people, not an intra-psychic phenomenon. Even if a person is behaving or reflecting with no one else present, their understanding of what they see, read or think is within contexts developed with others. Each of one's own ideas or behaviors also sets conditions for the next. You know the meaning when "you know how to go on" (Wittgenstein, 1953; Harre and Tissaw, 2005). In CMM, meaning is never finished because responsive action points into the future.

The CMM Diagram

The CMM diagram is used to suggest questions and organize data. Diagrams and partial diagrams are revised as new information is obtained by interview and observation. The diagrams are heuristic devices to help us understand how persons create experience together.

The Hierarchy of Stories

In CMM applications we describe experience as a hierarchically organized set of stories. There is no set list of stories and no universal organization. There are many ways that stories are organized for situated use. We highlight hierarchical organization for practical purposes. The hierarchy is a partial hypothesis about which story contains information another story needs to made sense. These contextual stories are not fixed. They evolve in the course of communication where they are created, developed, and/or changed. We think of experience as organized stories because a story has both detail and a temporal dimension, including a projection into the future. Beliefs are important but only as they have roles in stories. To illustrate, a participant in communication may at one moment be informed by stories about the organization in which she works, her identity, a particular relationship, and a story about the immediate episode in which she is engaged. These stories carry with them their own aesthetic possibilities. However, a particular aesthetic can only be achieved in joint action. Figure 6.1 is a hypothetical shorthand account of a person whose career story must be understood in light of his relationship to his boss. His identity story can be understood best in the context of his career. Finally, how he understands a particular ongoing episode depends on the other stories. These broader stories inform the three short stories that make up a speech act. For such a hypothetical employee the stories of who he is and his career would be highly threatened by a change in relationship to his boss.

The Three-Part Speech Act

CMM's account of a speech act includes 3 short stories within the hierarchy of contexts in figure 6.1. Here, CMM is consistent with the idea of Mead (1938). The three parts are: (1) A person's account of the immediate circumstances into which she or he is acting. Often, this is an interpretation of what another person says. (2) An actor's account of what he or she says she is doing in response. (3) A short account of what the actor desires or expects will happen next. All of these are interpretations and choices made within the broader contexts of figure 6.1. These interpretations may or may not be close to the other person's understanding.

The Interactive Diagram

CMM analysis usually (but not always) includes at least two persons in conversation. They are linked together as each takes account of what the other says and acts into that immediate condition as shown in figure 6.2. In the figure 6.2 hypothetical episode, the boss's utterance is interpreted by the employee as disrespect. The employee's act is meant, hopefully, to elicit guilt in the boss and get an apology, but he does not expect that. The boss interpreted what the employee says as irrelevant talk about the past and hopes that putting the employee in touch with present reality will induce him to resign. However, the boss does not actually expect that to happen. The employee only understood the comment as an insult. We used this model to interpret crucial moments in real episodes.

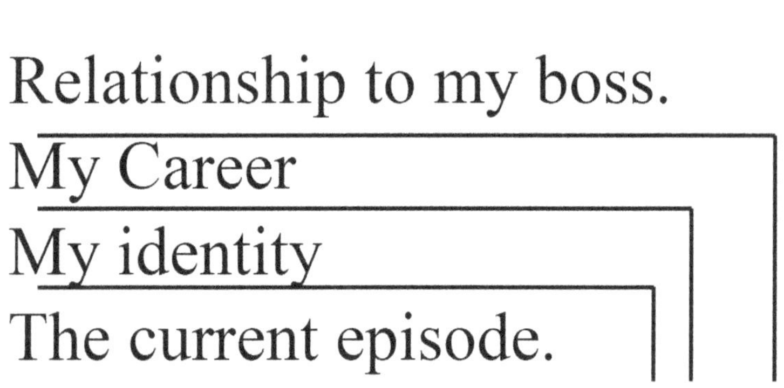

Figure 6.1. Example of a Hierarchical Arrangement of Four Stories. Note: Figure created by Cassandra Vinhateiro and Vernon E. Cronen

Exploring Connections in the Diagram

Using the CMM model we looked for the "logical forces" that connect elements of the model and assess their power. We looked for 5 such connections in each act.

1. Prefiguring Force: The degree to which contexts and interpretation of immediate circumstances constrain or open possibilities for interpretations, acts, and expectations.
2. Practical Force: The degree to which desire to get a particular response constrains or opens possibilities for interpretations, acts, and expectations.
3. Substantializing Force: How the process of acting affects contexts by using them in a new situation.
4. Reflexive Needs: How much a person needs a kind of response from another to develop or maintain contextualizing stories.
5. Reflexive Effects: How the responses one understands from the other sustain, develop, or change stories.

The cumulative effect of the logical forces created constraints and affordances for action. We are interested in whether a behavior or interpreta-

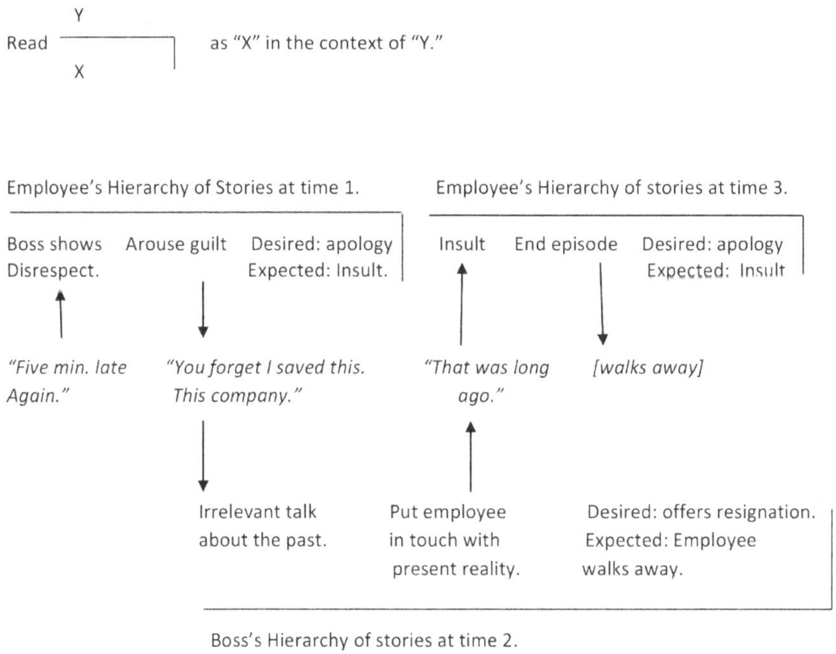

Figure 6.2. CMM interactive Diagram of a Hypothetical Episode. Note: Figure created by Cassandra Vinhateiro and Vernon E. Cronen

tion is constrained by the contexts as used. We are also interested in whether connections are conscious, that is, whether a person can report the connections to themselves or to another.

Person Position

In CMM work we also considered "person position" for each overt act and interpretation. Person position includes for whom a social actor speaks (themselves, a business, their community, etc.). It also includes whether a person is speaking or listening from a fully immersed first- or second-person position or a more removed, reflective third-person position.

Data Collection

To obtain the data, we used a method of inquiry called Circular Questions developed by the Milan Associates (Palazzoli, Boscolo, Cecchin & Prata, 1975) adapted to CMM (Cronen, Lang & Lang, 2014).[1] The interview was conducted on April 15, 2015, by the authors acting as co-inquirers. The interview lasted about one hour and thirty minutes and was conducted at the home of the second author. The first author was a friend of the interviewee, although they had not been in frequent contact for over two months. The second author had not met the interviewee prior to the interview. Permission for the interview was obtained five days prior. The interview was recorded with the interviewee's permission.

CASE BACKGROUND AND RAQUEL'S CONTEXTUAL STORIES

Two years before the interview Raquel left the community college to which she transferred from a four-year university. Her intention had been to transfer again to a four-year university. While attending community college she had worked part-time at a small second hand store. Raquel came to enjoy learning about and working in the business more than she enjoyed formal education. She enjoyed going to antique stores with her mother and looking at one-of-a-kind items since was a young girl. When the business at which she worked was put up for sale, Raquel contacted her parents who helped her to buy the business. The business was located in a small town on the outskirts of a larger city of about 100,000 inhabitants in the southeastern United States. With the financial backing of her parents, and only about a year of experience in the business, she became manager, marketer, sales person, and owner. Guided by CMM theory, we explored the crucial stories she has about her life as a young entrepreneur. From our interview data we identified five important stories:

Intertwined Stories: Raquel's Self, Store, and Mother-Daughter Relationship

Typically, our data allows us to distinguish between stories of personal identity, family relationships, and the business in which that person works. These stories are usually related, but distinguishable. Most frequently, someone's identity story has elements in it that are necessary to understand the story of the business. For example, an identity story might have been the higher order for understanding how to be an entrepreneur and run this particular business. In this case we think making a clear distinction between Raquel's story of the business and who she is would obscure the data. They have become one intertwined, very high-level story.

Raquel at a Crossroad: Becoming an Entrepreneur

We asked time-oriented questions about how she came to be a store owner. She said that two years ago she was "at a crossroads." She said she had "zero plans for where my life was going." She did enjoy her part-time job at a local second-hand store. Like her personal life she said the store was in "[r]eally bad shape." When the store was put up for sale she decided to buy it with some financial help from her family. Realizing what a big undertaking it was, she dropped out of school. Raquel said it was "[n]othing more than a leap of faith . . . sounds cheesy to say, but I always go with my heart. I really get passionate about something. . . . Fortunately, it worked out." Raquel said she started out with just a general idea. She was nineteen years old when she purchased the business. She discussed a future in which the store may move to a larger city and after that perhaps a second location.

The Challenges of Youth

This was a major theme in the interview. At many points Raquel referred to her age as a problem. Asked about "the most difficult obstacles she had to overcome," she said, "managing the expectations of others." When asked "in what specific situations was managing expectations of others an obstacle" she discussed the problems of being taken seriously by customers and by the vendors with whom she worked. She looked young and obviously had little experience. "Being young," said Raquel, "hinders what other people think you are capable of doing, and prevents them from taking you seriously."

We asked if youth gave her any advantages. She answered that it gives her a "dual perspective." She and her mother shared an interest in antiques and hand-made items since her childhood. They went to antique shops and secondhand stores together. So "I know what someone my age wants and what someone my mother's age wants." At many points in the interview Raquel referred to her mother and their trips to secondhand and antique stores.

The Transformation of Raquel

Raquel said, "I am nothing like who I was two years ago." She described the effort she makes to be respected. In IMC terms, she strived to integrate her ways of communicating with the identity of her new store:

> It is the small things, ya know. The average person has normal expectations and can very casually act themselves. [I must be careful about] little things, speech habits , not saying "like" all of the time. Looking really nice. I have to stretch a little bit to not only make myself comfortable but, but to make others comfortable around me.

The vendors with whom she works are typically about thirty-five to forty-five years old. Raquel dropped two vendors with whom she had continuing relationships. To do so she learned how take such actions, "[b]eing decisive without creating a reputation as insensitive." Responding to our questions about other ways she is different now, Raquel included:

"I changed the way I talk to my friends."
"The things that are important to me are very different now."
"I get up in the morning on time."
"What I get all depends on me."
"Always being on time."

Raquel summed up her situation and said, "I am a better person now." Raquel expects to continue maturing and becoming a well-respected business person.

Constant Self-Awareness

Raquel puts great stress on being "[s]elf-aware, extremely self-aware." Asked how she would describe herself now, her immediate response was, "[s]elf-aware, very self-aware." Indeed, she said, "It would be better if everyone was more self-aware." But she also said, "it's hard sometimes. I am so young."

Personal Continuities

There are, of course, important elements of continuity Raquel recognized in her life. Raquel described herself as always being "a really visual person." She remembered how, as a child, she enjoyed making scrapbooks and collages. She said she has, "an eye for what looks right." Her interest in antiques and one-of-a-kind second hand things was also part of her experiences with her mother. Since she was a young child she liked to look at catalogues and still gains inspiration from them. "If it looks great, I really want to have that. I am a visual person, hands on."

The Transformation of Self and Store

About one year after taking over the business, Raquel rebranded the store and herself. The store's new name was carefully chosen to show the change from a "flea market look," to a more "sophisticated business." The building itself is not attractive. It is not an old mansion, just a 10,000-square-foot metal building; In coping with what changed, she made sure that the merchandise was attractive and the store was so organized that the building did not distract. She has been very successful. Her store changed from a marginal business just surviving to a thriving business. A typical sale used to be about five dollars. Now, it's fifty dollars.

Reflecting on how Raquel presented herself aesthetically during the interview, she was professionally dressed, seemed approachable, and not stern, rigid, or tense. She was eager to tell her story with an engaging style. When she began to talk about dealing with vendors her demeanor changed. She became more upright and had a more authoritative tone of voice. We were struck by the fact that all of the personal transformations Raquel made were in response to her new position as the store owner. The store is an extension of her and she is an extension of the store.

Raquel's Story About Her Relationship with Her Mother

The kind of entrepreneur Raquel's becoming makes her sense of being her mother's daughter more and more salient. She frequently refers back to times they used to shop together for secondhand treasures. Her mother was highly pleased with what Raquel was doing and very supportive of her. As we will explain later, Raquel saw much of her mother in the kind of older customer she wanted to attract. Raquel expects that in the future her relationship with her mother will continue to be strong as her career is based on a common interest. However, as we will show later, this story is threatened by her concern for managing her identity in the age of social media.

Raquel's Story About Her Customers

Raquel said at one point, "I am my ideal customer. If I see something I like and I want to have it, I will get it for the store." At another time she said that her mother was her ideal customer. This was no contradiction. She developed her aesthetic sense with her mother and referred to her often. She purchased an item for the store that she believed her mother would like. Raquel was making a major effort to attract more customers her mother's age because they have more financial resources. It was evident how the higher-level context of relationship to her mother informed Raquel's story about the kind of older customer she wanted.

Raquel also wanted to attract customers who shared a love for interesting, one-of-a-kind items, similarly to her and her mother. Such customers, like herself, would be "[i]nterested in where an item came from and who made it." An ideal customer would be one who comes back and has a story to tell about having the item in her home, how it is used, and how a guest commented on it. The stories need not be greatly significant. The point is having a story to tell and sharing it with Raquel. Raquel hoped to attract more such customers who will enjoy the experience at the store and tell others about it.

Raquel's Story About Social Media

Raquel recognized the importance of social media. She was also aware that social media made it very difficult to separate herself from the store and nearly impossible to have a life outside the store.

Raquel said, "Nothing is as effective as social media and you don't have to play around with it long to realize it. " It is crucial to have, "A constant on-line presence." Instagram allows for the rapid addition of an item to a page so that a customer can see the item and come right to the store before another person purchases it. "Everything has to be really fast." She had a web page but did away with it. Instagram allowed her to create a catalogue of inventory in real time. "Customers want to know what you have and how much it is, they want to see a great picture of it and then they want to come in and get it." The store has one-of-a-kind items, so there is a sense of urgency when a prospective customer sees something they like. Instagram was the platform that she said works best for creating the aesthetic she wanted to present. She can stage an item, take a picture of it on her phone, and use the photo editing features on the phone and on Instagram to create a great picture. She posts pictures on her Instagram page to Facebook. Facebook reaches an older, larger, and wealthier audience. Most of her customers are reached by Facebook.

There was a negative side to social media presence for Raquel. We asked Raquel how she kept a boundary between her business life and her social life. She said, "It's hard." This was a phrase she repeated. Her problem was not limited to having a posting on social media meant for one person being sent to others without her knowledge. Raquel was highly aware that anything she said face–to–face can be rapidly spread by social media. When that happens something she said can appear in a context she cannot control and the changed context can change the meaning. Boyd (2014) calls this the problem of "collapsing contexts." Because she is the face of the store, she feels she must be constantly aware that all of her own actions must be consistent with what IMC calls the "branding." She avoids presenting herself in a way that undermines the image she wants to present. This is especially important to her, she said, "Because of my age." Her self-monitoring extends to all of her relationships. She said she must constantly monitor what she says face–to–face at a family dinner, to her friends, and to her boyfriend. As a result, Raquel goes to her family home less frequently and has less contact with her mother and other family members. She has little time for her boyfriend and must be careful what she says to him. Listening to Raquel's account of self-awareness and constant self-monitoring, we are keenly aware of how vulnerable she thinks her stories are.

STORIES IN ACTION: TWO EPISODES

Having insight into someone's stories is important. However, stories are created in joint action and are developed, changed, and amplified in joint action. Raquel was well aware of that so she monitored carefully how she responded in all conversations. In this part of our paper we show how Raquel's stories are used and developed in two episodes. Both of the episodes are related to the aesthetic dimension of communication. The first episode includes what Dewey (1934) calls a consummatory moment. It explores a conversation that Raquel identified as one of the kind that gives her "the most joy." The second is selected because it offers a theory-based account of constructing an art object. This entails communication without a live respondent.

Episode 1: A Consummatory Moment in Experience: Making More Than a Sale

In Raquel's stories about her customers, she emphasized episodes in her store in which stories were exchanged about a purchased item. The story itself need not be remarkable. What was important to Raquel was to join in telling a story about the item that makes the episode more than just a simple business transaction. This kind of episode has an aesthetic feel that she desired and that feeling is intrinsic to the episode going as she wanted: Raquel and her older customer created a conversation about where the item came from, who made it, how Raquel came to have it, how the customer will use it, and what they both liked about it. Aesthetically, this episode has much of the visceral feel Raquel remembered from many episodes talking to her mother about an item they came across together years ago in a secondhand store. This episode also has the comfortable feeling of being competent and respected while conversing with this older customer.

Nearing the end of the episode, Raquel experienced a "moment of joy" that Dewey called "a consummatory moment." In Dewey's words, that kind of moment was identifiable as "an experience." It a part of the episode having a beginning and an end. In Bateson's (1972, 1979) terminology, the moment of joy is a punctuation within the episode. A second feature of a consummatory moment is that it harmonizes various stories. In this case the stories are not discordant, but they are very much in-process, vulnerable, and vital to her. Their integration means that the vulnerability of the highest level context creates vulnerability for all. Their harmony needs reconfirmation and development for this young entrepreneur and her new store. Raquel must show in this episode that she is knowledgeable, mature, and shares the older customer's interests and can talk in a way they both find comfortable. In other words, her self-presentation must be integrated with the look of the store, the merchandise, and the social media posting. The harmony she needs to create is not simply a matter of logical fit. It is deeply felt. An important feature of a consummatory moment is that the harmony points into the future, creating and possibly closing opportunities (Dewey,1925). Here, the future is hopefully one in which Raquel and the store are successful. The episode is one in which the older customer acted very much like her mother. That mother-daughter relationship is maintained and harmonized with other stories in that consummatory moment. For the more immediate future, the customer may return and will tell her friends about the store and Raquel.

Now, we look at this episode in detail using the CMM heuristic to organize our data. The diagram in figure 6.3 is a "systemic hypothesis" that can be modified by later research. A middle-aged customer came into the store and told Raquel that she was interested in buying a cabinet Raquel posted on Instagram and Facebook earlier that day. After examining the cabinet the customer came to the store counter and told Raquel that she wanted to buy it. She handed Raquel her credit card and the episode began like this:

Customer:	"I just love this cabinet. I am so happy it is still here. I saw it on Facebook. [Tentatively] Do you know where it came from?
Raquel:	"Yes. It came from a nineteenth century mansion in rural Indiana."
Customer:	[Excited] "Do you know who made it? I have never seen one like it."
Raquel:	" [feeling a moment of joy]. Yes, I do. It was made by. . . ."

Hierarchy of Contexts

In figure 6.3 the fragment of dialogue appears in italics running horizontally between the context indicators for Raquel and for the customer.

Raquel's contexts are above and the customer's below. We will start with Raquel's contexts at the top. (See figure 6.3.) As Raquel joined in the conversation, her highest context is her intertwined story of the store and who she is. In figure 6.3 we refer to this highest context by the shorthand reference: "Evolving Store—Identity Story." The next level of context is Raquel's story about her relationship to her mother and then in descending order, stories about ideal customers, this customer, choice of media platform, and the emerging episode. The episode evolved with their conversation in a way Raquel desired it to. It moves into the right aesthetic feel. It involved the content and embodied responsiveness that Raquel wanted. It did not start that way, but it rapidly evolved as Raquel and the customer created both the episodic content and ambiance in responsive joint action.

Speech Acts

Next consider the particular speech acts. Look at Raquel's "short stories" in figure 6.3. These data are the result of taking Raquel through the conversation, asking how she interpreted each act, her own and those of the customer. Raquel interpreted the customer's first question and tentative style as both a request for information and a test of her competence. In Raquel's responsive act she said she provided information, showed her knowledge, interest, and maturity. The response Raquel desired is for the customer to show confidence in her by asking more about the cabinet and no longer being tentative. The customer's next act was, according to Raquel, a show of confidence in her knowledge as much as it was a request for more information.

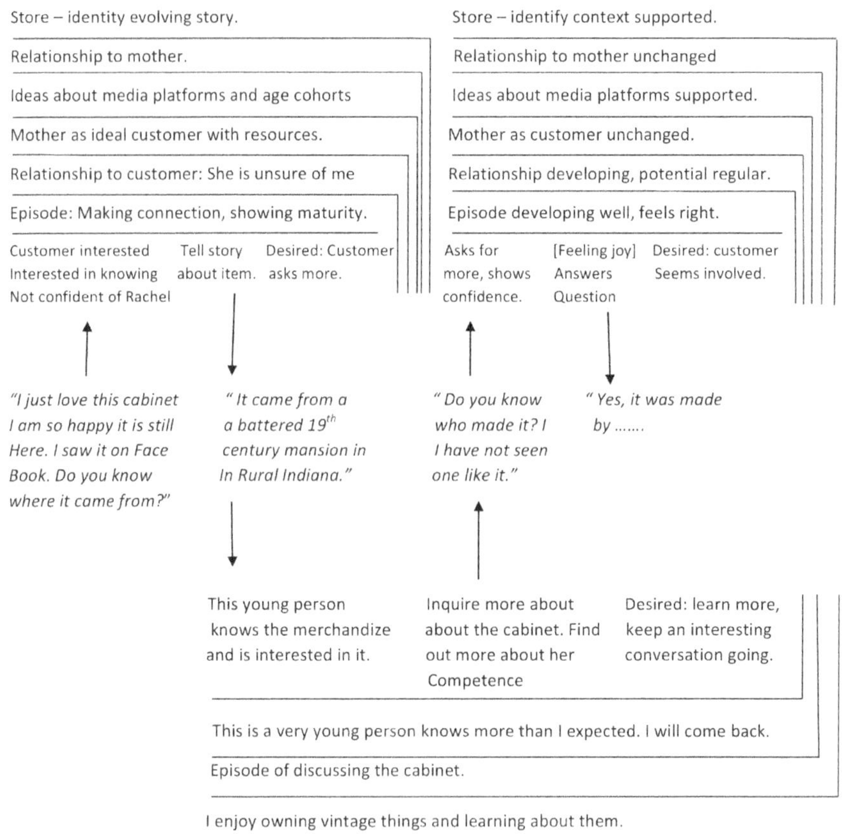

Figure 6.3. A Consummatory Moment In A Sales Episode. Note: Figure created by Cassandra Vinhateiro and Vernon E. Cronen

In a study devoted to assessing the success or failure of a sales person's participation, we wanted to interview the customer as well and examine more closely their interpretations, stories, and logical forces. Here we are inferring them from what the customer said as shown in figure 6.3.

Logical Forces

To more fully explain how the theory points us to connections, we need to describe what is happening with reference to the logical forces described earlier. Raquel's stories about herself, the store, ideal customers, this customer, and the episode at each moment "prefigured" Raquel's interpretations of the customer's immediate and desired future acts. She listened for signs that the customer had or did not have the right image of her. These connections strongly obligated the kinds of responses Raquel gave and could not give. They prohibited showing disinterest, appearing uninformed, being tentative or showing immaturity. Raquel said she has worked diligently to "eliminate using the word 'like' so much." In her language choices it is obligatory for her to act so that she is taken seriously as someone who shares the customer's passion for the item by responding with information in a way that shows her enthusiasm. These contexts, particularly the "Identity-Store" context, prefigure the aesthetics dimension of her responses as well as their instrumental dimension. Raquel's responses were strategic. They strongly articulated to the kinds of responses she wanted to hear. This is what in CMM we call "Practical Force."

Raquel's story of herself and the store are vulnerable stories, therefore there was a strong "reflexive need" to sustain them. The customer's responses reflexively supported the development of Raquel's still vulnerable stories, especially the highest level one. That is the "reflexive effect." Raquel felt support for the evolution of her own and her store's identity. In addition, the responses supported Raquel's stories about customers and the way she hopes the episode will develop. Raquel's response to the customer's second comment provided two things. It answered the next question and, in doing so, facilitated Raquel having that "joyous [consummatory] moment." Notice that Raquel cannot have this experience unless her postings attract customers like this whose actions and responses reflexively confirm and develop important stories. The fact that this middle-aged customer learned about the store and the cabinet from Facebook supports Raquel's ideas about media platforms. It is probably the fact that responses support a vulnerable and very high-level story that facilitated the consummatory moment. As shown in figure 6.3 reflexive effects from what the customer says also facilitated Raquel's developing a story about this particular customer. The middle-aged woman may now be a future customer and store promoter as well as a pleasant conversation partner in the future.

Responding to each new customer and situation developed Raquel's abilities for participating in episodes like this. Her abilities developed as she responded to new customers. Raquel also sees herself as still developing her abilities. No two customers and no two conversations will be exactly the same. The more Raquel deals with customers, the better equipped she will be for the next situation. She learns and develops her stories in the course of using them. This is "substantializing force."

Person Position

Raquel reiterated at several points in the interview that she has learned to be "self-aware" during almost every episode. She monitored herself from a third-person position. However, to feel the aesthetic experience, she must at moments take a first- or second-person position being fully immersed in what is going on. The movement from one position to another is a crucial skill for aesthetic experience.

Consummatory Moments and the Future

Like all events in the process of communication these moments have the quality of pointing into the future. They are distinguished from emotional experience by their lack of a clear linguistic label and by the power and scope of their consequences. In this case that future is the continuing path of development for Raquel as an entrepreneur, as an individual, and as her mother's daughter. She does this with increasing self-confidence and increasing ability to create more such moments of joy. Without these consummatory moments her work might become a regimen that is too difficult to bear.

Joint Action Focus

The customer was a necessary part of this episode. Without advertising that reaches and attracts customers who share her interest in these items and can afford them, such episodes could not happen and no support for Raquel's still fragile stories would be provided. Notice that the customer's first hesitant comment containing a question creates a space for Raquel to show who she is. The aesthetic dimension of the customer's next response facilitated Raquel responding in an enthusiastic way. If the customer asked nothing, it would be harder for Raquel to respond as she does in the style she used. Of course, the customer's responses were facilitated by what Raquel said and by the contexts the customer brings to a moment of conversation. The customer's story about Raquel and the store seem to develop in the course of the conversation.

We could do an equally detailed analysis of the customer and what the customer brings to the conversation by interviewing her too. It is inferred from the customer's change in tone and continuing inquiry that her story about Raquel is changing as she hears Raquel's enthusiasm and knowledgeable responses. However, our purposes are served by the partial analysis we have presented, focusing, as it does, on Raquel.

Forms of Life

From a CMM perspective it may be important to consider multiple episodes. Sequences of episodes are what Wittgenstein (1953) called a "form of life." Raquel told us about a moment of joy when on one Saturday morning she looked out her store window and saw her very large parking lot filled with cars. Raquel told this story with excitement and enthusiasm. She called her brother and sent a picture to him on her phone, "All these people taking time out of their Saturday mornings to come to my store!"

Episode 2: Creating Material for Social Media: The Artist and the Art Object

We included this episode to illustrate how CMM can be used to understand the creation of an art object when there is no human respondent. Dewey (1934) described creating a painting or a sculpture as a process much like any other instance of communication.

The artist acted out of a context that guides their actions and responses. These contexts may include a mental picture of the finished work, a desire to please a patron, being consistent with the product branding, identity as a great artist, and so on. Each act such as a paint brush stroke, a cut with a chisel, or a move on a computer screen takes into account the larger contexts and the mark just made. Together with the larger contexts, it creates conditions for the next act (prefiguring forces). Each move is made to facilitate the next (practical force). Each move in the artistic creation needs to facilitate the development of the object (reflexive needs). Of course, it can either develop the original plan or give the artist a wholly new vision of what to create (reflexive effects). The artist's skill developed as she worked out of and into these contexts (substantializing effects). The artist may also take a step back to look at the developing work or choose to view it from a different angle (person position).

Raquel Constructs an Art Object

Raquel had a new item to sell, a bureau. She knew that in her business success depends on rapid turnover, so she acted quickly to add a picture of it to her Instagram page and then posted it to Facebook. The following is a typical episode in which she crafted the addition to the Instagram page (see figure 6.4). She used her phone to take a picture of the cabinet. How she managed the photo before posting is influenced first by her broader contexts of experience.

The highest level of context included the integrated stories about her own and the store's identity (the brand). Also important is her story about ideal customers, who they are and what they would like. That story contained some strong prohibitions (logical force) on what can be shown. Concerned about her age, she will not take a photo that has her own image in it and her own image is absent in all previous postings. Concerned about the look of the store, her photos will show as little of the inside of the store as possible, and no image of the outside of the store. On the constructive side, Raquel brings to the moment of posting her aesthetic sense, including her self-description as an artistic person. That sensitivity is part of who she is and what the store is. Raquel did not have a name for the aesthetic she seeks, but that is typical of aesthetic experience. Aesthetic experience is powerful but largely ineffable. The desired aesthetic must be shown more than said. Raquel understood what fits her aesthetic and what does not.

A second level of context, subordinate to the highest one, is Raquel's sense of her customers. Recall that for her, she and her mother are the ideal customers and they share an aesthetic vision. How will the photo look to them? How would her mother respond to it? Someone looking for a mass-produced item such as could be found at Target would not be attracted to the page Raquel is creating for this item.

Raquel had posted a photo many times before. She knew the order of action (the episode) with which to create the posting. These three levels of context together informed Raquel's choice of Instagram as the media platform on which she will create the image. Choosing Instagram is a crucial part of the creative episode, just as a painter's choice of oils or water colors are intrinsic to his or her creative action. In our account of Raquel's story about social media we quoted Raquel as saying that in the act of creating the image she has a feeling of power; she can create the image of the store.

Like a painter, Raquel tried different ways to sight the camera and manage the image. Her aesthetic sense guided the way she took and managed the photo of the new bureau. When she took the picture she chose the position of the cabinet and the angle of the camera. Using Instagram she has many options to choose, including lighting and cropping. The options are why she uses Instagram. Instagram is intrinsic to the kind of episode she wanted to create. It is no mere channel for moving an inner idea to an action. There could be no such episode without Instagram and her phone. Raquel's mental images of the finished product are inseparable from her experiences with Instagram, Facebook, and her phone.

Each time she looks at the image in her camera and makes a change she does so in the light of the broad contexts, how the image presently looks, what she will do, and how the image will change in response to each of her actions. A moment from this episode can be diagrammed as in figure 6.4.

SUMMARY AND IMPLICATIONS

Our first general research question (RQ1) was, "What does CMM offer to IMC?" An IMC marketing plan sometimes involves representatives of an organization engaging in face–to–face conversation with clients or customers. CMM offers a way to analyze conversations in a way that explores the multiple stories that persons create and use in conversations. Such case studies can show where and how such conversations succeed

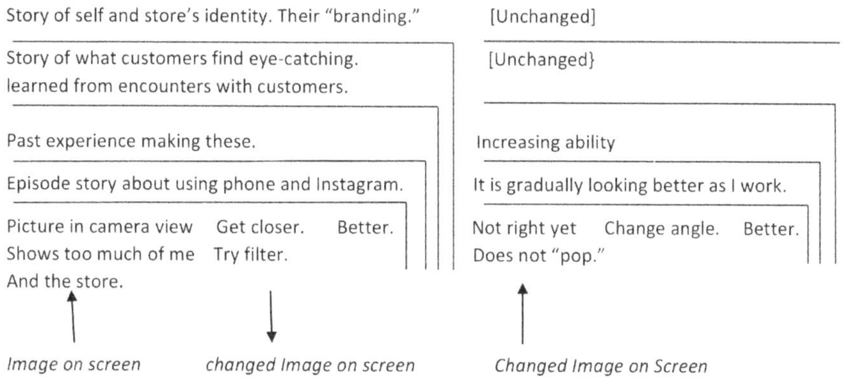

Figure 6.4. Creating a Artistic image as Interaction. Note: Figure created by Cassandra Vinhateiro and Vernon E. Cronen

or fail. In CMM-based work the meaning of a brand and other aspects of the sales message are co-constructions not fully under the control of any one participant. This provides a stronger focus on the co-participation of marketers and customers in the construction of meaning called for by Finne & Gronroos (2009). The hierarchical feature of CMM invites the exploration of what stories customers may have that lead to a particular understanding of what the representatives say. It is a tool for asking whether there are high-level stories that must change before stories about a product or business can change. It also directs us to explore the processes of communication that perpetuate those stories. CMM case analyses can supplement the more general findings of survey data to assess the effectiveness of an IMC plan and can also be used to develop the plan. Within an organization the CMM approach can be used to explore what stories employees have that inhibit their willingness to come "on board" with the IMC plan.

CMM is not limited in application to interpersonal situations. In an earlier study, Cronen (2004) showed how CMM can be used to study persons watching television. It is similar to examining how Raquel created an art object, responding to something that does not talk back.

Whatever the media, whether the focus is inside the organization or outside it, CMM directs attention to the future. For example, in creating a media campaign ask what stories would you hope viewers will tell about the product after viewing advertising material? How would we want the story to be different? To whom would they tell it? How will the change in context affect the next exposure?

CMM includes the idea of "substantializing force" which, along with "reflexive effects" directs attention to how the people responsible for creating the IMC plan are changed by the experience. In our case study the process of creating social media content involved change in the producer herself. In classroom teaching of IMC this learning is stressed as part of the educational process. However, outside of the classroom it is also important to consider how engagement in the creation of an IMC campaign functions to foster learning in the organization (Senge, 1990). Is the process of keeping everyone "onboard" the IMC plan promoting what Thorstein Veblen (1914) called, "Trained Incapacity," or does the process promote an openness to learning beyond the techniques involved in a particular campaign?

RQ1a was, "Can CMM illuminate the relationship of interpersonal communication and social media use for IMC practitioners?" The ability of CMM to do this is illustrated in both case studies. Social media can attract people to face–to–face communication as shown in Case Study 1) Ideas promoted on social media can become contexts for face–to–face talk. Of course, one–on–one communication is carried on using social media all the time. The adaptation needed is to take into account the unique features and norms of particular media platforms and how they enter into the conduct of an episode.

RQ1b was, "Is CMM useful to explore the aesthetic dimension of communication for IMC practitioners? We have demonstrated how this is done in both case studies. No one need tell marketing professionals that the aesthetic dimension of communication is important. In this paper we showed how important it can be to create consummatory moments in experience. In case study 1 we emphasized their importance for the sellers, however, we could have focused on the buyer by inquiring into the aesthetics of her conversations with friends about her purchases. Did she have some "consummatory moments" when she showed her purchase to friends? Are these moments important to her so that she will come back to the store that sold her the object? Clearly some ads do show viewers how neighbors may react when they see the new car and how they themselves may feel when they see that reaction. Concern for aesthetics and for the promotion of creativity are related. If members of an organization find work boring and repetitive, they are not engaged in stimulating, creative work. As Dewey (1925) once said, the enemy of art is not science or technology, it is the humdrum.

There is much encouragement for young people as individuals to strike out on their own as entrepreneurs. RQ2 was, "Does CMM identify any unique problems for the single entrepreneur with an IMC perspective in the age of social media? For our young entrepreneur, surely it does. When one person is the integrated face of the organization, her or his reputation and image are vulnerable to the spread of unwanted text, pictures, and so on. We worry about whether Raquel's concern for collapsing contexts—loss of control of where words and images will go—is taking the richness and joy out of life, costing her many important kinds of relationships. Hopefully, over time, she will have sufficient confidence in the reputation of her store, herself, and their image so that a single problematic tweet or image will not be a catastrophe for her. Perhaps, over time, her new style will become second nature to her so she will need less self-monitoring. At the time of this study, however, in Raquel' own words, "it's hard."[2]

NOTES

1. An full explanation of the interview method we use is beyond the scope of this paper. However, it is available elsewhere. (See Cronen, Lang & Lang; 2014.). Circular questions are so named because they make connections among people and among their stories and acts. The user takes a stance of curiosity. In addition to generating data for CMM systemic hypotheses, these questions are used to reframe actions and thereby open spaces for creative change. For example, suppose an organization member and her colleague gets into an argument over how to develop an IMC plan. Someone using Circular Questions might try to change the negative stories they use by reframing aggressive acts of mutual criticism in the negative stories. One kind of reframing might be to describe the intensity of the disagreement as an expression of how much they both care about making a good decision. Future-oriented questions might include, "If this argument continues for a week, how will that affect the company and yourselves?" The diagrams help us identify where to focus reframing efforts. With Circular Questions the goal is making new connections, not finding out who is right and who is wrong. If a better pattern of conversation is created, the question of who is right becomes irrelevant.

2. As a joke we discussed with our colleagues the possibility that we had discovered a new "mental disorder" to which we gave the Latin name, "Ruentis Terroris Contextibus" (terror of collapsing contexts). Later we discovered anecdotally that Raquel is not the only person tightly limiting their conversation because they fear collapsing contexts. Sherry Turkel (2015) like Boyd (2014) reports a concern among many users of social media about how their social media messages may be disseminated, leading to a reluctance to communicate. Our work suggests an extension of this idea to include face-to-face communication because that too can be reported by others via social media.

REFERENCES

Bakhtin, Mikhail. 1973. *Marxism and the Philosophy of Language*. New York: Seminar Press.

Bateson, Gregory. 1979. *Mind and Nature: A Necessary Unity*. New York: Bantam

Bateson, Gregory. 1972. *Steps To An Ecology of Mind*. New York: Ballantine.

Boyd, Danah. 2014. *It's Complicated: The Social Lives of Networked Teens*. New Haven: Yale.

Chetro-Szivos, John. 2006. *Talking Acadian: Communication, Work and culture*. New York: YBK.

Cronen, Vernon. 1995. Coordinated Management of Meaning: The Consequentiality of Communication and the Recapturing of Experience. In S.. Sigman, Ed., *The Consequentiality of Communication*, New York: Lawrence Erlbaum, pp. 17-66.

Cronen, Vernon. 2004. Something Old, Something New: CMM and Mass Communication. *Human Systems*. 15, 165-178.

Cronen Vernon. & Pearce, W. Barnett. (1981) Logical Force: A New Concept of Necessity In Communication Theory. *Communication*. 6, 5-68.

.ronen, Vernon & Chetro-Szivos, John. (2002) Pragmatism as a way of inquiring with special reference of a theory of communication and the general form of social theory. In David K. Perry (Ed.) *American Pragmatism and Communication Research*. New Jersey: Erlbaum.
Cronen, Vernon, Lang. Peter. & Lang, S. (2014) Circular Questions and Coordinated Management of Meaning. *Human Systems* . 2014, 7-34.
Cronen, Vernon. & Chetro Szivos, John. (2002) Consummatory Moments in Organizational Life. In C. Dalgaar, T. Meisner, & K. Voetmann (Eds.) *Forvandling* . Copenhagen: Danish University Press.
Dewey, John. (1938) *Experience and Education*. New York: Collier.
Dewey, John. (1934) *Art as Experience*. New York: Minton Balsh.
Dewey, John. (1925) *Experience and Nature*. Chicago: Open Court.
Finne, Åke & Grönroos, Christian. 2009. Rethinking Marketing Comunication: From Integrated Marketing Communication to Relationship Communication, *Journal of Marketing Communications*. 15: 179 – 195.
Garmany, Laura. (2014) Grunts 'n Groans. Unpublished paper, Communications Studies Department, UNCW
Harrre, Rom and Tissaw, Michael A. (2005) *Wittgenstein and psychology: A Practical Guide*. Burlington, VT: Ashgate.
James, William. (1905) Is Radical Empiricism Solipsistic? *Journal of Philosophy, Psychology and Scientific Methods*. Reprinted in R. B. Kerry (Ed.) William James*: Essays in radical empiricism*. Lincoln: University of Nebraska.
Mead, George Herbert. (1938) *The Philosophy of the Act*. Chicago: University of Chicago Press.
Palazzoli, Mara Selvini, Cecchin, Gianfranco, Boscolo, Luigi, & Prata, Giulana. 2004. *Paradox and Counter Paradox*. Lanham, MD: Rowman & Littlefield.
Pearce, W. Barnett, & Cronen, Vernon. 1980. *Communication, Action, and Meaning*. New York: Praeger.
Persuit, Jeanne M. 2013. *Social Media and Integrated Marketing Communication: A Rhetorical Approach*. Lanham, MD: Lexington Books.
Schultz, Don E. & Kitchen, Philip. 2000. *Communicating Globally: An Integrated Marketing Approach*. Chicago: NTC Publishing Group.
Shultz, Don E, Tannenbaum, Stanley I. and Lauterborn, Robert F. 2003. *Integrated Marketing Communications: Putting It Together and Making It Work*. Chicago: NTC Publishing,
Senge, Peter. (1990) *The Fifth Discipline: The Art and Practice of Learning Organizations*. London: Doubleday.
Shusterman, Richard. (2000) *Pragmatist Aesthetics: Living Beauty, Rethinking Art*. Lanham, MD: Rowman & Littlefield.
Torp, Simon. (2009) Integrated Marketing Communications: From One Look To Normative Consistency. *Corporate Communications: An International Journal*. 14:190.
Turkle, Sherry. 2015. Reclaiming Conversation: the Power of Talk in a Digital Age. New York: Penguin Press.
Veblen, Thorstein. (1914) *The Instinct of Workmanship and the Industial Arts*. New York: MacMillan.
Wittgenstein, Ludwig. (1953) *Philosophical Investigations*. Trans. G.E.M. Anscombe. New York: MacMillan.

SEVEN

Integrated Marketing Communication and Public Health Campaigns

Let's Quit Together

Kelli L. Fellows

In 1929, Edward Bernays, the "putative father of modern North American public relations practice" leveraged his creativity and forged the interconnectivity between corporate and social campaigns (Ewen 1996, 3 as cited in Parsons 2007, 268). How did he do this? "[B]y staging what appeared to be a spontaneous Easter parade of New York City women doing something that up until then was considered socially unacceptable: they strolled down Fifth Avenue smoking in public" (Parson 2007, 268). This momentous event's outcomes endure. Contemporary public relations strategies support product marketing goals and illuminate inherent potential to effectively shape a new market. However with such power, a distorted reality may emerge in the new marketplace. As corporate business and public health campaigns share a thematic commonality (e.g., anti-tobacco), the interplay of creativity and communication may blur the motivational boundaries between corporate business and public health goals (Parsons 2007, 268) and distort the view of the emergent marketplace.

In February 2014, CVS announced plans to "quit smoking." Facing a $2 billion revenue loss associated with removal of cigarettes and associated products from 7,600 stores by October 1, the announcement was the organization's metaphorical line in the sand.

Over 2014, CVS experienced considerable media attention yet kept their strategic campaign hushed. In September, CVS unveiled their "Let's

Quit Together" campaign concurrently with a name change from CVS Caremark to CVS Health. To fully appreciate the complexity of these organizational choices and their subsequent rhetorical role in shaping the marketplace, this case will explore consumer health behavior, public health campaigns, organizations in the public sphere, and the ethical implications of organizational decision making. Specifically, the case is constructed as interpretive inquiry analyzed through a tripartite theoretical foundation: social and role identity, relational strategies of organizing, and principles of integrated marketing communication (IMC). The CVS campaign "Let's Quit Together" utilizes an IMC-identity approach that engages business and public health goals of promoting a healthy lifestyle—facilitating the construction of a new meaning and behavioral enactment. In addition, this chapter will illustrate opportunities for engagement with audiences on two issues of public health that may lead to behavioral *and* attitudinal change directly affected by CVS, pharmacies, and tobacco.

Healthcare represents approximately one-fifth of the U.S. economy (Furchtgott-Roth 2014). CVS, as a pharmacy chain, is an essential part of the health care system in the United States. However, unlike in Canada, pharmacies are legally allowed to sell tobacco products. Jha and Blum (2014) note the paradoxical nature of tobacco sales in pharmacies, offering consumers conflicting behavioral messages regarding healthy lifestyle choices. Koh (2014) acknowledges the paradox and suggests CVS's decision to remove tobacco facilitates the creation of a "new social norm" (1719), calling for "committed leadership through every sector of society that rejects the status quo and envisions a healthier future" (1720) (i.e., a tobacco-free marketplace). The point is that framing marketing health information in an understandable and actionable manner for the public is important so that it becomes institutionalized into the daily psyche (Ratzan 2001, 212).

CONSUMER HEALTH BEHAVIOR

Fellows and Rubin (2006) note, "Cigarette smoking is a learned behavior," (266; Everett, Schnuth, and Tribble 1998; Wetterer and von Troschke 1986) that continues to increase despite extensive research linking it to a spectrum of disparate health conditions (Ezzati and Lopez 2003; Garrett et al. 2004; Hall, Madden, and Lynskey 2002; Thrush, Fife-Schaw, and Breakwell 1999). Further, once entrenched, "the habit remains consistent over time," (Fellows and Rubin 2006, 266). This consistency encompasses physiological, psychological, and psychosocial forms. Subsequently, smoking may become engrained in an individual's identity, evolving into an integral component of smokers' perceptions of themselves individually and collectively—social and role identities (Fellows and Rubin 2006, 266).

Consideration of identity at an organizational level encompasses individual stakeholders' spectrum of social and role identities, generally, and identities related to or informed by the organization (Fellows 2013, 29). This approach recognizes stakeholders may have individual organizational identities, and the organization overall may have an organizational identity (e.g., reflective of brand, market share, organizational mission). Identity is a socially constructed phenomenon (Lloyd, Lucas, and Holland 1998). It encompasses an array of complex intrapersonal processes of engagement and relationship with oneself (Breakwell 1983; Ting-Toomey 2010). Notably, identity is a perpetually evolving co-constructed process influenced by contextual variables (e.g., historical; cultural; geographic; Mokros 2003) and his or her previous experiences (Breakwell 1983; Brewer 1991, 1999; MacDonald, Sulsky, and Brown 2008; Fellows and Rubin 2006). Applied to individuals, social identity (Tajfel and Turner 1979) and role identity (Stryker 1987) are pertinent. Consideration of identity at an organizational level encompasses individual stakeholders' spectrum of social and role identities, generally, and identities related to or informed by the organization. This approach recognizes stakeholders may have individual organizational identities, and the organization overall may have an organizational identity (e.g., reflective of brand, market share, organizational mission).

Relational Strategies for Organizing

Human beings are social creatures innately driven toward group membership (Goedde, Fellows, and Scwichtenberg; Fellows 2014; Hogg 2001; Hogg and Terry 2000). This drive manifests as relational engagement—with individuals or organizations. The identity construct is woven throughout this desire, reflecting individuals' fundamental drive for acceptance and belonging. Thus, identity is a relational process that informs organizational membership, commitment, and sensemaking. Given the multiplicity of identities each individual represents, relational development, maintenance, or dissolution contributes to identity relevance and salience. "By extension, individuals may metaphorically expand or contract as variables of influence change, unfolding dynamics across the organizational context," (Fellows, Goedde, and Schwichtenberg 2014, 15). Observed identity status, then, may reflect a transient rather than entrenched identity state.

PRINCIPLES OF INTEGRATED MARKETING COMMUNICATION IN HEALTH COMMUNICATION

Porcu, Barrio-Garcia, and Kitchen (2012, 326) define integrated marketing communication as "the interactive and systemic process of *cross-functional planning* and optimization of messages to stakeholders with the aim of communicating with *coherence* and *transparency* to achieve synergies and encourage *profitable relationships* in the short, medium and long-term" (326). Utilizing an IMC approach facilitates organizational sensemaking and synchronized movement across the organization toward business goal attainment (Fellows 2013, 122). Further, organizations' strategic appreciation of the primacy of communication may synergistically leverage stakeholder relationships in the forms of brand equity and financial performance (Porcu, Barrio-Garcia, and Kitchen 2012, 314), while enhancing organizational agility in meeting target audiences' needs (Stokes 2009, 346). Thus, IMC is a strategic business process (Porcu, Barrio-Garcia, and Kitchen 2012, 322). Optimal business effects span gaining competitive advantage (Porcu, Barrio-Garcia, and Kitchen 2012, 3338), increasing market share (Parsons 2007, 267), or return on investment (ROI) optimization while concurrently minimizing waste (e.g., financial; time; 125).

Five dimensions characterize an IMC approach (Shimp and Andrews 2013, 12; as cited in Fellows 2013, 122):

1. identifying and focusing on the customer or prospect at the onset
2. utilizing any (and all) available points of contact and influence
3. speaking with a consistent, unified voice
4. developing, nurturing, and building stakeholder relationships, and
5. identifying an action-based behavioral response. (122)

Kotler (2005) defines brand positioning as "the specific meaning for a brand in the consumer's mind" (11). What goes on in their minds is the result of a number of strategies that include words, images, and associations resulting in a consumer identifying with that brand and not necessarily with the specific product it represents. Since "the symbolic aspect of the brand exists in the perceptual space of the consumer" (Sarkar and Singh 2005, 80), the consumer is able to identify personally with that brand" (Parsons 2007, 270).

Developed by Siegel & Gale agency, the CVS campaign used retail tobacco removal as an enterprise-wide springboard to unveil CVS Health and its four business units—CVS/pharmacy, CVS/specialty, CVS/minuteclinic and CVS/caremark. Through an IMC approach, CVS could reposition the organizational brand and unify the organizational business unit's role in multifaceted health service delivery (see http://www.siegelgale.com/case-study/cvs-health/). The campaign spanned from April to September 2014, culminating in the removal of tobacco products from over 7,600 retail locations.

The campaign momentum continued into 2015, as *PR Week* notes, "Overall, CVS Health earned 347 million media impressions, and, in the first week of February [2015] alone, the brand saw 200,000 social media mentions. The effort's launch garnered 129 million print and broadcast media impressions, along with more than 117,000 social media posts" (March 20, 2015, http://www.prweek.com/article/1310741/cvs-onegoodreason-social-effort-draws-high-level-support-twitter). Additionally, the campaign received two prestigious awards: the *AIGA 2015 Cased Competition* award (see http://www.aiga.org/cased-2015-winner-cvs-health-identity/) and *PR Week's* Corporate Branding Campaign of the Year (www.prweek.com/article/1338002/corporate-branding-campaign-year-2015).

Appreciating the campaign's IMC approach entails examination of the campaign across conceptualization, development, and implementation according to Shimp and Andrews' five dimensions of IMC. The subsequent sections scrutinize the "Let's Quit Together" campaign across these five aforementioned IMC dimensions.

Identify and Focus on Customer or Prospect at the Onset

According to Siegel & Gale, campaign conceptualization centered around stakeholders of the four business units and the development of a unifying corporate narrative—positioning the CVS Health brand and the seemingly limitless ways stakeholders could engage with the organization toward their healthy lifestyle goals (see http://www.siegelgale.com/case-study/cvs-health/). Central to this process, Siegel & Gale focused on "telling the brand story in an authentic and compelling voice." The brand's personality—"leading with heart"—the nucleus of the narrative, guided subsequent linguistic choices tailored to the specific stakeholders (e.g., shareholders; clients; members; patients; see http://www.siegelgale.com/case-study/cvs-health/).

Utilizing any (and all) available points of Contact and Influence

"The path to becoming smoke free doesn't start in the same place for everyone. That's why our program is designed to offer the 'interested quitter' many ways to interact with our services," says Helena Foulkes, President of CVS Pharmacy. "Our integrated business model, that includes CVS Pharmacy, CVS Caremark, CVS MinuteClinic and CVS Specialty, allows us to reinforce important resources at every venue and touch point" (CVS Health 2014). This approach especially required attention to points of contact such as point of purchase, healthcare providers, and advertising.

Speaking with a Consistent, Unified Voice

Hedgecock (2014) characterized the kickoff event as:

> A dozen or so "ambassadors" in khaki pants and branded shirts and ballcaps stood around the display and at park entrances giving out promotional materials. The handouts stayed true to the theme of the event: lollipops in the heart shape of the new CVS logo, packs of birthday candles (to celebrate years added to the life of a person who quits smoking), and tobacco-quitting kits packed into faux cigarette boxes. The ambassadors repeatedly emphasized that the latter were intended for passers-by to give to friends who might be smokers. Although the big lollipops were only occasionally seen in the hands (or mouths) of people walking by, the quitting packs were everywhere. Multiple people even asked for more.

Through this approach, CVS defined a new social norm and emergent healthy lifestyle meaning, and positioned itself as an integral partner in a contemporary health identity.

Identifying an Action-based Behavioral Response

The CVS website demonstrates the IMC-informed campaign that reinforces the campaign slogan and facilitates consumer action at each of the organization's four organizational touchpoints. Additionally, the Quitting Tips section is organized according to public health campaign stages of change theory: precontemplation, contemplation, preparation, which are covered in the "Prepare to Quit" section; action, in the "Manage Quitting" section, and maintenance, in the "Stay Smoke-Free" section (Slater 1999). Of course, the initial action required is the consumer purposefully connecting to the CVS website. Based on this behavioral choice, the website design provides an intuitive and engaging site to meet the customer dialogically at where she or he is in the smoking cessation process. The CVS smoking cessation micro-site categories (see http://www.cvs.com/quit-smoking/) expands on the initial "Let's Quit Together" campaign through affirming language and multiple health identity roles the individual site visitor may enact. The prominent headline, "Keep That Resolution," provides a definitive action for the visitor. Subsequent text exudes a narrative, collaborative tone, positioning CVS as a knowledgeable partner at the ready to quit with the customer through guidance and customer cessation success stories, and extends their supportive presence into the future shape of the customer's cessation and tobacco-free lifestyle. This site features nuanced approaches to consumer engagement, behavioral choice enactment, and CVS's partnering role throughout while achieving CVS Health's integrated enterprise brand strategy. This argument supports and extends CVS's strategy of releasing information prior to the specific campaign and cigarette removal action date. Through this approach, CVS "inoculates" the customer base, as explained in inoculation theory: "McGuire (1964) contended that by exposing individuals to a persuasive message that contains weakened arguments against an established attitude (e.g., a two-sided message, or a message that presents both counterarguments and refutations of those counterarguments), individuals would develop resistance against stronger, future persuasive attacks" (Compton, Jackson, and Dimmock 2016) and, consistent with relational development, who recognizes and addresses individuals general resistance to change.

Identifying an Action-Based Behavioral Response

The CVS "Let's Quit Together" campaign illuminates an IMC approach grounded in identity, which includes cognition, affect, and behavior.

Cognition

External communication artifacts frame CVS's organizational narrative as a health-centered organization. Consumers who previously purchased tobacco products at CVS now see "Let's Quit Together" campaign materials in their place. The removal of tobacco products provides visual rhetoric affirming CVS as a health-related facility, minimizing potential cognitive dissonance that may manifest amid smokers and non-smokers for a conflicting health message. Additionally, the simplicity of the message, "Let's Quit Together" provides varying degrees of cognitive engagement, scrutiny, and consideration of the meaning of the phrase. Holistically, the message personalizes the organization and the journey toward health-centered lifestyles. Essentially, the organization becomes a personified accountability partner—someone to go through the struggles of smoking cessation, specifically, and change, generally.

Affect

Consumers' intrapersonal examination of feelings provided by the campaign slogan is intriguing. Through the linguistic choices, CVS established a degree of relatability with the smoker. While CVS inoculated consumers over the course of nine months with the forthcoming tobacco removal, they affirmed the impact of the decision as challenging as well. This communicative engagement with smokers creates a bond of group affiliation. In this regard, the organization affirms to smokers they are not ostracizing them by no longer selling tobacco. Rather, they are offering a new identity co-creation opportunity. Through a co-constructive approach through "Let's Quit Together," CVS encouraged current customers on the quitting journey to share their personal stories via social media. The #OneGoodReason hashtag facilitated both active engagement and encouragement, co-constructing the narrative and creating a shared meaning and exemplification of the meaning of "Let's Quit Together"—creating a social context and a group of like others who shared a common goal of quitting smoking. This strategy personified the organization through its customers; CVS started the conversation with an invitation and customers participated both actively and passively, perpetuating and expanding the sense of community and defining "together" in transcendent means.

Behavior

Overt behavioral change is exhibited on the part of CVS and consumers. The visual rhetoric associated with no tobacco products signals the consumer to a change in behavior—that is, "Oh yeah, I can't buy cigarettes at CVS anymore." For some, this organizational behavior change may deter the individual from shopping at CVS. Alternatively, if smoking consumers decide to embark on the quitting journey, then purchasing products from CVS may be perceived as preferable because the temptation to backslide is minimized—that is, out of sight, out of mind. Further, individuals may develop additional messages intrapersonally to encourage themselves to continue smoking cessation. For example, "If CVS can take the financial hit, I can follow their lead; it hurt their bottom line significantly, and it can benefit my bottom line from quitting."

This intrapersonal discourse may extend the relatability of the campaign strategy concurrently with social media announcements, updates, or new identity artifacts. Co-dependent relationships may emerge, as Stokes (2009, 355) notes, "having more choices does not necessarily equal having more agency." Through the linguistic choices made, the campaign slogan "Let's Quit Together" engenders a level of connectedness that positions the retailer as the leader to follow toward a healthy lifestyle right now, which means we will both quit smoking. The question remains, though, as this trust, confidence, or partnership associated in the individual's mind may enhance their receptivity to subsequent messages from CVS and ultimately could create a state of learned helplessness or co-dependence as the individual's sensemaking and meaning: making become centered on or informed by CVS as the primary authority: "they supported me with quitting smoking" or removing a contrary health message: "clearly they have my best interest at heart."

CVS'S "LET'S QUIT TOGETHER" CAMPAIGN ANALYSIS

Smoking, as a public health concern, clearly represents an overt behavior that yields negative health outcomes. Notably, it is the leading cause of preventable morbidity and mortality influence factors. Further, research consistently notes it is a learned behavior, and once entrenched, remains consistent over time. This observation supports the tenets of social learning theory and provides a theoretical framework transcending the individuated reasons why smokers initiated or sustained their behavioral choices.

The fundamental corollary across smokers that binds smokers collectively is behavior-related commonality; a social group connection or an identity that may reduce uncertainty, affirm empowered sense of choice regarding individuals' own choices, and a level of connectivity, and a relationship with others who they may not nor need to personally know to exist. If individuals learn through observation, the presence or absence of a stimuli may trigger awareness to enact behavioral choices associated with the broader identity. Examples include product placement in television shows, product signage, placement, and displays in retail outlets, or signage specifying where the behavior is or is not allowed.

In the CVS case, the absence of cigarettes may accomplish a tripartite goal. First, its absence may support or reinforce the acceptability or possibility of life without the product. This reinforces attributes of a "healthy lifestyle" through observation of its absence. Second, the absence maintains the individual's ability to construct his or her own meaning of what the phrase "healthy lifestyle" means—interpreted cognitively, affectively, and behaviorally. This nuanced cognitive engagement may lead the individual to associate the retailer as a relational partner in the process of a healthy lifestyle, thus, co-constructing a new reality. The third and final goal is the preservation of choice to create a new meaning of a healthy lifestyle. Rather than enacting a paternalistic approach—telling the individual what he or she may or may not do vis-à-vis rules, restrictions, or punitive consequences—CVS's approach reflects a preservation of individual choice and rhetorical space to construct the meaning of a "healthy lifestyle" without demand for customers to maintain the same view.

"Let's Quit Together" and the associated campaign collateral materials (signage, logo, slogan) humanizes the organization. Rather than a directive, the slogan is an invitation—a relational endeavor where the organization is attempting to quit and they want to share the journey with its customers. This slogan personifies the organization's choice, and in its simplicity, opens the possibility for co-construction of meaning of experiential variables associated with the process of quitting: financial implications, withdrawal, new identity construction, shedding former behavior. In this regard, the CVS campaign achieves what most anti-smoking or smoking cessation endeavors miss: there is simply no "one size fits all" solution to encourage or facilitate individuals to smoking cessation or smoking initiation prevention.

Dependent on the anti-tobacco campaign du jour, paternalistic reinforcement appears through mass media and medical facilities' encounters. For example, recent focus centers on the financial costs of smoking and quantifies the financial gains if the behavior ceases. While this argument is factual, it may fail to resonate with the target audience because the financial aspect may simply be benign: an accepted cost associated with the individuals' preferred behavioral choice of smoking. Additionally, such a focused message design, even disseminated through an IMC-aligned framework, may fail to reach the audience. It fails to acknowledge that smoking is more complex than a costly behavior. There is no accounting for the perceived relational benefits (e.g., connectivity with smokers as a group) or psychologically facilitated notions of companionship through the behavioral enactment of smoking—essentially, the smoker identity.

Identity, Social Learning Theory, and "Learning to Play the Part"

Identity is socially constructed. According to Fellows and Rubin (2006), "when exploring the context of smoking, the role of group members in memory construction and maintenance is important to consider" (267). Public health campaigns focus on highlighting core attributes of a healthy lifestyle at both a macro- and micro-level approach enacted. Focus may center on chronic conditions (e.g., diabetes; sexually transmitted diseases) that may emerge from risky behavior. Regardless, the public health's system level thematic goal (purpose) is to generate awareness of the risk associated with a variety of daily choices that may impact individuals' proactive or reactive behavioral responses. The theory and practice of public health holistically strives to change behavior and influence decision making across individuals and in the public sphere. Recognizing the co-existence and interdependence, behavior change is proposed and reinforced across the level of communication: intrapersonal, interpersonal, small group, organizational, and marketplace.

Public health campaign efforts will significantly benefit from having intimate knowledge of smoking and the array of representation it is for individual smokers. Rather than elitist portrayals that reinforce the "us versus them" or ingroups versus outgroups (Fellows and Rubin 2006, 268) mentality—tones of compassion or understanding may resonate more deeply and facilitate long-term behavior change. CVS's campaign "Let's Quit Together" created a powerful relational rhetoric that illuminated a positive equitable relationship. Previous and ongoing public health campaigns are reminiscent of paternalistic or abusive relationships, fraught with one relational partner as the authority: knowing all, removing the capacity for choice, criticizing choices made that do not align with the asserted "correct way" to achieve a healthy lifestyle. They separate and further isolate the individual and exacerbate the critical dependence on the relational partner for sustained existence.

Such isolation may elicit reactance arousal, comparable with punitive consequence or restricted access. Psychologically, individuals may desire the behavior more when faced with limitations or restrictions—when their ability to choose is limited or removed (perceived or actualized), reactance arousal suggests the intended message behavior change goal may boomerang, further entrenching behavioral demonstration commitment (that is, smoking more).

Behaviorally, smoking implies a degree of connectivity with a specific group of others within the public sphere. This perceived connectivity reflects a relational dimension. A counter argument could easily suggest this relational dimension separates or isolates smokers from non-smokers, relegating them to an "outsider" status, consistent with identity—ascribed and associated—that reinforces the notion of us versus them; ingroups and outgroups. CVS' campaign neutralizes this separatist view through linguistic positioning of "together." At a system level, this personification is IMC relational-oriented behavior change. However, on the intra- or interpersonal levels experiential dimension, minimal consideration is given to frontline employee/customer interaction. For example, how or were front-line employees instructed to disseminate the removal of tobacco to customers? Beyond wearing logo marked buttons and stickers, was their discourse scripted to bring awareness? Were they trained on handling or diffusing angry customers?

A final dimension involves the passing of time and message salience. All relationships experience significant events, referred to as turning points. These events may be positive or negative, and the serves as "markers of time" along the relationship's development, sustainment, or dissolution. Removing cigarettes could be construed as a relational turning point for both smoker and non-smoker customers. Through inoculation, CVS eased customers into the approaching turning point, skillfully facilitating a new construction of meaning of CVS as a retailer, a pharmacy, a relational partner, and a part of the healthy lifestyle conceptualization. This gradual movement mirrors the organic nature of relational development, gradual rather than abrupt, that encourages rational versus emotion-based reactions and associated decision making. The ultimate removal of the prescribed day marked the future relational anniversary—the "quit date"—a memorial referent to reminisce about at a future time. Memorializing the event, in the future, provides an indicator of relational growth, accomplishment, and fortitude. The sentiments of a Barry Manilow song capture the relationship between the retailer CVS and the customer. This long-term relational possibility may or may not be actualized. Some turning points provide opportunities to celebrate victories, "Looks like we made it"—it was difficult, the struggle was real, but we slayed the dragon. Such analysis affirms previous choices and supports ego-driven needs such as success, victory, and being right.

Celebrating this turning point may not resonate across stakeholders. The sentiment of "that was then and this is now" comes to mind. If the new co-constructed relationship is not solely defined by the abandoned behavior specifically, then careful attention focused on development of new health opportunities and new relational turning points supporting healthy lifestyle demonstration opportunities is warranted. Looking back is not necessarily nurturing the relationship to elicit future behavior change or consistency. The slogan "Let's Quit Together" limits the relational development because it fails to illuminate a continued need for the relationship—a task defined relationship/mission centered, need based relationship—short-term. Once the novelty of the campaign fades, removal of cigarettes occurred, the need for or the strength of the relationship may fade as well. Reminiscent of recovering alcoholics—some love and need the meetings—it morphs into an identity through going to meetings while others find it a constant trigger, a symbolic tribute to the former life and behavioral enactment they are trying to be free from holistically.

Public health campaigns target population level segments to promote and drive better health outcomes than presently observed at a given moment in time. In this manner, the targeting is limited (generalized) still even within specific target audiences (e.g., by risk factors; behavioral indicators) or focused on behavior reinforcement or prevention. One criticism of public health campaigns, even at a local level, centers on the lack of individualization. IMC strategies employed by health sector retailers may bridge this gap through potential reinforcement of public health campaigns—ongoing addressing of social and role identity concurrently.

CVS Campaign Components and Implications

Carland (2001) notes the influence of delivery on how a message is received (43). Specifically, he asserts, "great care should be taken when delivering it," (43). While the "Let's Quit Together" campaign evidences the five dimensions of an integrated marketing communication approach, emergent questions require critical consideration of the new health reality created in the campaign's wake. While an exposition on business ethics and morals exceeds the scope of the present chapter, three emergent artifacts warrant critical examination. These include (1) the new identity, (2) better living through pharmaceuticals and consumerism, and (3) follow the ethical (?) organizational leader. The subsequent sections briefly explore each category.

The New Health Identity

Fellows (2013, 129) notes the perils associated with identity-grounded project development and implementation. Specifically, the question of "what identity they desire to create and replicate" is relevant to the CVS "Let's Quit Together" campaign. On one hand, the organization's choice to remove cigarettes and associated campaign focus on the CVS brand

and customers' identity centered around positive health choices—creating the new health identity.

Within the healthcare realm, Parsons (2007) notes, "Taking a consumer's set of medical signs and symptoms and providing a label is a good example of helping to shape a self-identity" (245). However, the pharmacy continues to sell processed foods, sugary confections, and a spectrum of products an individual may need for daily life—which are not related to health (e.g., office supplies; garden decorations; makeup). This approach reinforces the notion of consumerism—which in turn supports or extends a different identity. Haddad (2007) asserts even "telling the truth can be misleading," and claims individuals may not readily make "the distinction between information and persuasion" (62). From an IMC approach, these assertions are troubling. While the five dimensions of IMC provide a framework designed to optimize organizational communication, the infrastructure does not necessitate or ensure ethical or moral appropriateness of the brand created or messages disseminated.

Better Living Through Pharmaceuticalism and Consumerism

While removing tobacco products is laudable and reinforces the CVS brand as a partner in healthy lifestyle attainment, the implied message of accomplishment lies within their role of facilitating it through pharmaceuticalism and consumerism. Their general positioning as a source of pharmaceuticals and consumer goods toward business mission and goal attainment undermines public health campaigns in other less overt areas. For example, ready access to sugary or processed foods (fueling consumer convenience) and the general absence of fruits and vegetables shapes the meaning of "healthy lifestyle" and the associated potential behavioral enactments therein.

One counterargument to this assertion is the recent partnership of CVS and Target. The alignment of two non-tobacco retailers reinforces the healthy lifestyle brand and in some "Super Target stores" consumers may acquire fruits and vegetables, comparable with traditional grocery stores. With respect to tobacco products, though, this move focuses on a specific consumer base that does not necessarily align with demographics of smokers, who tend to be lower income populations. This partnership perpetuates CVS's organizational commitment to quit smoking and extends the behavior reinforcement and enactment by partnering with another retail organization.

Follow the "Ethical" Organizational Health Leader

The present moment in time is in the wake of "corporate scandals and crashes and the subsequent demand by society for higher business standards and ethics. The growth reflects a decisive shift in public opinion concerning the moral responsibility of corporations" (Haddad, 2007, 56). Nowadays, corporations are expected to be morally responsible for a variety of issues including the environment, gender and race issues, product and workplace safety and health (Paine, 2003; as cited in Haddad 2007, 56). McGill (2014) notes, "questions remain as to how influential the CVS Caremark decision will be in the fight against tobacco, whether it will change behaviors and if other retailers will follow suit" (1).

As CVS leads the tobacco-free, health centered retailer movement, mindful consideration of emergent markets to fill the tobacco void is warranted. Further, this attention should note both tobacco (for example, cigarettes) and the positioning of e-cigarettes (for example, vapes; vaping) as the new socially acceptable form of smoking. Examining the relationship between smoking cessation campaigns and e-cigarette marketing is a fruitful avenue for further research.

CVS Identity Construction

Through social media, CVS neutralized potential critical observations that the campaign was merely selling hope with false platitudes of relational commitment and investment. You, the customer, want to believe the organization cares about you and your well-being. By extension, you will interpret these data through this confirming lens of evidentiary support. The methodical integration of social media gave voice to both the organization and its customers, creating the appearance, if not a reality, of dialogic engagement.

The slogan approaches smokers on an equitable, "we are in this together" approach, rather than paternalistic approaches that blame the individual for his or her current situation because of poor health choices in the past. Public health campaigns targeting tobacco cessation have notoriously used this approach. Carland (2011) suggests the interconnectivity of blame and choice, "Perhaps the problem lies with the activity of blaming. . . . there is something aggressive and unkind about it. It sets up a situation in which it becomes difficult to move forward under the burdensome feelings of shame and guilt that arise. It also puts the resolution of our pain in the hands of someone other than us. Ultimately, we cannot insist that someone else take responsibility for their actions; only they can make that choice when they are ready" (71).

CONCLUSION

The CVS "Let's Quit Together" campaign case study illuminates the intricate connections of IMC strategic approaches. CVS's decision marks them as the first major retailor to answer U.S. Attorneys General's requests to remove tobacco (Estrel 2014). While their commitment to a health-centered goal is laudable, critical consumers may question how the organization will recoup lost revenue. McLeod (2014) notes their primacy of response yielded significant public relations attention and increased consumer sales, specifically in pharmaceuticals. Essentially, McLeod (2014) observes, "they have a strategic advantage because they create the new marketplace."

This new marketplace comes at a price—the reemergence of "the war on smokers" (Robb, 2014)—and associated stigmatic behavior (Miller, Fellows, & Kizito 2007). Examination of the "Let's Quit Together" campaign exemplifies IMC at its best—employing consistency, coherence, strategic integration across channels and message construction. However, is this accomplishment merely reframing the organization's true goal, revenue, through more socially acceptable means of pharmaceuticalism and consumerism?

REFERENCES

AIGA. 2015. Cased 2015 Winner: CVS Health Identity. http://www.aiga.org/cased-2015-winner-cvs-health-identity/

Breakwell, Glynis M. 1986. *Coping with threatened identities*. London and New York: Methuen.

Brewer, Marilyn B. 1991. The social self: On being the same and different at the same time. *Personality and Social Psychology Bulletin* 17: 475–482.

---. 1999. Multiple identities and identity transition: Implications for Hong Kong. *International Journal of Intercultural Relations* 23:187–197.

Carland, Trey. (2011). *A Seeker's Guide to Inner Peace: Notes to Self*. Whitney Press.

Compton, Josh, Jackson, Ben, and Dimmock, James A. 2016. Persuading Others to Avoid Persuasion: Inoculation Theory and Resistant Health Attitudes. *Frontiers in Psychology* 7: 122. http://doi.org/10.3389/fpsyg.2016.00122

Esterl, Mike. March 17, 2014. Attorneys General Urge Major Retailers to Stop Selling Tobacco Products. *Wall Street Journal*. http://www.wsj.com/articles/SB10001424052702303563304579445072945287860

Evans, W. Douglas. 2006. How Social Marketing Works in Health Care. *BMJ: British Medical Journal* 332(7551): 1207-1210.

Everett, Sherry A., Ray L Schnuth, R. L. and Joanne L. Tribble. 1998. "Tobacco and Alcohol use in Top-grossing American Films." *Journal of Community Health* 23: 317–324.

Fellows, Kelli L. 2013. Ethically constructing *Common Grounds* one cyber latte at a time: A thought leadership examination of emergent ethical dilemmas in designing technologically based nontraditional graduate student social support. *Journal of Scholastic Inquiry: Education* 1:120-137.

Fellows, Kelli L., & Rubin, Don L. 2006. Identities for sale: How the tobacco industry construed Asians, Asian Americans, and Pacific Islanders. *Journal of Intercultural Communication Research* 35(3): 265-292.

Furchtgott-Roth, Diana. September 9, 2014. "*The 'Coincidence' of CVS and Tobacco*" http://www.realclearmarkets.com/articles/2014/09/09/the_coincidence_of_cvs_and_tobacco_101267.html

Garrett, Nancy, A., Nina L. Alesci, Monica M. Schultz, Steven S. Foldes, Sanne Magnan and Mark W. Manley. 2004. The Relationship of Stage of Change for Smoking Cessation to Stage of Change for Fruit and Vegetable Consumption and Physical

Activity in a Health Plan Population." *American Journal of Health Promotion* 19: 118–126.
Goedde, Sascha Dennis, Fellows, Kelli L., and Schwichtenberg, Elisabeth Jasmin. 2014. What's your CQ? A thought leadership exploration of cultural intelligence in contemporary institutions of higher learning. *Romanian Journal of Communication and Public Relations (Revista Română de Comunicare şi Relaţii Publice)* 2:13-34.
Haddad, Louis. 2007. The Ethics of Business and the Business of Ethics. *The Middle East Business and Economic Review* 19(1): 56-67.
Hall, Wayne, Pamela Madden and Michael Lynskey. 2002. "The Genetics of Tobacco use: Methods, Findings and Policy Implications." *Tobacco Control* 11: 119–124.
Hogg, Michael A. 2001. A social identity theory of leadership. *Personality and Social Psychology Review* 5:184–200.
Hogg, Michael A. & Terry, Deborah I. 2000. Social identity and self-categorization processes in organizational contexts. *Academy of Management Review* 25:121–140.
Hong, Patrick. September 11, 2014. CVS rebrands, asks customers to share #OneGoodReason to quit tobacco. *Momentology.* http://www.momentology.com/936-cvs-rebrands-asks-customers-to-share-onegoodreason-to-quit-tobacco/
Jha, Vinayak. and Blum, Alan. April 3, 2014. Op-Ed: Health Groups Fail to Exert Influence for Tobacco-Free Pharmacies. *Drug Channels: Expert Insights on Pharmaceutical Economics and the Drug Distribution System.* http://www.drugchannels.net/2014/04/health-groups-fail-to-exert-influence.html
Koh, Howard K.(2014). It Shouldn't Take Another 50 Years: Accelerating Momentum to End the Tobacco Epidemic. *Clincal Cancer Research*, 20(7): 1719-1720.
Kotler, Philip and Gary Armstrong. 2005. *Principles of Marketing*. Upper Saddle River, NJ: Pearson/Prentice-Hall, 11th edition.
Lloyd, Barbara, Lucas, Kevin, Holland, Janet, McGrellis, Sheena, and Arnold, Sean. 1998. *Smoking in Adolescence: Images and Identities.* Oxford and New York: Routledge.
MacDonald, Heather A., Sulsky, Lorne M., and Brown, Douglas J. 2008. Leadership and perceiver cognition: Examining the role of self-identity in implicit leadership theories. *Human Performance* 21: 333–353. DOI: 10.1080/08959280802347031
McGill, Natalie. 2014. Advocates call on all health retailers to stop selling tobacco: Sign APHA petition. *The Nation's Health* 44(3): 1-12.
McLeod, Lisa E. February 4, 2015. Doing the Right Thing Makes You Money. If You Go First. https://www.linkedin.com/pulse/doing-right-thing-makes-you-money-go-first-lisa-earle-mcleod
Miller, Ann Neville, Fellows, Kelli L., & Kizito, Mary N. 2007. The impact of onset controllability on stigmatization and supportive communication goals toward persons with HIV/AIDS versus lung cancer: A comparison between Kenyan and U.S. participants. *Health Communication* 22: 207-219.
Mokros, Hartmut B. 2003. A constitutive approach to identity. *Identity Matters: Communication-based Explorations and Explanations* p. 3-28.
Naeem, Bilal, Muhammad Bilal and Uzma Naz. 2013. "Integrated Marketing Communication: A Review Paper." *Interdisciplinary Journal of Contemporary Research in Business* 5(5): 122-133.
Nichols, Laura. (September 3, 2014). *CVS #OneGoodReason Social Effort Draws High-Level Support on Twitter.* http://www.prweek.com/article/1310741/cvs-onegoodreason-social-effort-draws-high-level-support-twitter
Parsons, Patricia. 2007. Integrating Ethics With Strategy: Analyzing Disease-Branding. *Corporate Communications* 12(3):267-279.
Porcu, Lucia, del Barrio-Garcia, Salvador, Kitchen, Phillip J. 2012. How Integrated Marketing Communications (IMC) works? A theoretical review and an analysis of its main drivers and effects. *Comunicación y Sociedad* 25(1): 313-348.
PR Week, (March 20, 2015). *Corporate Branding Campaign of the Year.* http://www.prweek.com/article/1338002/corporate-branding-campaign-year-2015#Hqc4W9ucDVBxufQW.99

Ratzan, Scott. 2001. "Health Literacy: Communication for the Public Good." *Health Promotion International* 16 (2): 207-214.

Robb, Alice. February 10, 2014. *Let's not wage war on smokers: Quitting smoking is good. Stigmatizing smokers isn't.* http://www.newrepublic.com/article/116553/smoking-and-stigma-war-smoking-has-gone-too-far

Slater, Michael D. 1999. Integrating application of media effects, persuasion, and behavior change theories to communication campaigns: A stages-of-change framework." *Health Communication* 11(4): 335-354.

Stokes Quesinberry, Ashli. 2009. Living the sweet (d) Life: public relations, IMC, and diabetes. *Journal of Communication Management* 13(4): 343-361.

Stryker, Sheldon. 1987. Identity theory: Developments and extensions. In Krysia Yardley & Terry Honess (Eds.), *Self and identity: Psychosocial perspectives*. Chichester, England: Wiley, pp. 89–103.

Tajfel, Henri, and John C. Turner. 1979. "An integrative theory of intergroup conflict." *The social psychology of intergroup relations* 33:(47), 74.

Thrush, Diana, Chris Fife-Schaw and Glynis M. Breakwell. 1999. "Evaluation of Interventions to Reduce Smoking." *Swiss Journal of Psychology* 58: 85–100.

Ting-Toomey, Stella. 2010. Mindfulness. In *Encyclopedia of Identity*. Ronald L. Jackson, II, ed. Thousand Oaks, CA: SAGE Publications, pp.455-458.

Tybout, Alice and Calkins, Tim, eds. 2005. *Kellogg on Branding: The Marketing Faculty of the Kellogg School of Management.* Hoboken, NJ: John Wiley & Sons.

Wetterer, Angelika and Jürgen von Troschke. 1986. *Smoker Motivation: A Review of Contemporary Literature.* Berlin, Heidelberg: Springer Verlag.

EIGHT

Integrated Marketing Communication and Crisis Communication

The American Red Cross

Amanda G. McKendree

In *The Women of Katrina: How Gender, Race, and Class Matter in an American Disaster*, authors David and Enarson (2012) pose the following questions: whose experiences do disasters reveal, and whose experiences do they neglect? The interplay of integrated marketing communication (IMC) and crisis communication offers one approach for exploring these questions and creates a space that gives voice to marginalized publics. By using the American Red Cross as a case study, this chapter relies on the IMC metaphors of "discourse," "system," and "practice" (Cornelissen, Christensen, and Vijn 2006), to investigate the internal and external communicative strategies that drive the organization's work. This metaphorical perspective concludes by detailing how the American Red Cross collaborates with stakeholders to better understand the populations it serves and identify the "forgotten publics" (Waymer and Heath 2007) who could benefit the most from its programs and resources.

COMMUNICATING ABOUT CRISES

Major public crisis events help establish best and worst communication practices. Whether communications professionals are faced with a Flint Water Crisis, Hurricane Katrina, Canadian wildfire, or refugee crisis, they are responsible for gathering, organizing, and disseminating information to key stakeholder groups. A crisis is defined as "an unusual event of overwhelmingly negative significance that carries a high level of risk, harm, and opportunity for further loss" (Seeger, Sellnow, and Ulmer 2003, 4). A crisis can also refer to "the perception of an unpredictable event that threatens important expectancies of stakeholders and can seriously impact an organization's performance and generate negative outcomes" (Coombs 2012, 2). Whether real or perceived, a crisis poses challenges for gathering, interpreting, and disseminating information before, during, and after the event. Just ask any Red Cross disaster mental health manager about the most critical aspect of a crisis and he or she will tell you that "information is currency in a situation like this because trauma builds from the lack of information" (Costa 2016). The complex, ambiguous, and uncertain nature of crisis demands a response that is contextually relevant and, simultaneously, static. Crisis mandates an emphasis on theory and action, short- and long-term horizons, and stakeholders within and outside of an organization. Crisis response plans must consider the appropriate type of communication message, key stakeholders, crisis communication plans, and communication strategies. They must allow for a range of challenges that might be presented by particular events or constituents as the crisis evolves.

According to Seeger, Sellnow, and Ulmer (2003), "communication is essential for sensing risk, for coordinated and effective response, for reducing uncertainty, for apologizing, for memorializing, and for returning to normalcy" (82). Crisis communication can take on a variety of forms during a crisis. For example, it is often defined as "an exercise in public relations" (Mitroff and Gus 2001, 7). Organizations that adopt this definition tend to focus their efforts on communicating effectively with the media "after a crisis occurs" (Mitroff and Gus 2001, 7). Kathleen Fearn-Banks (2007) defines crisis communication as a process of "verbal, visual, and/or written interaction between the organization and its publics (often through the news media) prior to, during, and after the negative occurrence" (480). The organization's communication practices after the crisis fall within the organization's crisis response strategy.

Crisis communication involves gathering, organizing, and making information available to others. These tasks bring about two significant challenges for organizations. First, the information-related challenge is to identify the "truth" around crisis events. Organizational leaders must internally collect and process information to determine what is known and unknown about a given crisis event. In addition, externally, the organization must inform stakeholders about the crisis and take actions to address their concerns. The second challenge in crisis communication focuses on the audience's ability to interpret issues in a time of high stress. Crisis communication typically transpires in times of stress when the stakeholders' ability to process information is reduced.

Coombs (2012) suggests that the content of crisis messages should include instructing information, adjusting information, and reputation management. An organization's ability to protect or repair its reputation rests with its ability to offer both instructing and adjusting information in crisis response messages. Instructing information offers advice for stakeholders on how to protect themselves in the crisis or details on how the crisis affects business operations. For example, in April 2016, the Red Cross offered advice on tornado safety and what to do before, during, and after a tornado. In this case, instructing information might include how to evacuate and how to find shelter. The logical places for posting instructing information include discussion boards, blogs, and social networking sites. According to Coombs (2012), "adjusting information helps stakeholders cope psychologically with the crisis" (148). By sharing details on the events of the crisis, stakeholders experience reduced psychological stress and reduced uncertainty. Reputation management suggests that organizations can use "words and actions to affect how stakeholders perceive the organization in a crisis" (Coombs 2012, 152). Only after an organization adequately addresses instructing and adjusting information can it begin to address reputational issues. Stakeholders expect organizations to share action-oriented communication, not just specific statements aimed at protecting their reputation.

When examining the effectiveness of an organization's response, external stakeholders can consider the content, medium, and timing of crisis messages. At the same time, the organization is evaluating its own crisis communication strategy. For external stakeholders and the organization, a crisis brings about a struggle for control and calls for interpretation, understanding, and a coordinated, but not always agreed upon, response. Given the highly complex and contingent nature of the response, an equally complex and nuanced approach is necessary for examining its effectiveness. Integrated Marketing Communication (IMC) offers a multi-faceted perspective for further examining organizational crisis communication.

THE INTERPLAY OF IMC AND CRISIS COMMUNICATION

Integrated communication can be defined as the notion and the practice of aligning symbols, messages, procedures, and behaviors for an organization to communicate with consistency, coherence, clarity and continuity within and across formal organizational boundaries (Christensen et al. 2008). In times of crisis, consistent, coherent, clear, and continuous communication removes the risk and uncertainty associated with crisis events. These qualities also help the organization to portray a sense of control over the crisis. Rather than allowing external stakeholders to define the crisis and evaluate the crisis response, the company is framing its own perception of the crisis and crisis response strategies. Communications professionals interpret and apply the concepts of IMC in a variety of ways. However, it is these diverse interpretations and ambiguous definitions that contribute to the richness of the marketing and management fields (Cornelissen, Christensen, and Vijn 2006).

IMC is an approach for navigating change and ambiguity to build strong communication plans (Groom, 2008). IMC assumes that communications must adapt and change as the environment changes. This approach is attentive to a more fluid enactment of communication activities, especially when applied to changing crisis scenarios. Research suggests that "disaster preparedness and mitigation depend on how well governments and service organisations communicate and coordinate with one another" (Curtis 2015, 611). The content and process of communication is central to achieving this coordinated response. The strength of crisis response relies upon action—in particular, coordinated, although not always agreed upon, action. Coordinated action results from a shared understanding of the best actions to take to address the crisis situation.

To illustrate the interplay of IMC and crisis communication, the following section details the work of the American Red Cross. This large and complex organization was selected for this chapter because it regularly responds to major public crisis events. Waymer and Heath (2007) suggest, "natural disasters can be considered bona fide crisis situations that need to be addressed and managed" (90). In fact, the Red Cross responds to approximately 70,000 disasters in the United States every year that include home fires and natural disasters (What We Do 2016). In addition, the Red Cross is an exemplar for illustrating coordination and integration. The Red Cross works in partnership with other agencies, organizations, and networks that provide services to disaster victims around the world. For example, the Red Cross partners with the Federal Emergency Management Agency (FEMA) to assist government agencies and community organizations plan, coordinate, and provide feeding, sheltering, and family reunification services for people affected by disasters. An IMC perspective textures and nuances the communication strategies of the Red Cross as it carries out its mission internationally.

CASE STUDY: THE AMERICAN RED CROSS

The Red Cross is a not-for-profit organization that depends on volunteers and public donations to carry out its mission. There are approximately 2,800 American Red Cross chapters throughout the United States educating their local communities about how to prepare for disasters and identify available resources. The American Red Cross is governed by a Board of Governors, "which has all powers of governing and directing, and of overseeing the management of the business and affairs of the organization" (Governance 2016). The organization's corporate governance principles are found in the Congressional Charter of the American Red Cross and a series of documents "that are reviewed periodically to ensure they continue to meet the needs of the organization and reflect current industry best practices" (Governance 2016). The work of the Red Cross is primarily done through local chapters and the coordinated efforts of multiple chapters when responding to large-scale disasters.

The organization was founded in 1881 by Clara Barton and friends in Washington, DC. The organization's charter includes the responsibilities of "giving relief to and serving as a medium of communication between members of the American armed forces and their families and providing national and international disaster relief and mitigation" (Brief History 2016). Currently, the American Red Cross focuses on people affected by disasters in America; support for members of the military and their families; blood collection, processing, and distribution; health and safety education and training, and international relief and development.

The Red Cross has achieved success in these areas in that it is the largest single supplier of blood and blood products in the U.S. Each year, nearly 4 million people donate blood through the Red Cross, helping to provide more than 40% of America's blood supply (What We Do 2016). The Red Cross is also the nation's leading provider of health and safety courses, such as CPR, First Aid, and Lifeguard training. Each year, more than 9 million Americans participate in training programs, including first responders, educators, babysitters, and people who want to be prepared to help others in an emergency (What We Do 2016). On an international scale, the American Red Cross is part of the world's largest humanitarian network with 13 million volunteers in 187 countries. Each year, the organization reaches an average of more than 100 million people around the world (What We Do 2016).

The American Red Cross is part of the global Red Cross/Red Crescent network. The international Red Cross and Red Crescent network is the largest humanitarian network in the world with a presence and activities in almost every country (Global Red Cross Network 2016). The network is made up of all the national and international organizations around the world. The three parts of the Global Red Cross network are the International Committee of the Red Cross (ICRC), the International Federation of Red Cross and Red Crescent Societies (IFRC) and the more than 185 national societies (Global Red Cross Network 2016). The International Committee of the Red Cross helps victims of armed conflicts while the International Federation of Red Cross and Red Crescent Societies works with national societies to respond to catastrophes and health emergencies and prepare communities for disasters.

Red Cross Communication Strategies

A large and complex organization like the Red Cross relies upon coordination and communication to effectively respond to crisis events. Organizations are able to coordinate more effectively when they develop an inter-organizational language, mission and protocol with a network of other responding organizations (Curtis 2015). Crisis response requires coordination among several agencies. For example, 91 organizations and departments were involved in the Hurricane Katrina relief effort (Curtis 2015). The success of the response depends upon all of these components working together. For example, the Canadian Red Cross collaborates with national and local emergency management authorities to implement emergency preparedness and response initiatives. When responding to a crisis, the Canadian Red Cross relies on a network of more than 6,000 trained disaster response volunteers across Canada.

Communication is integral to disaster and emergency management and response (Curtis 2015; Houston et al. 2016). The Red Cross develops communication strategies appropriate for before, during, and after a public disaster. The before stage consists of disaster education and preparation initiatives that can be defined as "a concerted effort to inform people about hazards and what to do if a disaster should occur" (McEntire 2007, 430). Disaster education initiatives involve outreach to individuals, schools, organizations and families. The Red Cross believes that being prepared can help mitigate the impact disasters have on people, families, and communities.

More recently, the Red Cross began using smart phone applications to provide disaster education. The Canadian Red Cross designed the Be Ready app to help people prepare for emergency situations. The app gives users instant access to the information needed to prepare for different emergency situations and to take action when a disaster strikes. The Be Ready app includes live weather feeds as well as interactive learning tools that educate Canadians on how to prepare their homes and families before, during, and after disasters and emergencies. For example, the Be Ready app connects to the Weather Network and sends users alerts for emergency events in their area. If an area is experiencing extreme heat, then people will receive an alert on their phones with information on what to do in extreme heat conditions. The app is free and once it is downloaded it does not need an internet connection to send alerts or to share information. The Red Cross hopes that the Be Ready app will encourage people to create an overall preparation plan that also include an emergency supply kit and an alternative source of water that might be necessary in a crisis. The supply kit should contain items that would allow people to be self-sufficient for up to 72 hours in the event of a disaster or up to two weeks in a health emergency.

Communication related to weather emergencies will often include what to do before, during, and after a major weather emergency like a tornado. The Red Cross's preparation communication includes information on reviewing and discussing an emergency plan, collecting supplies, and checking a safe room. They also instruct people to move items inside that could be picked up by the wind such as lawn furniture, trash cans, and hanging plants. The Red Cross recommends that people become familiar with their community's tornado warning system and stay informed about any watches or warnings that might be issued. The Red Cross also includes information on how to identify tornado danger signs that include dark clouds, large hail, or a roaring noise.

In addition to pre-crisis preparation communication, the Red Cross also focuses on communicating what to do during and after a crisis. During a weather related emergency, such as a tornado, the Red Cross communicates information related to finding underground shelter in a basement or storm cellar or even an interior closet, hallway, or bathroom. The Red Cross communicates instructing information for people on what to do if caught outdoors or driving during the tornado. After the storm, the Red Cross offers may ways to let family and friends know that you are safe that include registering at the Red Cross website or updating Facebook and Twitter status through the Safe and Well website. Another example of Red Cross after-crisis communication occurred in response to the 2013 Boston Marathon bombings. After this crisis, the American Red Cross conducted a campaign to publicly communicate coping strategies, including recommendations to limit exposure to media coverage of the bombings to reduce the psychological stress associated with the tragic event.

These examples illustrate the diverse set of communication practices that the Red Cross employs before, during, and after a crisis event. Because of the multiplicity of crises and communication practices, the Red Cross cannot approach its communication functions in a template fashion or as one individual model. An IMC approach captures the multiplicity and diversity of crises and communication strategies. In particular, the IMC metaphors, "discourse," "system," and "practices," create a variety of starting points for describing the communication activities of the Red Cross. In addition, examining the communication strategies of the Red Cross through these three metaphors allows the organization to be structured enough to implement an appropriate response strategy, but flexible enough to adapt to the dynamic nature of crisis response. The interplay of the "discourse," "system," and "practices" metaphors is useful for navigating the tension between structure and flexibility.

The IMC metaphors, "discourse," "system," and "practices," describe three different interpretations of IMC for communications professionals. The IMC as discourse approach describes IMC as "a specific way of talking about marketing communication phenomena that sensitizes the attention of managers to certain characteristics of the market while justifying the (temporary) ignorance of others" (Cornelissen, Christensen, and Vijn 2006, p. 9). The IMC as system metaphor suggests that communication activities adopt a holistic, integrated systems approach. The IMC as practice perspective differs from the discourse and system perspectives by focusing on the day-to-day practices of communication professionals. Rather than focusing on the organization's structure, the practice perspective considers specific processes and activities for "aligning, coordinating, and ultimately 'integrating' the activities of various communication professionals" (Cornelissen, Christensen and Vijn 2006, 16). IMC is constituted by practices of communications professionals.

The IMC as discourse interpretation emphasizes consistency and coherence as one way to address the fragmented and disjointed messages that an organization might communicate. With thousands of chapters, volunteers, and donors communicating on behalf of the Red Cross, the notions of consistency and coherence are difficult to imagine. In fact, miscommunication can occur when "two or more organizations exchange false information, spread rumors or exaggerate scenarios either directly or through a third party" (Curtis 2015, 614).

The IMC as system interpretation emphasizes how the local chapters of the Red Cross interact with the National Office and other chapters not only in routine times, but times of crisis, as well. The systems approach suggests that integration at the Red Cross occurs at many levels, including between the various communication activities, other business functions, other chapters, and the National Office. In essence, the local chapters function within the larger system of the organization. According to Curtis (2015), "Coordination takes place when organizations work together toward a common purpose and each entity involved is aware of its own role and the role of others" (615). One example is Emergency Preparedness Week, a national event coordinated by Public Safety Canada with support from provinces, municipalities, and the Canadian Red Cross. The purpose of the coordinated initiative is to raise awareness about the importance of preparing for emergencies. When responding to large-scale crises like tsunamis, hurricanes, and tornadoes, the Red Cross relies upon its national and international networks to best meet the needs of affected populations. Miscommunication within the networks can be detrimental to not only the Red Cross, but all of the entities that rely upon the Red Cross for information during crisis response. Miscommunication can contribute to an ineffective response from organizations that are best positioned to assist the crisis response efforts.

The IMC as practice interpretation focuses on the coordinated work activities of American Red Cross communication professionals. The best example of this coordination is the Red Cross's engagement with social media platforms. The American Red Cross uses social media to connect with various stakeholder groups, show appreciation to donors, and communicate its mission. Social media are important for building relationships with volunteers, the media, and the larger community (Briones et al. 2010). The Red Cross created the "#ChooseYourDay" campaign to encourage blood donation during the summer months, a time of decline in regular donors and student donor populations. This campaign is designed to raise awareness about blood donation shortages and encourage donations by offering free promotional items that include t-shirts, baseball caps, beach towels, and coolers. Red Cross communications professionals have also created a blood donor app for individuals to schedule an appointment, track donations, earn rewards, and store health history information (Corrigan 2016).

Social media platforms can also be used to update constituents during a crisis situation. For example, when three Red Cross workers were captured in northeastern Mali in April 2016, the International Committee of the Red Cross (ICRC) announced when they were freed by using Twitter. The news was then confirmed by an ICRC spokesperson. Social media creates a more complex delivery channel that can be used before, during, and after a disaster. The extent of social media depends on the crisis situation, the target stakeholders, and the crisis response message. A 2012 study of Red Cross communication professionals suggested that Twitter is the most useful social media tool for their chapters because it is easy to use and can be updated using cellphones. In this same study, Facebook was cited as helpful because it is easy to monitor, update, and has a broader user base than Twitter. A small number of communications professionals reported that YouTube and Flickr are useful in both routine and crisis times. Local chapters also monitor the Red Cross's National Headquarters daily social media update to identify trending Red Cross topics. Social media can build relationships with volunteers and the media that provide support in times of crises (Liu et al. 2012). Red Cross local chapters and National Headquarters departments interact with social media content creators and practice preliminary pre-crisis strategic intervention. According to Liu and associates (2012), "most of these responses are based on sending corrective information via the social media platform in which the issue emerged in order to address the issue with source credibility and information authority" (365). Liu and associates (2012) found that monitoring social media is critical during routine times as well as during crises because they are low-cost tools to generate and maintain volunteers and donors, attract and maintain media attention, and educate the general public about Red Cross services. Liu and associates (2012) also found that the American Red Cross faces a few challenges when using social media channels as part of its communication strategies. Three primary obstacles include: (1) time and human resources (2) learning curve and/or reticence of volunteers and management to use social media tools, and (3) the scope of the blogosphere. The most significant challenge is finding the time and staff to monitor social media channels.

REACHING AT-RISK POPULATIONS

As Red Cross staff members respond to disasters, they recognize that within communities, the capacities of people to cope with disasters may differ, depending on socio-economic status, location of residence, cultural peculiarities, nature of employment, and age, among other factors. Groups of individuals prone to disasters and "those who are least able to deal with their impact are known as *special populations*," (McEntire 2007, 284). Crisis events can have a disproportionate negative impact on these special populations. Waymer and Heath (2007) suggest that little or no attention is given to the voices of the affected publics, those whose interests are part or most of the reason why the subject organization is suffering a crisis and in need of responding to public and media inquiry.

Tierney writes that disaster research is characterized by "critical disjunctures," the neglect of some issues in preference for others resulting in discontinuities in research. Critical disjunctures just come with territory of disaster research. It was not until the 1970s and 1980s that issues of inequality in evacuation and disaster response began to emerge. Up until this point, disaster research emphasized males' perspectives, partly because most first responders were male. The challenge for the Red Cross to meet the needs of diverse stakeholders is grounded in a history of disaster management that relies upon a strongly privileged male, white perspective.

To address this challenge, the Red Cross has several programs in place to reach diverse populations. These populations might be unaware of the types of hazards that can threaten their communities and might not know how to prepare for them or avoid them. Additionally, the population might not know what actions to undertake in case of disaster (McEntire 2007). The Red Cross reaches out to assisted living and nursing homes to conduct senior citizen resiliency programs that include evacuation strategies and emergency kits (Brooke Riester, pers. comm.). To reach kids, Red Cross volunteers conduct a preparedness education program for children in third through fifth grade. This program, known as the Pillowcase Project, teaches children about personal and family preparedness, local hazards, and basic coping skills (Pillowcase Project 2016). When students complete this program, they receive a pillowcase to hold their emergency supplies. Within the broader community, Red Cross volunteers in collaboration with local fire departments, visit homes, install smoke alarms, distribute fire safety materials, and map out evacuation plans. One challenge for the Red Cross is that people do not often think about fire safety and may not even have smoke alarms. The goal of the Red Cross is to focus on preparation in hopes of avoiding the fire call (Brooke Riester, pers. comm.). Another challenge is to identify individuals who hold expertise in disaster mental health and the appropriate state licensing. These individuals can help console families who are victim to fires. They are prepared to deal with the range of emotions that emerge as a result of a crisis event. Disaster mental health professionals can also focus on staff and volunteer wellness and address any emotional concerns that these stakeholder groups may have as they provide support to victims of crisis.

Another population that the Red Cross tries to reach is the Latino population. Depending on the particular chapter's resources, the Red Cross can use the Spanish television station to reach this population. For example, one Midwest local chapter participates in interviews on local shows to share information on upcoming events and resources in the region. This chapter has also identified translators who are on call in case of a crisis. They also recruit Spanish-speaking volunteers and form partnerships with Latino organizations in the region (Brooke Riester, pers. comm.).

A 2013 study conducted by a student research team and a Midwest chapter of the American Red Cross found that an engagement strategy for connecting with vulnerable populations should include education and outreach (Alvarez et al. 2013). In this study, the elderly and the Latino community were two groups identified as needing special concern and attention.

This study also recommended cultivating relationships among key agencies serving the elderly and Latino communities surrounding the Midwest chapter. The study also recommended helpful resources to assist the elderly in planning for emergencies and disasters. In the area of education, this study recommended that the local chapter of the Red Cross use social media as the main point of engagement with the broader public, along with targeted individual efforts for agencies and businesses associated with the two target populations. The research team developed an Excel spreadsheet of the main agencies and businesses serving these target groups that arose during the research project.

In the area of outreach, the research team identified a need for developing a strategy for the targeted communities, which will help them prepare for possible disasters, in addition to helping the local chapter create a more effective network to respond to disasters (Alvarez et al. 2013). To effectively maintain the emergency management programs and succeed in post-disaster operations it is vital to identify available internal and external resources in advance (McEntire 2007, 417). The research team recommended that the local chapter form relationships with existing media outlets, organizations, and businesses. The research team members identified available community resources and best practices for accessing those resources. They also contacted appropriate vendors to begin the conversation of establishing an agreement on estimates for certain services that might be necessary in times of crisis. The team created sample correspondence templates in both English and Spanish that could be used to find food, shelter, clothing, and general supplies. McEntire (2007) recommends that any type of resource lists should be updated at least once a year so that resources can be easily accessed in a time of crisis. In addition to being constantly updated, the resource lists should also be evaluated for "needed information that is not part of [the] previously assembled crisis database" (Coombs 2012, 132). The stronger the networks are, and the more extensive the information about each resource, the easier it will be to gather information for obtaining a more accurate understanding of problems arising from a crisis (Coombs 2012).

The research team found that one aim of individuals working within the emergency management field is to provide access, warnings, and notifications in case of disaster, especially to those with disabilities and functional needs (Alvarez et al. 2013). Through education and outreach activities, the Red Cross determines what makes certain populations vulnerable to disasters and what these populations do throughout the disaster cycle to reduce their own vulnerability and that of their families, neighborhoods, and communities. Through integration and coordination, both governmental and not-for-profit organizations like the Red Cross can better serve these populations most affected by crisis events. Although IMC offers an approach that contributes positively to the field of crisis communication, the following section addresses the critiques of integration and coordination as key components of the communication strategy.

Limitations of an IMC Approach

When examining crises through an IMC lens we are attending to the coherent, cohesive, clear, and consistent nature of the response. However, giving such focused attention to certain aspects of the response necessarily means that we are overlooking others. For example, no matter how hard a communications team strives for coherent, cohesive, clear, and consistent communication, crisis events are fraught with information that is highly contextual and highly temporal. As the crisis unfolds, the information shifts and changes, requiring a response that addresses the incoherent, fragmented, unclear, and inconsistent nature of crisis. These particular qualities of crisis are not necessarily negative. In fact, they can often prompt reflection and learning within the organization.

An IMC lens also suggests that we're considering the practices of integration and coordination to achieve the communication strategy goals. IMC is appealing to communications professionals because it implies a sense of organization and structure for communication activities. The fundamental belief is that organizations should centralize their communications into one department (Christensen, Morsing, and Cheney

2008). For a large and complex organization like the Red Cross, this task is difficult, if not impossible. With so many disaster program specialists and disasters assistance workers speaking to the media, and so many Red Cross entities operating nationally and internationally, the notion of an integrated, centralized communication effort is misleading. Essentially, the theory of IMC is inconsistent with the actual practices of IMC within organizations.

These limitations are a note of caution for communications professionals. Unreflectively applying an IMC approach or any other approach when communicating with stakeholders or within the communications team can create problems for the crisis response. Communications professionals with the Red Cross can exacerbate the crisis by choosing inappropriate or inadequate communication strategies.

REFERENCES

Ahmed, Baba. 2016. "International Red Cross Workers Freed in North Mali." April 21. Accessed April 22, 2016. http://abcnews.go.com/International/wireStory/extremists-north-mali-free-intl-red-cross-workers-38591658.

Alvarez, Karla, Baisubanova, Daniya, Flynn, Laura, and Courtney Sippo. 2013. "Disaster Preparedness and Response for Special Populations: Report for the Saint Joseph County American Red Cross." Crisis & Community Course. University of Notre Dame.

Associated Press. 2016. "Three Red Cross Employees Abducted in Eastern Congo." May 3. Accessed May 3, 2016. http://www.foxnews.com/world/2016/05/03/3-red-cross-employees-abducted-in-eastern-congo.html.

A Brief History of the American Red Cross. 2016. "A Brief History of the American Red Cross." Accessed May 15, 2016. http://www.redcross.org/about-us/who-we-are/history.

Briones, Rowena L., Kuch, Beth, Liu,Brooke Fisher, and Yan Jin. 2011. "Keeping Up with the Digital Age: How the American Red Cross Uses Social Media to Build Relationships." Public Relations Review 37: 37-43.

Canadian Red Cross. 2016. "Red Cross Launches New App to Help Canadians Keep Themselves and Their Families Safe During Emergencies." May 1. Accessed May 1, 2006. http://www.redcross.ca/about-us/news-room/news-releases/latest-news/-red-cross-launches-new-app-to-help-canadians-keep-themselves-and-their-families-safe-during-emergen.

Christensen, Lars Thoger, Morsing Mette, and George Cheney. 2008. *Corporate Communications: Convention, Complexity, and Critique*. Los Angeles: Sage Publications.

Curtis, Christopher A. 2015. "Understanding Communication and Coordination Among Government and Service Organisations After a Disaster." *Disasters* 39: 611-625.

Coombs, W. Timothy. 2012. *Ongoing Crisis Communication: Planning, Managing, and Responding*. Thousand Oaks, CA: Sage Publications.

Cornelissen, Joep P, Christensen, Lars Thoger, and & PieterVijn. 2006. "Understanding the Development and Diffusion of Integrated Marketing Communications (IMC): A Metaphorical Perspective." Nyenrode Research Group (NRG) 06-02: 1-32.

Corrigan, John. 2016. "Red Cross Recruits Summer Donors with Promo Products." May 18. Accessed May 19. http://www.asicentral.com/news/web-exclusive/may-2016/red-cross-recruits-summer-donors-with-promo-products/.

Costa, Chris. 2016. "Cumberland Country First Responders Train for Emergency."
David, Emmanuel, and Elaine Enarson. 2012. *The Women of Katrina: How Gender, Race, and Class Matter in an American Disaster*. Nashville, TN: Vanderbilt University Press.
Fearn-Banks, Kathleen. 2007. *Crisis Communication: A Casebook Approach*. New Jersey: Lawrence Erlbaum Associates.
The Global Red Cross Network. 2016. "The Global Red Cross Network." Accessed May 15, 2016. http://www.redcross.org/about-us/history/global-red-cross-network.
Governance. 2016. "Governance: Achieving Excellence in Corporate Governance." Accessed May 16, 2016. http://www.redcross.org/about-us/who-we-are/governance.
Groom, S. Alyssa. 2008. "Integrated Marketing Communication: Anticipating the 'Age of Engage.'" *Communication Research Trends* 27: 3-19.
Houston, J. Brian, First, Jennifer, Spialek, Matthew L., Sorenson, Mary E., and Megan Koch. 2016. "Public Disaster Communication and Child and Family Disaster Mental Health: A Review of Theoretical Frameworks and Empirical Evidence." *Current Psychiatry Reports*, 18: 54.
Kake News. 2016. "Red Cross Prepares Severe Weather Response." April 26. Accessed April 26, 2016. http://www.kake.com/home/headlines/Red-Cross-prepares-severe-weather-response-377137531.html.
Liu, Brook Fisher, Jin Yan, Briones, Rowena, and Beth Kuch. 2012. "Managing Turbulence in the Blogosphere: Evaluating the Blog-Mediated Crisis Communication Model with the American Red Cross." *Journal of Public Relations Research*, 24: 353-370.
McEntire, David A. 2007. *Disaster Response and Recovery*. Hoboken, NJ: John Wiley & Sons.
Mitroff, Ian I., and Gus Anagnos. 2001. *Managing Crises Before They Happen: What Every Executive and Manager Needs to Know About Crisis Management*. New York: AMACOM.
Seeger, Matthew, Timothy Sellnow and Robert Ulmer. 2003. *Communication and Organizational Crisis*. Westport, CT: Greenwood Publishing Group, Inc.
News 24. 2016. "Three Red Cross Staff Kidnapped in Mali Now Free." April 22. Accessed April 22, 2016. http://www.news24.com/Africa/News/three-red-cross-staff-kidnapped-in-mali-now-free-20160422.
The Pillowcase Project. 2016. "The Pillowcase Project." Accessed May 15, 2016. http://www.redcross.org/get-help/prepare-for-emergencies/resources-for-schools#/The-Pillowcase Project.
Tierney, Kathleen. 2012. Critical Disjunctures: Disaster Research, Social Inequality, Gender and Hurricane Katrina. In D. Emmanuel and E. Enarson (Eds.), *The Women of Katrina: How Gender, Race and Class Matter in an American Disaster*. Nashville: Vanderbilt University Press.
Waymer, Damion, and Robert L. Heath. 2007. "Emergent Agents: The Forgotten Publics in Crisis Communication and Issues Management Research." *Journal of Applied Communication Research*, 35: 88-108.
What We Do. 2016. "What We Do." Accessed May 15, 2016. http://www.redcross.org/what-we-do.

NINE

Integrated Marketing Communication and Demarketing

The Demand for Weber and Rationality

Jeremy Langett

The inception of Integrated Marketing Communication (IMC) in the late twentieth century dismantled a product-oriented communication strategy in favor of an audience-centric approach. Schultz, Tannenbaum, and Lauterborn (1994) described the key to IMC as "realigning communications to look at it the way the customer sees it—as a flow of information from indistinguishable sources" (xvii) while Duncan (2002) viewed the activity as "a process for managing the customer relationships that drive brand value" (Duncan qtd. in Kitchen and De Pelsmacker, 7). Considered by Schultz and Schultz (2004) as a strategic and coordinated practice, IMC maintains the ability to influence customer behavior to meet organizational objectives. While this activity may attempt to increase customer purchases to reach sales goals, IMC may also be explored as a means to decrease consumption or dissuade patronage to ensure scalable operations in a process known as demarketing.

Kotler and Levy (1971) articulate the imbalanced relationship possibilities between production and consumption in a free market as a catalyst for introducing "demarketing" (74) in their article, "Demarketing, yes, Demarketing." Initially perceived as a contradiction—organizations traditionally have endeavored to bolster demand for a product or service—demarketing ushered in an opportunity for scalable, efficient practices that are aligned with the realities of the market. In their article, Kotler and Levy describe four different types of demarketing:

> (1) General demarketing, which is required when a company wants to shrink to the level of total demand; (2) Selective demarketing, which is required when a company wants to discourage the demand from certain customer classes; (3) Ostensible demarketing, which involves the appearance of demarketing as a device for actually increasing it; and (4) Unintentional demarketing, which is a negative practice that unintentionally drives customers away. (Bradley and Blythe, 2014)

While each type relates to the label of demarketing, ostensible demarketing covertly maintains an intention to increase demand for a product or service while unintentional demarketing is an unfortunate outcome for organizations attempting to grow demand but conversely reduce it. Bradley and Blythe (2014) expand Kotler and Levy's four types into six, which include the additional concepts of synchromarketing, an effort to manipulate the market to align with an organization's production schedule, and counter-marketing, which seeks to counteract a pressure to buy products associated with health warnings. No matter the overarching demarketing strategy employed, the authors contend that traditional marketing tools may be used to diminish demand just as easily as they are used to increase it. This contention may be examined through Weber's understanding of rationality in the social and economic implications of demarketing as a viable and grounded practice.

As equal parts economist, sociologist, and critical theorist, Max Weber embraced a subjectivist viewpoint in a world that was presented in scientific and mechanical language. Described by Parsons (1947) as "critical" (9) to an understanding of the world from a historical position, Weber advances two points that undergird his conception of a dynamic human-social and nature-scientific sphere. The first suggests that "generalized theoretical categories are as essential to the proof of causal relationships in the human and cultural field as they are in the natural sciences" (Parsons qtd. in Weber 1947, 9). Second, Weber contends that "empirical knowledge is in the nature of the case abstract," which disallows an investigator to attain a complete picture of a phenomenon (Parsons qtd. in Weber 1947, 9).

These conclusions place Weber in a challenging methodological vortex—the explanation of social material vis-à-vis theoretical categories working within a systematic framework, but without an opportunity to fully grasp the essence of a concept experienced in the natural world. Consequently, Weber posits two kinds of "meaning" that may be understood from this orientation: The first as "actually existing . . . to a concrete individual or actor" and a second as the "theoretically conceived pure type of subjective meaning" (Parsons qtd. in Weber 1947, 13). The latter type, considered "ideal," is representative of what Weber believed to be the closest to "typical" (Parsons qtd. in Weber 1947, 13).

Despite the splintered characteristics of Weber's understanding of the human-social and nature-scientific worlds, he does find a unifying factor in his conceptual scheme: rational action emerging from normative patterns working toward an ends. According to Parsons (1947), "the actor is treated not merely responding to stimuli, but as making an effort to conform to a certain ideal, rather than actual, patterns of conduct" (12). While the normatively ideal course lends itself to a variety of influences and unforeseen circumstances, the intention of conforming to procedures aligned with reaching a desired end marks a commitment to a presumption of rationality. In this way, support is gathered for a desired outcome regardless of the perception within an actual/existing or ideal/theoretically substantiated orientation.

Weber's dynamic schema of human-social and natural-scientific action showcases a system of "ultimate ends to the choice of means," which provides an inroad to exploring demarketing as a proactive activity with multiple means to potentially inverted ends (Parsons qtd. in Weber 1947, 14). From a Weberian perspective, demarketing spans several conceptual thresholds that call for a closer analysis of its rationality. Accordingly, this article seeks to ground demarketing as an activity in a Weberian foundation of formal and substantive rationality in an effort to clarify its meaning on the economic and social landscape. A brief explanation of demarketing types will offer context to this discussion.

TYPES OF DEMARKETING

Nigel Bradley and Jim Blythe's (2014) description of demarketing as an attempt "to reduce demand for a product, sometimes overall, sometimes from 'undesirable customers' and sometimes at specific times," introduces a variety of ways to diminish demand (1). No matter the scenario, the core function of demarketing is demand diminishment or cessation. Noting that the demarketing description at first glance offers an unusual proposition, Bradley and Blythe compile a variety of essays explaining different types in their 2014 edition of *Demarketing* to elaborate upon this concept.

Maria Pilar Martinez-Ruiz (2014) shares insight into synchromarketing, which she describes as marketing management's job "to regulate the level, timing and character of demand for an organization's product in terms of its objectives at the time" (8). Developed in response to Kotler's understanding of "irregular demand," described as an imperfect temporal pattern affecting the supply of a product or service, synchromarketing seeks to "smooth demand to fit the existing structure of capital, personnel, finance and, in general, organizational resources" (Martinez-Ruiz 2014, 11). Such an example of synchromarketing would be offering sales promotions during off-peak seasons for major tourist destinations popular in particular months. In addition to synchromarketing, a second demarketing strategy is selective demarketing, which describes an organization's efforts to discourage demand from a particular customer group. Daisy Jing Tan (2014) provides a case study of Frizzell Insurance, which applies segmentation theory to target and serve a specific customer profile base. Following the realization that lifetime value of customers over age thirty-five provided greater financial rewards than prospecting new customers, Frizzell Insurance embraced a loyalty program that concentrated primarily on building relationships with existing customers rather than engaging new customers. The result was a reduction in inquiries about Frizzell Insurance, which freed up time and resources for Frizzell associates to serve the preferred customer profile segment.

While synchromarketing and selective demarketing aim to reduce demand, ostensible demarketing provides an appearance of discouraging demand but actually endeavors to increase it. This third strategy is arguably the most controversial of the demarketing strategies, as its objective is inverted from its appearance—a practice that lends itself to a rationality critique provided later in this chapter. Based on what Michael Brehm calls psychological reactance, ostensible demarketing operates under the assumption that when an item is withdrawn, audiences begin to believe that its value was better than they initially thought. Robin Croft (2014) articulates salient examples of ostensible demarketing in his weblog, "Ostensible Demarketing: Prohibition, Prevention & Power," that examines charities, musical/artistic works, and soft drinks that have leveraged this strategy despite appearing unintentional.

Rather than coalescing support for a product, the aim of the fourth demarketing strategy, countermarketing, is driven to reduce both the supply side and demand side of a product or service. Often referenced in the context of social marketing, countermarketing efforts attack issues that strain the wellbeing of a social system—the erosion of family structures, the inflation of health concerns and the production of an underground economy. Nigel Jones, Paul Baines, and Steve Welsh (2014) advocate for intervention strategies that curb the demand for products such as narcotics and increase policy formation that can quell drug trafficking within countries serving as major suppliers.

As countermarketing seeks to decrease demand intentionally, unintentional demarketing decreases demand accidentally. Kotler and Levy (1971) reference unintentional demarketing briefly in their seminal work as activities that seek to attract customers but actually drive them away. According to Theresa Kirchner (2014), unintentional demarketing may be defined as "a decrease in demand resulting from an abortive effort to increase demand" (183). Strategies that may lead to unintentional demarketing include: price increases that seek to indicate luxury but ultimately discriminate against lower income groups; elimination of discounts that lose customers who relied on lower prices; and availability reductions that seek to place a premium on goods or services but can alienate customers in the process (Kirchner 2014, 91). Various demarketing approaches may be described as either contradictory or integral to organizational functions (Koschnick 1995, 48). This disconnect is dependent on the description of marketing and its possible inverse result—an understanding that may be applied to Weber's lens of meaning. A review of the demand concept and its essential characteristics may assist in drawing these disparate conclusions.

The Demand Concept

According to Theresa Kirchner (2014) "although the idea of 'demand' is central to Kotler and Levy's definition of 'marketing,' the current American Marketing Association definition of marketing does not include the word 'demand' or any other strong synonym" (182). Rather, the AMA defines marketing as "the activity, set of institutions, and processes for creating, communicating, delivering, and exchanging offerings that have value for customers, clients, partners and society at large." However, the AMA's definition of demarketing does address the concept of demand through an economic understanding of the word, "a term used to describe a marketing strategy when the objective is to decrease the consumption of a product," and a social understanding of the word, "the process of reducing the demand for products and services believed to be harmful to society" (Kirchner 2014, 182).

The inclusion or omission of demand from descriptions of marketing and demarketing provides an illustration of Weber's two meaning types. Theoretically, marketing presupposes a management, or at least an influence, of customers and prospects valuing or desiring a product or service, yet the explicit use of "demand" is only offered in a demarketing definition. In this sense, Weber's two-part position of conceiving generalized categories of causal relationships and their abstract nature is realized. For the theorist omitting the word "demand" in descriptions of marketing, an understanding of marketing is subjective and finds meaning in an ideal type. However, the organizational actor engaged in marketing is prospecting customers and building connections through creation of advertisements, communicating messages and maintaining current customer loyalty in an effort to elevate demand. In this way, marketing meaning is found in the actually existing mode of activity designed for a specific end.

Curiously, demarketing's definitional focus on the centrality of adjusting demand also falls under the umbrella of Weber's two-part position of conceiving generalized categories of causal relationships and their abstract nature. At first glance, the prefix "de-" would indicate the reversal of marketing activities. However, demarketing's focus on reducing demand appears to influence a specific aspect of marketing, which either extends beyond a normative understanding of marketing or marginalizes its effects on a desired outcome. Once again, Weber's categories of meaning as ideal or actually existing are necessary to delineate, this time in an effort to understand the connection between marketing and demand. In theory, demarketing as a function of reducing demand may be viewed ideally as a clearly established objective. However, the implementation of demarketing activities may extend beyond the scope of reducing demand and actually exist to increase demand, as in the case of an ostensible strategy. Or even more simply, engaging in demarketing may fail to impact levels of demand, leading to a discrepancy between Weber's ideal understanding of the concept and what actually exists.

The application of demarketing strategy may be illustrated in Medway and Warnaby's (2008) study of place marketing. Suggesting that places are "increasingly perceived as being in competition," (641) Medway and Warnaby (2008) contend that enhancing negative aspects about a place may frequently assist in reducing demand, but sometimes result in the opposite effect, and increase the place's popularity. If implemented for this particular objective, the latter strategy is coined "perverse place marketing" and may be surmised as an ostensible demarketing strategy (Medway & Warnaby 2008, 643). In addition, place marketers may elect to incorporate selective demarketing strategies for venues that already maintain a desired customer base, such as the elite, upper-class clientele of the French Riviera. These strategies may be implemented passively, such as the end of controlled message development for a particular destination, or actively, such as disseminating messages that suggest a lack of vacancy or capacity for guests who do not meet a particular socioeconomic criterion.

Rational Economic Action

Max Weber's observation of economic action suggests that individuals attempt to conform to a certain ideal, which may be generalized as acting rationally. Despite this conclusion, Weber posits that "rationality is a variable and a fundamental one at that" (Vanagunas 1989, 395). To account for its variability, Weber divides economic behavior into several categories; chief among them *wertrational,* which may translate to "worth," described as a formal and calculative understanding, and *zweckrational,* which may translate to "purpose," described as a substantive and values-laden understanding (Parsons qtd. in Weber 1947, 14). Despite the perceived necessity of retaining formal and substantive rationality within an organization, Weber contends that these rationality types "are always in principle in conflict" (Weber 1947, 212). Indeed, contemporary organizations only concerned with formal accounting practices and other calculative activities may lose their understanding of a greater purpose built from an agreed-upon culture or set of core values. An entity without an identity has no mechanism for effective communication and is without a sturdy foundation on which to operate. Similarly, organizations without formal practices facilitating a "systematic process for the valuation and verification of opportunities for profit and of the success of profit-making activity," will not successfully manage organizational operations despite a robust and meaningful organizational culture (Weber qtd. in Vanagunas 1989, 395). Balancing the resources to manage both formal rational and substantive rational activities is a responsibility tasked to organizational leaders, which may lead to political and bureaucratic challenges among various constituent groups. However, it is understandable that both forms of rational action maintain indispensable value to organizations seeking to exist in an economic capacity, which can be influenced by marketing/demarketing activities. Determining the rationality of marketing/demarketing as a formal or substantive practice may elucidate both the "actually existing" concrete type and "theoretically conceived" ideal type of these activities to an organization's goals.

Wertrational: *Demarketing as Formalized Activity*

The consideration of demarketing as *wertrational* entails several characteristics that would indicate its practice as specific, measurable and accountable. First, demarketing must have a conceptual framework in economic theory, preferably law. Given demarketing's AMA-defined relationship with the demand concept, The *American Journal of Economics & Sociology* offers the first law of economic demand as "the quantity demanded of any commodity will be greater or at least never less at a lower price" (L.S.M. 1997, 285). Typically, the first law of economic demand holds true with commodities, although the designation of "law" would assume that this is an incontrovertible truth among all commodities at all times. Such is the requirement for a *wertrational* activity that lends itself to calculation and valued as worth. Exemplifying the understanding of this static proof would be the use of the word "widget" to designate commodities in economic descriptions. Immune from sociopolitical, geographic or cultural factors inhabiting the marketplace, widgets are calculable based on the laws applied to them. Typically—or ideally—a Weberian understanding would perceive the price of widgets to escalate as demand increases. Should demand for widgets overwhelm the production capacity of a firm, strategies may be employed to reduce the demand in a calculated manner. This is an example of demarketing perceived under the characterization of *wertrational* and responsive to the laws of the economic landscape. If demarketing is effective according to *wertrational*, its ends will reflect a reduction in demand for a targeted time and maintain the production efficiency of an organization.

Zweckrational: *Demarketing as Substantive Activity*

Despite the ideal perception of demarketing as a *wertrational* activity, this practice may also characterize itself as a *zweckrational* activity that offers substantive, purposive value to an organization. Demarketing perceived as a *zweckrational* activity embraces the dynamic factors affecting an increase or decrease in demand while acknowledging the potential of demarketing for all goods—not just commodities. As the characterization most likely embraced by marketing managers and agents, demarketing as *zweckrational* maintains a fluid understanding of the first law of economic demand and focuses its ends on content-related, subjective means that extend beyond formal calculation.

An example of demarketing as *zweckrational* may be the case of luxury coffee. Considered a commodity in economic texts, coffee brands have catapulted into luxury status due to a variety of sociopolitical and cultural factors that are recognized by a substantive rationality. Some of these factors include a manipulation of demand as a result of targeted messaging, visual identity, product location availability and a positioning that affects social status. Despite higher prices, coffee of this branded variety may be demanded in much greater quantity than coffee of a basic variety at a lower cost, thus violating the first rule of economic demand. Inconsistent with a *wertrational* understanding of demand, the case of branded coffee follows a *zweckrational* understanding of the substantive value the coffee brings to consumers. Marketing managers faced with the challenge of supplying this higher-demanded coffee may initiate demarketing activities to reduce the volume sold at a particular time or location in an effort to provide equal access opportunity to the customer base.

Conclusions from a Wertrational *and* Zweckrational *Analysis of Demarketing*

An analysis of demarketing as *wertrational* and *zweckrational* offers several conclusions that may be drawn from each category of rationality. Given Weber's understanding that categories remain generalized and abstract, these conclusions may be advanced as points of discussion but are particularly challenging to solidify into concrete theory. Nevertheless, both categories offer support and critique to the demarketing concept.

Reviewing demarketing from a *wertrational* perspective grounds the practice in a calculable and accountable foundation. In an ideal scenario, an organization employing demarketing can select the appropriate strategy to curb demand from one time to another (synchromarketing), from a particular audience (selective demarketing), or from use of a particular product in general (countermarketing). Each approach abides by the first law of economic demand and can be characterized as an effective means to reach efficient ends. Problematic to the *wertrational* idea, ostensible demarketing does not seek to curb demand and endeavors toward different ends—increasing demand. Similarly, unintentional demarketing does not incorporate means to diminish demand but produces an ends consistent with demarketing—reducing demand. From a *wertrational* standpoint, the disruption of the linear and similar means-to-end function of ostensible demarketing and unintended demarketing obstructs the perception of an ideal rational action.

Given the problems identified through the lens of *wertrational* with ostensible demarketing and unintentional demarketing, the use of the demand concept as a foundation may be misleading. Although demand is central to the first law of economic demand, the reality of ostensible demarketing manipulates demand to intentionally reach an organizational objective, which may be perceived as "purpose" or *zweckrational*. The objective takes precedence over demand, which leads to an ability to pursue overt demarketing practices (synchromarketing, selective demarketing and countermarketing) and covert marketing practices (ostensible demarketing). Organizations that establish marketing objectives apply the traditional four Ps of marketing—product, price, placement and promotion—opportunities to adjust demand toward a desired outcome. Unlike the *wertrational* practice of a calculable and linear activity abiding to the first law of economic demand, a practice built on *zweckrational* escalates or reduces demand for the goal of obtaining an objective, as exemplified by the idea of the luxury item equal in quality to a commodity but promoted in a unique way that resonates emotionally with a target audience.

Characterizing demarketing as a purpose-laden *zweckrational* activity may relate to an organization's objectives, but demarketing's relationship to demand remains puzzling, given the variable consequences of many of these strategies addressed in Kirchner's diagram. According to Vanagunas (1989), "it is realized that within the domain of economic behavior, purely rational, ideal-type economic action is extremely rare" (396). Therefore it can be expected for demarketing to feature aspects of *zweckrational* as the purpose—or objective—of organizations easier than the calculable and accountable features of a *wertrational* activity.

However, the meaning derived from this *zweckrational* activity may question its incorporation of the "de" prefix of demarketing. This issue becomes particularly relevant when demarketing is implemented with the intention to increase demand, such as the case of an ostensible demarketing strategy, or fail to reach any objective at all as in the case of an unintentional demarketing strategy. In either case, the concept of demand stays constant; no formulation of de-demand (diminished demand) is offered in congruence with the activity seeking to diminish it, demarketing. The rhetorical construction of demarketing may be analyzed as a way to ascertain the intent of organizational managers and the consequence of these activities—some of which may be unintended and inverse to the "de" prefix.

Deconstructing the Rhetoric of Demarketing

The unpredictability of a demand outcome following the implementation of demarketing activities may warrant a closer inspection of the "de" prefix associated with activities attempting to reduce demand. If demarketing follows a *wertrational* path, the intention and outcome of reducing demand stays constant for synchromarketing, selective demarketing and countermarketing. However, an understanding of demarketing as *wertrational* activity would be found in what Weber recognizes as the "theoretically conceived" arena and elude the "actually existing" mode of meaning perceived by individuals. For the concrete actor seeking to manage demand in some capacity, demarketing appears in a form closer to *zweckrational,* as a means to reach a desired purpose—either to increase or decrease demand through strategies labeled as "demarketing," which might be labeled more appropriately as simply "marketing." The inclusion of "de" in demarketing responds to Weber's notion that generalized theoretical categories are essential to demonstrate causal relationships. From Weber's perspective, organizational actors attempting to reduce demand will incorporate demarketing strategies and move toward achieving that end. As Parsons (1974) suggests, these efforts will conform to reaching the ideal—a reduction in demand—but may be influenced or manipulated toward reaching different ends. The strategies of synchromarketing, perverse place demarketing and unplanned ostensible demarketing all maintain the potential for this result, leading to an abstractness of demarketing concept Weber asserts in his theory of social and economic organization. The abstractness of this phenomenon may accommodate the "de" prefix without upending the meaning of how these activities are rationally oriented. Demarketing as *wertrational* aligns with the first law of economic demand and is a calculable function while demarketing as *zweckrational* accepts market influences and adjusts its course based on objectives for sustaining a purpose.

Given this understanding, the decision to incorporate the "de" prefix in demarketing becomes perceptually rhetorical. The art of persuasion is implicitly tied with marketing, which lends itself to the same critique of practices that indicate causal relationships but remain far more abstract than what a systematic social scientific approach may yield. Although framing demarketing as *wertrational* or *zweckrational* attempts to explain the conforming of demand-reducing activities to an ideal, neither orientation of rational action can perfectly account for the dynamic economic and market forces affecting the ultimate outcome. In this way, Weber's perceptually convoluted two-part meaning structure, the "actually existing . . . to a concrete individual" and the "theoretically conceived pure type" offers surprising clarity to the demarketing concept that can be intended to accomplish a specific end but experiences an inverse result (Parsons qtd. in Weber 1947, 13). An illustration of the demarketing concept rooted in Weberian rationality may be the Coca-Cola Company's introduction of a new formula in 1985.

The Rationality of (De)Marketing Coca-Cola®

The Coca-Cola Company's introduction of a new formula in 1985 has served as both a case study for marketing blunders as well as marketing brilliance (Croft 2014; Haig 2011; Haoues 2015; Ringold 1988). Asserting that the company sought to "re-energize its Coca-Cola brand," chief executive officer Roberto Goizueta oversaw the reformulation of the classic cola after 200,000 consumers indicated a taste preference for the "new" Coke® compared with the old (The Real Story of New Coke, 2012). The result was a consumer panic that led to the hoarding of the original formula as well as the formation of several protest groups that coalesced around the love of what was affectionately and commercially known as the Real Thing™. Less than three months later, the Coca-Cola Company announced the return of the "old" Coca-Cola following the customer reactions that evangelized the original formula—"suddenly everyone was talking about Coca-Cola, realizing what an important role it played in his or her life," leading to the reintroduction of the original formula that appeared in "network newscasts" and front page stories of "virtually every major newspaper" (The Real Story of New Coke, 2012). The removal and reintroduction of a loved brand appeared to accomplish Mr. Goizueta's reenergizing objective, although the CEO maintained that the means used to accomplish this objective were unintended. According to Ringgold (1988), the new Coke story exemplified psychological reactance within a demarketing strategy, although former Coca-Cola president Donald Keough indicated that "we're not that smart" when asked if the event was strategically planned (Clifford 2009).

Weber's conception of rational action imbues the Coca-Cola (de)marketing campaign with several important economic and social considerations as well as an explanation for the mystery of its diverse perceptions as a success or failure. First, market competition enabled Coca-Cola to work toward a desired end, a rational action that would precipitate a means to advance in the Cola Wars. A *wertrational* understanding of this rational action illustrates the development and launch of New Coke, which emerged from calculable data indicating a taste preference over the traditional formula from more than 200,000 consumers. Launching a *wertrational*-based product provided Coca-Cola managers with a theoretically conceived, ideal type of meaning to the marketing—a quantitatively supported action verified in taste preference results that would assumedly lead to greater demand. What actually existed to the marketers, however, was a consumer response built on *zweckrational*—the substantive, values-laden type of meaning to the marketing that incited consumer outcries, protests and stockpiling of the original formula given the emotional attachment customers shared with the Real Thing™. Ideally, framing the introduction of New Coke as an ostensible demarketing strategy is theoretically sound and follows a linear logic identified in a *wertrational* approach. What actually resulted, however, was a denial of any preconceived strategy to employ ostensible demarketing and trigger a *wertrational* customer reaction, which ultimately propelled Coke's market share to 17.6 percent in 2014 and a clear winner of the contemporary Cola Wars (Peterson 2015). Despite the denial of an ostensible demarketing strategy, Coca-Cola's achievement of soda serendipity can be examined without the public rhetoric that accompanied its veiled marketing efforts by returning to conclusions drawn from Weber's *wertrational* and *zweckrational* action.

Coca-Cola's sensible decision to move forward with a reformulated cola that was supported with data appears as a means to escalate demand. However, this *wertrational* appearance may fail to unearth Weber's conception of *zweckrational*, analyzed as a substance-driven, and not demand-driven, objective. Reflecting Weber's rational action, Coca-Cola exerted effort to conform to a certain ideal rather than a specific pattern of conduct. A reformulation of the cola may have served as a stimulus appearing as an ostensible demarketing strategy; however, the response embraced the purpose-laden *zweckrational* that exposed the veneer of reducing demand for the purposes of increasing it.

CONCLUSION

Weber's theory of rational and economic action provides an exploratory inroad to understanding the rhetoric of demarketing and the debate about Coca-Cola's planned or unplanned marketing success. Organizations, as rational actors, will move toward a desired ends while conforming to an ideal, which may appear within the domain of any number of diverse social and economic arenas. While public acknowledgement or denial to pursue a (de)marketing strategy to escalate demand allows for reflexive discourse, Weber's preference to view the subjectivity of these activities, such as a present duality of *wertrational* and *zweckrational*, rather than asserting a mechanical language explanation, such as a firm's decision to engage or not to engage an ostensible demarketing, reinforces his notion that "empirical knowledge is in the nature of the case abstract" (Parsons qtd. in Weber 1947, 9).

The abstractness of empirical knowledge is revealed in rhetorical constructions such as demarketing, which maintain multiple intended/unintended consequences and a "de" prefix that persuades audiences of a concerted effort to reduce. The category of communicating offers that have value for customers comprises multiple definitions that include components such as demand and strategy, which are frequently simplified into a binary of "marketing/demarketing" to indicate casual relationships and illustrate Weber's call for generalizing theoretical categories in a world that presents information mechanically. Nonetheless, given the variability of outcome and ostensible characteristics of some (de)marketing programs, a foundation in Weberian rationality is of greater utility to understand the success/failures of these activities rather than ascribing them to a popularized concept.

REFERENCES

Bradley, Nigel and Jim Blythe, eds. 2014. *Demarketing*. New York: Routledge.

Clifford, Stephanie. 2009. "Coca-Cola Deleting Classic from Coke Label." *New York Times*. January 31. http://www.nytimes.com/2009/01/31/business/media/31coke.html.

Croft, Robin. 2014. *Ostensible Demarketing: Prohibition, Prevention & Power* (blog). http://ostensible-demarketing.blogspot.com.

Duncan, Tom. 2002. *IMC: Using Advertising and Promotion to Build Brands*. Boston: McGraw-Hill.

Haig, Matt. 2011. *Brand Failures: The Truth about the 100 Biggest Branding Mistakes of All Time*. London: Kogan Page Publishers.

Haoues, Rachid. 2015. "30 Years ago Today, Coca-Cola Made its Worst Mistake." *CBS News*, April 23. http://www.cbsnews.com/news/30-years-ago-today-coca-cola-new-coke-failure/.

Jones, Nigel, Paul Baines and Steve Welsh. 2014. "Countermarketing in a Wicked Problem Context – The Case of Cocaine." In *Demarketing*, edited by N. Bradley and J. Blythe, 42-64. New York: Routledge.

Kirchner, Theresa A. 2014. "Unintentional Demarketing." In *Demarketing*, edited by N. Bradley and J. Blythe, 181-197. New York: Routledge.

Kitchen, Philip J. and Patrick De Pelsmacker. 2004. *Integrated Marketing Communications: A Primer*. London: Routledge.

Koschnick, W. J. 1995. *Dictionary of Marketing*. Gowder: Aldershot.

Kotler, Philip and Sidney J. Levy. 1971. "Demarketing, Yes, Demarketing." *Harvard Business Review* November/December, 74-80.

L.S.M. 1997. "Taking Max Weber's Proposal Seriously." *American Journal of Economics & Sociology*, 56(3): 285-286.

Martinez-Ruiz, Maria P. 2014. "Synchromarketing." In *Demarketing*, edited by N. Bradley & J.Blythe, 8-25. New York: Routledge.

Medway, Dominic and Gary Warnaby. 2008. "Alternative Perspectives on Marketing and the Place Brand." *European Journal of Marketing*, 42(5/6): 641-653.

Peterson, Hayley. 2015. "Pepsi Surpasses Diet Coke in Huge Soda Shift." *Business Insider*, March 26. http://www.businessinsider.com/pepsi-surpasses-diet-coke-in-soda-shift-2015-3

Ringgold, Debra J. 1988. "Consumer Response to Product Withdrawal: The reformulation of Coca-Cola." *Psychology and Marketing*, 5(3): 189-210.

Schultz, Don E. and Heidi Schultz. 2004. *IMC: The Next Generation*. Boston: McGraw-Hill.

Schultz, Don E, Stanley E. Tannenbaum and Robert F. Lauterborn. 1994. *Integrated Marketing Communications: Pulling it Together and Making it Work*. Chicago: NTC.

Tan, Jing. 2014. "Selective Demarketing Case Study – Frizzell Insurance." In *Demarketing*, edited by N. Bradley & J. Blythe, 138-149. New York: Routledge.

Vanagunas, Stanley. 1989. "Max Weber's Authority Models and the Theory of X-inefficiency." *American Journal of Economics & Sociology*, 48(4), 393-400.

Weber, Max. 1947. *The Theory of Social and Economic Organization*. Edited by Talcott Parsons (Ed.) New York: Free Press.

TEN

IMC in a Networked Society

Engaging Professionals and Educators

Kees van het Hof and David E. Weber

In a period of roughly three decades, integrated marketing communication (IMC) has become a prominent and consequential approach to launching, maintaining, refining and extending articulate encounters between organizations and customers, or potential customers. Laczniak and Patti (2005) observe that "IMC was [originally] about ensuring that all marketing communication messages had *one voice, one look*. It was soon discovered, however, that to accomplish this . . ., a new set of marketing principles and practices was required that would support an ongoing, interactive, cross-functional process" (6) by which flows of information relevant to the organization could be managed. Reid, Luxton, and Mavondo (2005), among others, have enumerated the benefits of this process, defined by Procu, del Barrío-Garca, and Kitchen (2012) as follows:

> the interactive and systemic process of cross-functional planning and optimization of messages to stakeholders, with the aim of communicating with coherence and transparency to achieve synergies and encourage profitable relationships in the short, medium and long term. (326)

Porcu, del Barrío-Garca, and Kitchen (2012) add that "'One voice' represents the core of [the] integration [project]" (326), and that "a common strategy must unify the activity of . . . public relations, advertising, sales promotions, [and] direct and interactive marketing . . . on- or off-line . . .. [in order to] set a constant dialogue between the organization and its constituencies" (326). To those four core IMC activities (PR, advertising, sales promotion, marketing), Kitchen and De Pelsmacker (2004) would add "sponsorship, internet or e-communications [and] relationship marketing" (27-28). The purpose and focus of IMC work, then, is to bring conceptual and thematic congruence and consistency to the results generated in a good half-a-dozen functions by which an organization may construct mutually beneficial relationships that, in various guises and configurations, involve "insiders" (i.e., members of an organization) and "outsiders" (e.g., clients, customers, consumers, prospects, regulators, members of the community in general).

For many IMC practitioners and scholars, the concept of brand is inseparable from IMC. For example, Reid, Luxton and Mavondo (2005) "view the . . . domain of IMC as being similar to that of brand orientation" (13). Similarly, Chen, Liu, and Huang (2015) aver, "the corporate brand should be the basis of . . . [an integrated] communication program and all . . . forms of [strategic or corporate cross-functional] communication should be integrated with this (100). Kliatchko (2008) places the concept of brand at the heart of his definition of IMC: "An audience-driven business process of strategically managing stakeholders, content, channels, and results of brand communication" (140).

What Kliatchko termed "content and channels" are remarkably unstable, especially within as generous (measured by the technology clock) a span of time as forty years or so, because change in one generates change in the other; and three or four decades offers plenty of time for such change to occur. Further, the rapidity of those changes means that the coherent cross-functional messaging that constitutes IMC will not be generated by the same tools all the time. New technologies and techniques for designing and delivering messages emerge; the contours of established ones change, or languish or even disappear. For example, each new photographic film format alters the act of taking a photograph; and digital photography has caused the use of chemically treated strips of acetate for capturing images to languish in any case. In turn, as channels change, content of those channels generate changes as well. So, staying with the example, what we photograph and how we do it has been in part shaped by what photography tools we have at our disposal. As an illustration, consider how the selfie is almost wholly a product of the inexpensive, portable, easily accessible smartphone and its photo-snapping function; this affordance can serve as an IMC application, as a private one.

Both authors are long-serving university faculty members in academic departments that offer strong applied communication programming. Accordingly, a final task to undertake in this report is to articulate its relevance for IMC pedagogy. Educators who train new cohorts of IMC specialists must familiarize students with the occupational concerns, interests and responsibilities of IMC professionals. They must also prepare students to navigate a future in which some tools of IMC do not even exist yet.

In this chapter, therefore, we aim to respond to one fundamental question: How may organizational professionals charged with integrating marketing communications (IMC)—specifically, the branding endeavor—make effective choices in praxis? We anchor our inquiry in the following sources of information: (a) relevant theoretic grounding; (b) our backgrounds, before entering the academy, as practitioners, particularly the first author's fifteen years' experience in managing IMC for several Dutch and international brands; (c) discoveries made in service-learning projects completed by undergraduates enrolled in the communications program of HAN University of Applied Sciences' Arnhem Business School, The Netherlands.

SUMMARY OF RELEVANT THEORETIC GROUNDING

The onset of personal computing and digital telecommunications began during roughly the same period of IMC's emergence as a credible approach to designing and managing corporate communications (Cornelissen, 2001; Persuit, 2013). The following ideas will ground our analysis and discussion of IMC, branding, and digital communication, as organizational praxis and the basis of IMC pedagogy for today.

TURNING POINTS—SOCIETIES 1.0, 2.0, AND 3.0

Digital communicating has produced a noetic reconfiguration (i.e., adjustments in consciousness, habits of thought, and modes of expression) of the human communicator. Ong (1982) has explicated the "original" shift—from orality to literacy. An example would be our ability to transform as writing words uttered orally. Tyner (1998), Johnson (1997), and Lanham (1993), among others, have done the same for the shift from the literate to the digital.

Human communication capacities developed during an earlier noetic epoch maintain some presence in a later one (Ong 1968, 1982; also, Farrell 1991). An example is our use of print terminology (folder, file, page, etc.) from the literate epoch for naming some digital phenomena. Similarly, earlier digital tools and forms of expression maintain a presence in the space of digital communication today. For example, we may as a population use email less heavily, or visit chat rooms less often, than we did in the recent past, thanks to the development of new modes of digital encounter. But we still use email and the chat function to a measurable extent—they have not disappeared as a communicator's options. From the noetic standpoint, the tension between mastering new digital tools and dealing with older ones (should they be adopted, or not? kept? altered? jettisoned?) is one humans have likely never before negotiated self-reflexively or consciously. Enactments of that negotiation play out during sociocultural moments called Society 1.0, Society 2.0, and Society 3.0 (cf. van den Hoff 2013).

Society 1.0: "One-Way" Communication

The conduit model of communication (Reddy, 1979) holds that communication consists of messages sent by a source and consumed by a receiver. In organizational terms, an organization originates and sends messages to stakeholders (i.e., members and customers, as well as third parties, such public officials, or private citizens affected by an organization's decisions) in a "one-way" process, i.e., one that unfolds with little or no feedback from or dialogue with audiences. As of the late 1970s or early 1980s, an "inserted" dialogue into the "conduit" traditional print artifacts as well as artifacts from electronic media such as television and radio; and, in some cases, media products generated by primitive or rudimentary, early-adoption digital communication. Society 1.0 is a name for this communication era.

Society 2.0: "Two-Way" Marketing Communication

The "post-Gutenberg" (Palmeri 1991, 57) habits of mind and manner privileged in Society 1.0 would, by the mid-1990s, be altered by the extent to which digital "technology [became] . . . intertwined in the way we interact with . . . the world" (De Roeck et al. 2012). This produced Society 2.0, an era characterized by "increasing dependence on information and communication technologies . . . in everyday life, both in our professional and private lives" (Verdegem 2011, 28). Between organizations and stakeholders, parasocial interaction and technologically constructed relations depended increasingly on refined digital information design, plus ease of stakeholder access to digital communication tools—which in the 1990s meant email primarily. Derksen (2011) observes that for a Society 2.0 organization, the extent of "two-way" interaction with stakeholders exceeds anything accomplished along those lines by Society 1.0 organization. Even so, a Society 2.0, organization still sought to remain in control of the communication process, despite more reciprocity than a 1.0 organization might seek.

Society 3.0: "Multi-Way" Communication—The Networked Society

Li and Bernoff (2008) explain that fast broadband connectivity, a variety of new communication tools (including stable, seemingly instantaneous connections to the Internet) and platforms, masses of people wanting to use those tools to interact with one another, to generate an almost incalculable amount of content launched a transition from Society 2.0 to

Society 3.0. To describe that phenomenon, Li and Bernoff use the term *groundswell*. Jenkins (2006) calls it "convergence," that is, access to and use of "multiple media platforms, the cooperation between multiple media industries, and the migratory behavior of media audiences" (2). He explains that the "circulation of media content—across different media systems, competing media economies, and national borders" (Jenkins 2006, 3)—constitutes a paradigm shift in how we interact, what we interact about, and how we make decisions.

In Society 3.0, this "multi-way" application of communication technologies illustrates *intermediality*—"phenomena that . . . in some way take place between media . . . [or] have to do with a crossing of borders between media" (Rajewsky 2005, 46). In Society 3.0—the networked society—communication practices accommodate a variety of personal networks, media, objectives and applications, each with its own dynamics, characteristics and atmospherics. Bastos and Levy (2012) declare that the artifacts of social media—tweets, snaps, yaks, updates, photos, videos, posts, comments, likes—"provide easy, inexpensive, quick and broad-reaching ways of conveying meanings, values, and views to one's social circle and beyond" (361).

In his reflections concerning the intersection of social theory and social science, Blumer (1954; cf. Bowen 2008) refers to *definitive* concepts, his term for "stable empirical contents [established] through precise procedures" (7); and in contradistinction to them, speaks of (b) *sensitizing* concepts, which provide "prescriptions of what to see . . . [and] suggest directions along which to look" (7). This report pivots on one particular definitive concept and a sensitizing concept, which we will now elucidate.

FROM PRODUCT PROMOTION TO "THE COMPANY BEHIND THE PRODUCT"

The definitive concept at the heart of this report is *brand*—operationalized as *branding*—which Bastos and Levy (2011) define as "the union of technology and aesthetics, the integration of the pragmatism of engineering and the elevation and elegance of art, addressed to the sociology and psychology of the intended audiences" (360). A "brand is an interdisciplinary creation" (Bastos and Levy 2012, 363) and "the backbone of marketing" (Bastos and Levy 2012, 363). An exploratory study by Reid (2005) identified a "positive relationship between the IMC process and brand outcomes" (47). Because the scholarly roots of our report lie in communication studies and rhetoric, a particularly salient aspect of branding is that: "the distinctiveness of a brand . . . is not a property of the actual product, but *a product of communication* [italics added] of the brand" (Reid, Luxton, and Mavondo 2005, 16).

Shifts in the Meaning of "Brand"

The story of branding is the story of a shift, over more than a century, from guiding audiences' thoughts and feelings about a product or service, to training outsiders how to view the organization associated with that product or service. Franzen (2006) has traced the history of branding, starting with its origins in the nineteenth century as a discipline with a more or less narrow focus on how to distinguish one product from another. Hatch and Schultz (2009) state that brands "were [at first] a means of dressing up products. Created and managed almost exclusively by marketers, they were a designed means" (117) of connecting customers with specific goods and services. By the 1950s, techniques for branding had become part of a marketing manager's or marketing unit's portfolio. Marketing professionals considered themselves to be in charge of what brands should look or feel like. They designed and transmitted messages to large, dispersed audiences consisting primarily of consumers and prospects. Only occasionally were stakeholders in the brand approached for input on how to best present a brand's story.

Over the next several decades, thanks to developments in the study of brand loyalty and brand personality, the concept of branding extended to the organization itself—as much as a product or service was branded, so too was the organization that produced or provided it (Bastos and Levy, 2012). Congruence between an organization's branding and that of its output was cultivated. By the early twenty-first century, the concept of *total branding* had gained purchase (Franzen 2006), and revolved around managing the integration of communication tools, and coordinating the use of media content in service to PR, marketing communications, and digital communication.

The financial crisis of 2007- 2008 increased awareness in organizations of their social responsibility (Franzen 2006). Now, in addition to making money for the benefit of members and investors, an organization was required to "make friends" with outsiders and the community. Accordingly, organizations began thinking of *corporate social responsibility* (CSR) as a reputation management imperative. Organizational elites ultimately recognized that creating consistent brand policy on a corporate level was necessary. Corporate identity has become a pillar of the corporate brand—"identity-based branding," designed "inside out" (i.e., originating in the aspirational discourses of organizational elites) instead of "outside in" (i.e., launched by market-driven perceptions of the organization) has become common. Wider applications of the concept of brand have recently come forth, with terms such as financial branding, employee branding, and internal communications branding, becoming part of strategic discourse.

The Meaning and Application of Gesamtkunstwerk

The key sensitizing concept in our chapter is *Gesamtkunstwerk*, which we use as a metaphor for how and why messages and tasks distinctive of branding, brand management, and IMC in general, are generated. A phrase often used synonymously with *Gesamtkunstwerk* is "total work of art." That certainly is a legitimate starting point for understanding the concept. We must generate additional insight and nuance in order to apply it to the IMC project.

A more sophisticated definition of *Gesamtkunstwerk*, then, is "a holistic, aesthetically elaborate combination of individual art forms" (Schmidt 2011, 157). Schmidt (2011) cites passages from a number of encyclopedia entries containing a definition of the term. From those passages emerges a theme in *Gesamtkunstwerk* of merging, or blurring of distinctions between or among, diverse art forms, in order to produce a particular composition—a harmony of "all individual artistic genres, especially orchestral music, mimic dance, and poetry . . . [in] mutually illuminating collaboration" (Goebel 2007, 494).

Fornoff (2004; quoted in Schmidt 2011; cf. Dobrenko's very brief summary in English of the Fornoff material) identifies "*vier Strukturmerkmale des Phänomens 'Gesamtkunstwerk'* [four formative characteristics of the *Gesamtkunstwerk* phenomenon]" (170-171), which Schmidt revises and reconceptualizes (175-177) as follows: (a) the practical design process by which various artistic or aesthetic elements or artifacts may be combined to form one entity; (b) the theoretic grounding for the design process; (c) the problem to be solved by the design; and to solve the problem, (d) a negotiation of the tension between art and reality, ideally conducted with "a revolutionary and utopian attitude" (Schröter 2011, 2) about the value of the new entity and the process of constructing it.

The term itself is most often linked with the works of German composer Richard Wagner (Goebel 2007; Rickert and Salvo 2006; Schmidt 2011; Scherer 1995; Schröter 2011). In his writings Wagner named *Gesamtkunstwerk* as "the foundation for the epic operatic genre" (Dobrenko 2016, 209) with which he is most closely associated. Menninger (2011) proposes that for Wagner, totality in a work of musical art pertained to the "total experience of the [audience member] . . . [as well as] a complete collaboration among artists" (98). The *Gesamtkunstwerk* concept has been deemed relevant outside the boundaries of music and music history. For example, Goebel (2007) refers to the city of Dresden, Germany, known for having been destroyed by bombing in February 1945, as "an urban *Gesamtkunstwerk*" (494) and observes that "the visual spectacle of Dresden as a *Gesamtkunstwerk* is . . . directly related to larger issues of history" (495); in the 1990s, German urban planner Hans Stimmann spoke similarly about reconfiguring certain historic precincts in Berlin (Staiger 2009).

Hinchman (2013; cf. Lewer 2011, and Peters 1998) describes early-twentieth-century interior designer Josef Hoffmann as an artisan with a "commitment to [incorporating the practice of] *Gesamtkunstwerk*, or total designed environment" (xiii) into his projects. German artist and environmentalist Joseph Beuys (fl. 1950s-1980s) believed that environmental "responsibility moved from scientific interest to public protest and alternative political organizations and then to the need to restructure society itself" (Adams 1992, 28); and "his approach to art developed from traditional objects to installations and performances and then to the idea of . . . involving everyone as an artist" (28). Beuys labeled this confluence of political action, art, and community an "ecological *Gesamtkunstwerk*" (Adams 1992, 28). Greber (2006), in analyzing literary themes in Russian novelist Boris Pasternak's work, proposes that Pasternak conceives of memory as a specific place that "represents architecture of the synthesis of arts (*Gesamtkunstwerk*)" (27).

SERVICE LEARNING AND IMC PEDAGOGY

By definition, *Gesamtkunstwerk* presupposes a holistic integration of forms to produce a harmonious and "mutually illuminating" (q. v. Schmidt 2011) result. Similarly, IMC's "cross-functional coherence and synergies" (q. v. Procu, del Barrío-Garca, and Kitchen 2012) imply a holistic sensibility about connecting organizations and stakeholders, as does the view of a brand as an "interdisciplinary" (q. v. Bastos and Levy 2012) phenomenon. The convergence and intermediality (q. v. Jenkins 2006, and Rajewsky 2005) of the networked society we inhabit further illustrate the theme of holism found in the theoretic underpinnings of this chpater. Accordingly, to teach IMC, an educator will do well to think of the subject matter as holistic, and favor holistic approaches to instructional development and course design. Enter service learning. Hironimus-Wendt and Lovell-Troy (1999) define service learning as a pedagogy that is relatively "structured in form, and . . . involves the deliberate integration of . . . [a] service activity into the course" (361). A typical service activity may involve assessing the needs of a client organization (very often a community-based organization) and then providing materials and artifacts, developmental intervention, coaching, research report, among other responses, to meet the needs (eee Easterling and Rudell 1997, and Petkus 2000, for brief descriptions of possible service-learning student roles and projects). Details vary from one course or instructor to another, but most service learning designs "engage students in service to the community in a way that is connected . . . to course or curricular goals" (Tacelosky 2008, 878). Normally, however, instruction focuses each student markedly, although not exclusively, on learning enough in the course to contribute effectively to the completion of a service activity, or suite of them; reflecting on the experience afterward; and ultimately declaring (orally or in writing) what, concerning the course curriculum, he or she learned from the process. Individual students working on their own, teams of class members, or course enrollees working as a plenary collective, may participate in the service component of the course.

Service learning has earned a reputation for effectiveness as a method of introducing students to topics that revolve around a call to think holistically about subject matter. In particular, when compared with education in other business disciplines, "marketing [education] may be best suited to this pedagogy" (Easterling and Rudell 1997, 60; cf. Petkus 2000). Martin (2015) concurs: "Service learning as a pedagogy is particularly beneficial for marketing" (109). For the client, benefits may include: "new ideas to improve organizational operations, and provide additional human resources" (Blouin and Perry 2009, 122); and "build[ing instrumental] relationships with academic institutions" (Easterling and Rudell 1997, 60).

WHAT A 3.0 ORGANIZATION LOOKS LIKE

The 7i Network Model (van Os et al. 2013) provides a framework for envisioning and facilitating the process of developing and implementing IMC activities that distinguish a 3.0 organization from a 1.0 or 2.0 entity. The model consists of seven critical aspects of an organization. No one of them functions independently of the others; and IMC professionals must manage all of them with great care and vision. The aspects are: *Identity*; *Internal Flexibility*; *Insights*; *Interaction*; *Inspiring Networks* and *Innovation* (the two will be combined in one discussion); and *Instruments*.

Identity

Although all seven aspects of organizations are vital to manage effectively, the *identity* aspect is *primus inter pares*. Here is the central question an executive or manager asks about the 3.0 organization's identity: "Is it clear?" If the answer is "No," the organization performs tasks that are branding tasks.

Branding was once regarded as a responsibility for advertising experts, agencies and communications specialists. In Society 2.0, brand managers, despite the use of some digital tools, ultimately closed a great deal of the branding process off from outsiders. Society 3.0 brand managers, however, blur functions and boundaries, and the assumptions underlying them. Outsiders to the organization feel in their own way as proprietary about their relationship with the brand as insiders do.

Consider the case (recounted in Jenkins, Ford, Green 2013) of Susan Boyle, the 2009 winner on the British reality-talent television show *Britain's Got Talent* (the inspiration for the U.S.A.'s *American Idol*) in 2009. One video of her performance, astonishingly good for an amateur, spread virally among multiple millions of individual consumers worldwide. Could the producers of the show rightly claim this high-profile accomplishment as theirs? Or was it a credit to those who distributed the video again and again on the Internet—even though they did not actually produce or underwrite it? Was value created; and if so, how was it created? In short: Who "owns" Boyle's triumph; who deserves (or does not deserve) to make money from it?

Legal permissions exist that provide more or less traditional answers to such questions, and to others involving intellectual property rights, communication protocols, and ownership of channels and content (Hatch & Schultz 2010; Jenkins, Ford and Green 2013); innovation (Jacobs 2007); and the brand itself (van den Hoff, 2015). For example, some legal controls exist that address the phenomenon of *brandjacking* (Hesseldahl 2007; Lee 2011; Ramsey 2010; Zeltser 2011), whereby an individual or a group "hijacks" a corporation's identity. Accomplished primarily in social media environments, to brandjack means to pretend to be communicating on behalf of a particular organization, hoping to realize some benefit from making an explicit or implicit claim of connection to or membership in that organization. But IMC professionals in 3.0 organizations think less in terms of "ownership" issues and more in terms of developing competences in cultivating meaningful relationships in order to facilitate negotiation in determining solutions to dilemmas that once would have been cut-and-dried violations of ownership rights. Hatch and Schultz (2010) suggest holding onto such rights "is not only unnecessary, it is also undesirable because it limits the use and usefulness of these channels [i.e., connections with stakeholders] for gathering information, and for cementing relationships and the loyalty that comes with them" (603).

Internal Flexibility

Internal flexibility concerns who and what the organization is, or should be, and the reason it exists (Sinek 2009), as well as the structuring of formal and informal culture and leadership, and the competence of individual members. The key question that launches enhancements of internal flexibility: "Is the organization as adaptable as it needs to be?" The organization must be sufficiently flexible to respond effectively to surprises—yet too much flexibility is as limiting as too little.

Insights

Insights pertain to knowledge and knowledge management. The key question that opens an organization up to high-quality insights is, "Can knowledge be acquired, stored, managed and used effectively by our organization?" Insight is generated by monitoring and responding to market and industry trends, inquiring into the organization's image, and discovering expectations held by outsiders. Such knowledge is acquired by relatively formal methods (e.g., surveys, focus groups, other research protocols), and equally meaningfully in informal contact with outsiders on a topic of interest to the organization.

Soliciting insights is facilitated by what is known as *horizontalization* (Ruiter 2015)—a development of particular relevance to the IMC and branding endeavors. Horizontalization refers to the tendency of society to be "flattening and equalizing. People move through different and multiple networks. There is less sense of hierarchy. People want to share experiences and opinions" (van Ruler 2015, 14). IMC professionals, managing the digital communication activities that horizontalization enables and invites, acquire insights from a large number of stakeholders in a short time.

Interaction

Ronald van den Hoff (2011) describes a 3.0 organization as one in which the connections between and among employees and other stakeholders are a focus of primary attention. This means that the organization is only as important as conversation members and stakeholders are valued. The key question insiders know to ask is: "Who is interacting with whom; and about what?" The networked society not only has a multiplicity of opportunities for organizational members and stakeholders to interact; interaction has been fundamentally redefined, in light of the digitization of the communication process. Quoted in van den Hoff (2015) is an observation by Marco Derksen, that a drive to instantiate "multi-way" communication "makes the distance between organizations and individuals continually smaller. In the 3.0 era, the hierarchical relations between organizations and individuals tend to disappear."

Inspiring Networks; Innovation

A 3.0 organization monitors and encourages conversations and interaction to form into networks of organization members and stakeholders, who inspire one another to co-create brand identity. The central question to ask is, "Who is taking us seriously, seeking to be an enduring part of our environment, and wanting to bring others into the setting?" *Inspired networks* consisting of members, managers and stakeholders who are committed to and enthusiastic about connecting with one another to the benefit of the organization fuel interaction, make sense out of information coming into and going out from the organization, and ultimately maintain relationships of instrumental value to the organization.

Absent such "inspiration" to take action, the various aspects of organization accounted for by the 7i Model would be inert ideas. It is the number and commitment of an organization's inspiring networks that push an organization into 3.0 status. The networks create opportunities for engaged partnerships (Hatch and Schultz 2010). For example, members of an engaged network could become partners in innovation by launching crowdsourcing opportunities outside-in to shepherd new ideas to market.

Instruments

Technical affordances such as hardware and software are *instruments*. So too are policies that facilitate and stimulate 3.0 interaction (conversation, partnership, connecting). Another instrument is executive- or management-level encouragement of entrepreneurialism in meeting the needs of constituents. The key question members know to ask about instruments is: "What tool do we need, and who must be able to wield it most effectively?" IMC in a 3.0 organization involves the use of tools that facilitate the "multi-way" communication.

TEACHING IMC: HOW IT'S DONE AT ONE DUTCH UNIVERSITY

IMC educators must teach students how to navigate the whitewater of a volatile organizational universe, in which insider and outsider roles are not sharply demarcated. The students will one day be charged with applying their skills as IMC practitioners to support an organization in achieving, maintaining or enhancing 3.0 status—never mind having one day to determine what *4.0* status may look like, and proposing how to get there. The curriculum and instruction favored at Arnhem Business School (ABS) of HAN University of Applied Sciences (where the first author has taught for almost two decades) illustrate how this may be accomplished.

ABS's advanced-level students who have completed internships and other service learning experiences have little interest in long-term projects, classic university lectures and standard testing; they have served as novice professionals and want more of that. On the client side, organizations are eager to work with students, but not solely or primarily as internship sponsors or as clients for semester-long interventions. So ABS has organized its curriculum around short-term projects that would throw all students, new or veteran, into the vortex of real organizational problems.

ABS's pedagogy is therefore unabashedly oriented to service learning. Students work with clients who seek real solutions to actual organizational problems. The students write functional communication plans, design social media strategies and campaigns, and develop search engine optimization processes for the clients. Many clients do not think strategically about IMC; all they know is that they are supposed to get current with social media. Accordingly, the students often must educate a client about what the client is inquiring into in the first place. They learn how to actually co-create and co-produce IMC results with clients.

The students, ABS faculty, clients (new, prospective, or former), and other interested parties, have formed an online community (www.toecomst.nl) where knowledge, ideas, solutions, queries, and concerns, may be shared. Students have uploaded documents and other deliverables from their projects, which can serve as a sort of portfolio for a student. Several dozen organizations have a presence on the website.

Beyond the website, ABS has organized "speed dating" events—"meet markets" designed to make salubrious connections between students and clients, and facilitate networking among ABS stakeholders (students, faculty members, potential internship sponsors, etc.). The event also enables students to pitch the possibility of interning at organizations of interest to them. Faculty members—most of whom came to the academic world after successful careers as practitioners—facilitate short courses and workshops, to acquaint stakeholders with the latest research.

CONCLUSION

The concept of *sharing* applies to the challenge of doing effective work in IMC (Le Meur 2013; Hendriks 2015). An IMC practitioner shares stories about the brand; he or she allows customers to share responses to the brand with other customers and with members of the organization. The concept dovetails well with the 7i Network Model aspect of interaction, in that an imperative to "share" implies a certain kind of co-equality of insiders and outsiders. Perhaps the concept of "brand-sharing" will become the theme of IMC in the future.

To meet the challenge of branding in Society 3.0, marketing communicators will do well to think of their challenge as creating a *Gesamtkunstwerk*. Surely many of the properties of a "total work of art" map across to conceptualizing and executing functions and operations that facilitate and manage "multi-way" communication about a brand.

Gesamtkunstwerk's four formative characteristics (q. v. Schmidt 2011) may with some "translation" be also seen as "formative" of IMC work. One of those characteristics is the practical design process by which artists produce their works. To generate their artifacts, IMC practitioners and brand managers make decisions according to an intentional design process, which could include informal steps (e.g., asking a colleague to review drafts of a marketing communication) or formal protocols, such as following a specific house style in formatting a white paper, in order to underscore "one look, one voice."

Related is the call to base design on solid theoretic grounding. Surely in the world of marketing praxis, a specialist will make allowances for choices that, say, intuition borne of experience may suggest (e.g., "I have a gut feeling that customers are going to want us to cut to a shot of the outer office. . ."). In her book-length exploration of the connection between social media and IMC, Persuit (2013) writes that her discussion will "situate social media as a human communication effort within an organizational context" (2) and that she intends to develop proposals "grounded in Cicero's rhetorical theory" (2). Persuit's declaration presupposes that, for the IMC endeavor—and by logical conceptual extension, the task of branding—the utility and applicability of discoveries made as a result of work in no fewer than three theory-building arenas: human communication and organizations; media theories; and Ciceronian rhetoric.

The third and fourth characteristics concern the problem to be solved by the communicator's choices. A *Gesamtkunstwerk* solves a problem that a "lightweight" or expressly commercial may not. Additionally, a *Gesamtkunstwerk* instantiates a tension with reality, and to negotiate that tension is to hold out revolutionary or utopian ends as possibilities. The goal of IMC may not be "utopian" per se; but the call to seek and privilege mutuality between customers and organization members is certainly an idealistic direction to walk in.

Finally, what tension is negotiated in the process of solving a branding problem? A brand manager must negotiate at least three tensions during the process. One is suggested by the question, "Are my claims about the brand accurate and defensible?" and mirrors the art-versus-reality tension residing in the *Gesamtkunstwerk*. A second tension concerns resources, as suggested by the question, "What is the most resourcing I can request or expect in order to get the highest-quality results?" ("Resourcing" may mean time, funds, personnel, training, materials, access to information, contact with key decision makers, or some combination of those affordances.) This points to a third tension: Organizational elites who manage and monitor resources are asking the brand manager, "What is the least resourcing you need in order to get the highest-quality results?"

For an organization wanting to acquire 3.0 status, the following anecdote may be an apposite cautionary tale (van Os, Delisse, Derksen & Jurriëns 2013). Students and faculty members of HAN University of Applied Sciences conducted research into IMC operations in seven healthcare organizations. The researchers conducted interviews of, and facilitated focus groups populated by, organization insiders. They inspected strategic plans, mission and vision statements, social media policies, and other instruments. From the vocabulary of the 7i Network Model, they designed data analysis procedures—which revealed that none of the organizations turned out to qualify as a 3.0 organization. Internal flexibility was meritorious, but deficiencies practices associated with insight, innovation, inspiring networks and interaction, were numerous. Also, marketing communications tended to be "one-" or "two-way" much more often than "multi-way." The researchers ultimately concluded that leaders and IMC managers should not underestimate how challenging it is to become a 3.0 organization.

REFERENCES

Adams, David. 1992. "Joseph Beuys: Pioneer of a Radical Ecology." *Art Journal*, 51 (2): 26-34.

Bastos, Wilson, and Sidney J. Levy. 2012. "A History of the Concept of Branding." *Journal of Historical Research in Marketing*, 4 (3): 347-368. doi: 10.1108/17557501211252934.

Blouin, David D., and Evelyn M. Perry. 2012. "Whom Does Service Learning Really Serve? Community-Based Organizations' Perspectives on Service Learning." *Teaching Sociology*, 37 (2): 120-135. http://www.jstor. org/stable/25593983.

Blumer, Herbert. 1954. "What is Wrong with Social Theory?" *American Sociological Review* 19 (1): 3-10.

Bowen, Glenn A. 2006. "Grounded Theory and Sensitizing Concepts." *International Journal of Qualitative Methods* 5 (3): 1-9.

Chen, Mei-Liang, Chu-Mei Liu, and Chien-Jung Huang. 2015. "Integrated Marketing Communication, Collaborative Marketing, and Global Brand Building in Taiwan." *International Journal of Organizational Innovation* 7 (4): 99-107.

Cornelissen, Joep P. 2001. "Integrated Marketing Communications and the Language of Marketing Development." *International Journal of Advertising* 20 (4): 483-498.

De Roeck, Dries, Achiel Standaert, Robert A. Paauwe, Stijn Verwulgen, Christiaan Baelus, and Pieter Jan Stappers. 2012. "Interweaving Digitality in the Fabric of Design." In *Design Education for Future Wellbeing: Proceedings of the 14th International Conference on Engineeering and Product Design Education, Antwerp (Belgium), September 6-7*. The Design Society, Institution of Engineering Designers.

Derksen, Marco. 2011. "How Do You Determine the Strategy of a Successful Network?" *Upstream* [blog]. http://www.upstream.nl/blog/bericht/hoe_bepaal_je_de_strategie_van_een_netwerkorganisatie/

Dobrenko, Evgeny. 2016. "Prigov and the *Gesamtkunstwerk*." *The Russian Review* 75 (2): 209, 219.

Easterling, Debbie, and Frederica Rudell. 1997. "Rationale, Benefits, and Methods of Service Learning in Marketing Education." *Journal of Education for Business* 73 (1): 58-61.

Farrell, Thomas J. 1991. "Secondary Orality and Consciousness Today." In *Media, Consciousness, and Culture: Explorations of Walter Ong's Thought*, edited by Bruce E. Gronbeck, Thomas J. Farrell, and Paul A. Soukoup, 194-209. Newbury Park: SAGE Publications.

Fornoff, Roger. 2004. *Die Sehnsucht nach dem Gesamtkunstwerk* [Nostalgia for Gesamtkunstwerk]. Hildesheim: Studien zu einer ästhetischen Konzeption der Moderne.

Franzen, G. 2006. *The SWOCC Book of Brand Management Models*. Amsterdam: SWOCC.

Goebel, Rolf J. 2007. "'*Gesamtkunstwerk*' Dresden: Official Urban Discourse and Durs Grünbein's Poetic Critique." *The German Quarterly* 80 (4): 492-510. http://www.jstor.org/stable/27676108.

Greber, Erika. 1997. "The Art of Memory in Boris Pasternak's Aesthetics." *Russian Literature*, 42 (1): 25-46.

——— and Majken Schultz. 2009. "Of Bricks and Bricks and Brands: From Corporate to Enterprise Branding." *Organizational Dynamics,* 38 (2): 117-130. doi: 10.1016/j.orgdyn.2009.02.008

Hendriks, Theo. 2015. "Verhalen: fantastisch gereedschap." In *Communicatie NU 2:* 86-89.

Hesseldahl, Arik. May 1, 2007. "'Brandjacking' on the Web." *Bloomberg* (business news). http://www.bloomberg.com/news/articles/2007-05-01/brandjacking-on-the-webbusinessweek-business-news-stock-market-and-financial-advice

Hinchman, Mark. 2013. "Interior Design History: Some Reflections." *Journal of Interior Design* 38 (1): ix-xxi.

Hironimus-Wendt, Robert J., and Larry Lovell-Troy. 1999. "Grounding Service-Learning in Social Theory." *Teaching Sociology,* 27 (4): 360-372. http"//www.jstor.org./stable/ 1319042.

Jacobs, Dany. 2007. *Adding values, the cultural side of innovation.* Arnhem, NLD: ArtEZ Press.

Jenkins, Henry. 2006. *Convergence Culture: Where Old and New Media Collide.* New York: New York University Press.

———, Sam Ford, and Joshua Green. 2013. *Spreadable Media: Creating Value and Meaning in a Networked Culture.* New York: New York University Press.

Johnson, Steven. 1997. *Interface Culture: How New Technology Transforms the Way We Create and Communicate.* New York: HarperEdge.

Kitchen, Philip J., and Patrick De Pelsmacker. 2004. *Integrated Marketing Communications: A Primer.* London: Routledge.

Kliatchko, Jerry. 2008. "Revisiting the IMC Construct: A Revised Definition and Four Pillars." *International Journal of Advertising* 27 (1): 133-160.

Laczniak, Russell N., and Charles Patti. 2005. "From the Editor." *Journal of Advertising* 34(4): 5-9. doi: 10.1080/00913367.2005.10639206

Lanham, Richard A. (1993). The Electronic Word: Democracy, Technology, and the Arts. Chicago: University of Chicago Press.

Lee, Dave. November 11, 2011. "Copy and #paste: How Brandjacking Stalks Companies Online" *BBC News--Business.* http://www.bbc.com/news/business-15647373.

Le Meur, Loïc. 2013. "The Sharing Economy" (PowerPoint presentation). *LinkedIn SlideShare.* http://www.slideshare.net/loiclemeur/sharing-economyforslideshare-20131145

Lewer, Deborah. 2011. "German Expressionism as 'Gesamtkunstwerk'?" Review of *Gesamtkunstwerk Expressionismus,* ed. Ralf Beil and Claudia Dillmann. *Art History,* 34 (5): 1065-1068. doi: 10.1111/j.1467-8365.2011.00863.x

Li, Charlene, and Josh Bernoff. 2008. *Groundswell: Winning in a World Transformed by Social Technologies.* Boston: Harvard Business Press.

Martin, Mary C. 2015. "Service Learning as Marketing Pedagogy: Practical, Theoretical and Institutional Perspectives." *Academy of Educational Leadership Journal* 19 (2): 109-127.

Menninger, Margaret E. 2011. "The Classroom as a 'Total Work of Art'—Pedagogy, Performance and 'Gesamtkunstwerk.'" *Ubiquitous Learning: An International Journal* 3 (3): 97-103.

Newton, Harry. 1979. "800 Lines—a Great Marketing Tool." *Telephone Engineer* 83 (18): 61.

Ong, Walter J. 1982. *Orality & Literacy: The Technololgizing of the Word.* London: Routledge.

———. 1967. *The Presence of the Word: Some Prologomena for Cultural and Religious History.* Minneapolis: University of Minnesota Press.

Palmeri, Anthony J. 1991. "Ramism, Ong, and Modern Rhetoric." In *Media, Consciousness, and Culture: Explorations of Walter Ong's Thought,* edited by Bruce E. Gronbeck, Thomas J. Farrell, and Paul A. Soukoup, 50-76. Newbury Park: SAGE Publications.

Persuit, Jeanne M. 2013. *Social Media and Integrated Marketing Communication: A Rhetorical Approach.* Lanham, MD: Lexington Books.

Petkus, Ed, Jr. 2000. "A Theoretical and Practical Framework for Service-Learning in Marketing: Kolb's Experiential Learning Cycle." *Journal of Marketing Education* 22 (1): 43-64-70.

Peters, Cynthia M. 1998. "*Gesamtkunstwerk* and the Vienna Secession." Honors thesis, University of North Carolina Wilmington.

Porcu, Lucia, Salvador del Barrio-García, and Philip J. Kitchen. 2012. "How Integrated Marketing Communications (IMC) Works—A Theoretical Review and an Analysis of its Main Drivers and Effects." *Comunicación y Sociedad*, 25 (1): 313-348.

Rajewsky, Irina O. 2005 (Autumn). "Intermeidality, Intertextuality, and Remediation: A Literary Perspective on Intermediality." *Intermédialités* 6: 43-64. http://cri.histart.umontreal.ca/cri/fr/intermedialites/p6/pdfs/p6_rajewsky_text.pdf.

Ramsey, Lisa P. 2010. "Brandjacking on Social Networks: Trademark Infringement by Impersonation of Markholders." Buffalo Law Review, 58 (4): 851-928. www.buffalolawreview.org/past_issues/58_4/Ramsey.pdf

Reddy, Michael. 1979. "The Conduit Metaphor: A Case of Frame Conflict in our Language about Language." In *Metaphor and Thought*, edited by A. Ortony. Cambridge: Cambridge University Press.

Reid, Mike. 2005. "Performance Auditing of Integrated Marketing Communication (IMC) Actions and Outcomes." *Journal of Advertising* 34 (4): 41-54.http://www.jstor.org.liblink.uncw. edu/stable/4189318

———, Sandra Luxton, and Felix Mavondo. 2005. "The Relationship Between Integrated Marketing Communication, Market Orientation, and Brand Orientation." *Journal of Advertising* 34 (4): 11-23. ProQuest document i.d. 236503116

Rickert, Thomas, and Michael Salvo. 2006. "The Distributed *Gesamtkunstwerk*: Sound, Worlding, and New Media Culture." *Computers and Composition*, 23 (3): 296-316. doi: 10.1016/ j.compsom.2006.05.001.

Ruiter, John, Aniek Gaveel, and Rik Wester. 2015. *Communicatiejaaronderzoek 2015.* https://www.communicatiepanel.nl/pdf/Trendonder-zoek%20Communicatiepanel%202015%20(definitief).pdf.

Schmidt, Wolf G. 2011. "*Was ist 'Gesamtkunstwerk'* ?" *Archiv für Musikwissenschaft* 68(2): 157-179. ProQuest Central document i.d. 877039029.

Scherer, Klaus R. 2011. "Expression of Emotion in Voice and Music." *Journal of Voice* 9 (3): 235-248.

Schröter, Jens G. 2011. "Discourses and Models of Intermediality." *CLCWeb: Comparative Literature and Culture* 13 (3): 1-7. http:/docs.lib.purdue.edu/clcweb/vol13/iss3/3.

Sinek, Simon. 2009. *Start With Why: How Great Leaders Inspire Everyone to Take Action.* New York: Penguin.

Solis, Brian. 2011. *The End of Business as Usual: Rewire the Way You Work to Succeed in the Consumer Revolution.* Hoboken, New Jersey: John Wiley.

Staiger, Uta. 2009. "Cities, Citizenship, Contested Cultures: Berlin's *Palace of the Republic* and the Politics of the Public Sphere." *Cultural Geographies* 16 (3): 309-327.

Tacelosky, Kathleen. 2008. "Service-Learning as a Way to Authentic Dialogue." *Hispania* 91(4): 877-886. . http"//www.jstor.org./stable/ 40648267.

"The Art of Management: Business Has Much to Learn from the Arts." February 17, 2011. *Schumpeter* (blog). http://www.economist.com/node/18175675

Tumin, Zachary, and Archon Fung. 2010. "From Government 2.0 to Society 2.0: Pathways to Engagement, Collaboration and Transformation." *John F. Kennedy School of Government, Belfer Center for Science and International Affairs Report* [report]. https://www.innovations.harvardedu/sites/default/files/1977353.pdf.

Tyner, Kathleen. 1998. *Literacy in a Digital Age.* Mahwah, NJ: Erlbaum.

van den Hoff, Ronald. 2011. *Society 3.0.* Lindonk & de Bres, 2011.

———. 2013. *Mastering the Global Transition on Our Way to Society 3.0.* N.p.: Society 3.0 http://www.society30.com/download_book/society30updated.pdf.

———. 2015. *Society 3.0: From Network Donnections to Value Networks.* N.p.: http://publish.society30.com/pubs/society30/book/
055_Van_netwerk_naar_waardenetwerk.

van Os, Renée, Janneke Delisse, and Jan Jurriëns. 2014. "Hoe een 3.0 organisatie in te richten?" *Holland Management Review* 158: 1-9.

———, Janneke Delisse, Marco Derksen, and Jan Jurriëns. 2013. "Het 7i-Netwerkmodel – 7 kritische succesfactoren voor een 3.0 organisatie." *Hogeschool van Arnhem en Nijmegen.* http://docplayer.nl/712603-Het-7i-netwerkmodel-7-kritische-succesfactoren-voor-een-3-0-organisatie.html.

van Riel, Cees. 2010. *Identiteit en imago* (e-book). N.p.: Academic Service.

van Ruler, Betteke (ed.). 2015. *Communicatie NU.* Amsterdam: Adfo.

Verdegem, Pieter. 2011. "Social Media for Digital and Social Inclusion: Challenges for Informaiton Society 2.0 Research & Policies" *TripleC* 9 (1): 28-38 https://uu.diva-portal.org/smash/get/diva2:388577/FULLTEXT01.pdf.

Zeltser, Lenny. November 22, 2011. "Brand Impersonations On Line: Brandjacking and Social Networks." *InfoSec Handlers Diary Blog.* https://isc.sans.edu/diary/Brand+Impersonations+On-Line%3A+Brandjacking+and+Social+Networks/9952

Conclusion

IMC Creating Spaces for Engagement

The origins of the word *engagement* trace to the early fifteenth century, a legal or moral obligation: French from *engager* (to pledge) (Merriam-Webster 2016). Over time the word has gone through a transformation from an obligation to a choice to be involved in a brand. The evolution of the term throughout history is truly an act of engagement itself. In the postmodern era, what it means to participate civically, elicit responses, make decisions, and cultivate identity is grounded by engagement. This capacity to engage through comparison, assertion, potential, and so on, makes the act a crucial and powerful societal facet.

We live in a complex time in which headlines are often driven by negative societal acts, but as you have read in the cases presented in this book, successful headlines do exist and make a significant impact on people. Clearly, IMC campaigns provide a frame of reference for consumers to advocate for brands; therefore, it is important to manage their impact, positive or negative. In this way, IMC is customer-centric, allowing the consumer to express himself/herself through engagement. IMC is about selling ideas and experience (not product driven), which can include the experience of creation; selling an actual product is a residual effect of these efforts.

This idea of making creations is brought to life through a brand that brick by brick all audiences (kids and adults) engage in imaginative play through LEGO®. Since its inception in the early 1930s, the LEGO brand has created spaces to engage fans. Contributing to the brand's success is its ability to tells stories, in multiple formats, reaching a variety of audiences in which the content creation that drives the sell (Pulizzi 2013). On the LEGO website it reads, "All LEGO products are based on this underlying philosophy of learning and development through play" (lego.com 2016). The company allows consumers to rethink the way they work (creatively and intellectually), which is why its content drives the social interaction. In the beginning, LEGO's primary audience consisted of children and parents, and not until the 2000s did the company realize a consumer base, traditionally ignored, was a key audience using their product—they were adults (O'Neil 2010). For years, adult fans had been going online starting discussion boards, sharing photos of creations, and setting up sites to buy and sell products (2010). At this moment, LEGO set out to build a personal relationship with LEGO fans of *all* ages, creating a space for engagement.

We use LEGO as an example because the company exemplifies how the intrinsic nature of IMC can create spaces for engagement—how a simple design has the potential to open up the possibility for dialogic conversations. Aakhus (2007) describes the phenomenon of communication design, which incorporates design thinking with communication questions of meaning, interaction, and coherence. When we apply design thinking to communication, we consider the potential for people to design the kinds of interactions in their relationships, shape the search for meaning in their lives, and endeavor to be coherent in their words and actions. Communication is designed to create spaces for engagement of customers, voters, volunteers, students, and other audiences. In his keynote address at the 3rd Biennial Integrated Marketing Communication Conference at the University of North Carolina Wilmington, J. Kevin Barge connected Aakhus' idea of communication as design to IMC, because in IMC we are trying to design communication that engenders behaviors, not just attitudes, that at best can foster engagement and dialogic communication (2015). According to Aakhus, design is a natural fact of communication; designs are hypotheses; and design is theoretical (2007, 113-15). All three of these aspects of design are seen in the cases and analyses in this book, but especially design as theoretical. In order to redeem IMC from technique-driven or emotivistic practices, we must seek theoretical ground for the practice of IMC. If design is theoretical, the way we design IMC efforts requires a praxis (theory-informed action) approach. The authors in this text have found a plethora of theoretical approaches from the social scientific and humanities roots of the study of communication to ground our understanding of IMC: from social identity theory to epideictic and kairotic rhetoric; from philosophy of communication to theories of civic engagement; and from Weberian economic theories to Coordinated Management of Meaning, these diverse approaches enable us to understand IMC as a vital form of human communication.

Throughout history we can see the transformation of the term engagement through the insights, observations, and ideas and concepts of people and places. IMC and engagement are inextricably linked. We offer ways to find balance between excesses and deficiencies—walking the "narrow ridge" (Buber 1948)—ways in which IMC can create spaces for engagement. Such spaces are enacted through actions that engage others, and it is our hope that after reading this book, you will consider how and why IMC changes your behavior; if you are a teacher, how you might engage your students in a productive, ethical approach to IMC; and, if you are an IMC scholar, how your scholarship might continue the conversation and create spaces for engagement.

REFERENCES

Aakhus, Mark. (2007). Communication as Design. *Communication Monographs*. Vol. 74, No. 1, pp. 112-117.

Barge, J. Kevin (2015). *Communicating Design, Designing Communication.* Keynote speech given at the 3rd Biennial Integrated Marketing Communication Conference, University of North Carolina Wilmington.

Buber, Martin (1948), *Israel and the World.* New York: Schocken.

O'Neill, Megan. (2010). *Then & Now. How Fans Changed the Face of LEGO's Marketing Strategy.* Accessed May 25, 2016: http://www.adweek.com/socialtimes/how-fans-changed-the-face-of-legos-marketing-strategy/15645

Pulizzi, Joseph. (2013). *Epic content marketing: How to tell a different story, break through the clutter, and win more customers by marketing less.* McGraw-Hill Education.

http://www.merriam-webster.com/dictionary/engage

http://www.lego.com/en-us/aboutus/lego-group

Index

About the Contributors

Daniel Assmus, Ph.D., is Professor of Marketing & Communication and MBA/International Business Program Coordinator at the IUBH School of Business and Management in Germany. He holds a Ph.D. in Rhetoric from Duquesne University, a B.Sc. in Business Administration/Marketing from West Virginia University, and a degree in International Management from Fulda University of Applied Sciences. Dr. Assmus' main research interest is in the area of consumer suspicion toward advertising and social media marketing. In addition to his academic activities, Dr. Assmus is vice chairman of the supervisory board for a retail, wholesale, and logistics company and he regularly delivers management workshops on marketing strategy and online communications.

Jill K. Burk, Ph.D., is an Instructor of Communication Arts & Sciences at Pennsylvania State University, Berks. Dr. Burk's research focuses on applied communication interests, including constructive approaches to public life and civic engagement, communication pedagogy, service-learning, and ethical communicative practices in integrated marketing communication. She is the editor of the *Undergraduate Journal of Service Learning & Community-Based Research*. Before entering academia, she worked in marketing and public relations. Dr. Burk teaches courses in rhetorical theory, communication ethics, community and civic engagement, organizational communication, and public speaking.

Vernon E. Cronen, Ph.D., is Professor Emeritus, University of Massachusetts, Amherst and Adjunct Faculty, Department of Communication Studies, University of North Carolina Wilmington. He is co-author of the theory Coordinated Management of Meaning (with Barnett Pearce). Dr. Cronen was Senior Consultant, KCC International, London (1984 – 2010). He lectures and presents workshops applying CMM theory in many countries for various contexts including organizational communication, leadership and family therapy. His work is widely published in national and international books and journals.

Kelli Lynn Fellows, Ph.D., is the Founder and Principal Consultant of *Cognitive Gymnastics*—a consulting group focused on business intelligence, creative inquiry, and transformational leadership. Additionally, she is an Associate Professor in *Pfeiffer University's* Graduate School of

Business and Leadership. She received her Ph.D. in Speech Communication from the University of Georgia, an M.S. in Speech Communication, and a B.S. in Public Relations from the University of Southern Mississippi. With over 25 years of professional organizational communications experience across corporate, non-profit, and academic contexts, Dr. Fellows utilizes a spectrum of quantitative and qualitative approaches to optimize business outcomes. Her research, consulting, and non-profit service interests include: identity construction and maintenance, risk and crisis communication, creative approaches to leadership optimization, change management, communication audits, and organizational stakeholder engagement.

Kees van het Hof, M.A., studied Communication at Radboud University in Nijmegen from 1982–1987 and graduated as a master in communication on image research at AMRO Bank (now ABN AMRO) in Amsterdam. Professor van het Hof worked for several national and international brands like Deloitte, De Hypotheker (a leading Dutch brand in retail mortgage advice), Reed Elsevier, and in the retail sector. His corporate experience expands 15 years on operational, strategic and executive levels in marketing communications. Since 2005, he has been a full-time faculty member and senior lecturer at HAN University of Applied Sciences in the Netherlands with a special interest in branding and media. He coordinates a minor in brand management where students work for real organizations, with real problems and questions that require real solutions. He utilizes his experiences as a professional in applied learning situations with his students.

Jeremy Langett, Ph.D., is assistant professor of communication studies at Lynchburg College in Virginia. He is a frequent presenter of original research at regional and national communication conferences and is published in *The International Journal of Strategic Communication, The Communication Law Review* and *The Journal of Mass Media Ethics*. Prior to his academic appointment, Dr. Langett worked for a marketing-communication firm in Pittsburgh representing clients in the education, technology and nonprofit sectors. He holds a B.S. in Journalism–Public Relations from the E.W. Scripps School of Journalism at Ohio University, an M.A. in Corporate Communication from Duquesne University and a Ph.D. in Rhetoric from Duquesne University.

Paul A. Lucas, Ph.D., is an Assistant Professor at the University of Pittsburgh at Johnstown. He has a Ph.D. in Rhetoric from Duquesne University. His research deals primarily with marketing, and he has presented at conferences such as the National Communication Association Conference, Eastern Communication Association Conference, Pennsylvania Communication Association Conference, and Biennial Integrated Marketing Communication Conference. He has published IMC/branding works in the *Communication Annual Journal of the Pennsylvania Communication Association*, and the *International Journal of Integrated Marketing Communications*.

Christina L. McDowell Marinchak, Ph.D., is an Assistant Professor of Business Communication and Marketing at the University of Alaska Anchorage in the College of Business and Public Policy. Dr. McDowell's research focuses on applied communication interests, including engaged scholarship, interpersonal communication, and ethical communicative practices in integrated marketing communication. She has presented papers at national, regional, and state conferences and is published in *Communication Research Trends*, the *Journal of Learning Community Research and Practice*, and the *Journal of the Association for Communication Administration*. Before entering academia she worked in account services for an integrated marketing communication firm. As an account manager, she was responsible for client relations, market research and database development, account management, event planning, copy-editing, marketing surveys, and collateral development.

Amanda G. McKendree, Ph.D., teaches management writing, management speaking, and management communication at the University of Notre Dame, where she is an Associate Teaching Professor of Management in the Fanning Center for Business Communication. Dr. McKendree's research examines crisis communication, conflict communication, and the influence of rhetoric on organizational identity. She is published in the *SAGE Encyclopedia of Identity, Business Communication Quarterly, Teaching Ideas for the Basic Communication Course*, and *Review of Communication*. She is the coauthor of *Conflict Between Persons: The Origins of Leadership* (Kendall Hunt Publishing Company, 2014).

Leeanne M. Bell McManus, Ph.D., associate professor in the Business Communication department at Stevenson University, received her Ph.D. in Rhetoric from Duquesne University and her M.A. in Communication Studies from West Virginia University. She has co-authored two books, *Communication Ethics Literacy: Dialogue and Difference* (Sage, 2009), and *Conflict between Persons: The Origins of Leadership* (Kendall Hunt, 2014). She is currently working on her third book, *Event Planning: Communicating Theory and Practice.* She has also published excerpts in *Exploring Communication Ethics: Interviews with Influential Scholars in the Field* and *The Encyclopedia of Social Identity*. Dr. Bell McManus has published in *Atlantic Journal of Communication, Communication Education, Communication Annual: Journal of the Pennsylvania Communication Association* and *Review of Communication*. In addition to her publications, she is a journal reviewer for *Communication Theory, Review of Communication, Communication and*

Religion, and *Qualitative Research Reports*. She is an active member of the National Communication Association, the Eastern Communication Association and the Southern Communication Association.

Jeanne M. Persuit received her Ph.D. from Duquesne University. She is associate professor in the Department of Communication Studies at the University of North Carolina Wilmington, where she teaches courses in integrated marketing communication, public relations, advertising, rhetorical theory, and communication ethics. With her co-author, Deborah A. Brunson, she has published a book chapter on the epideictic rhetoric and brand of Michelle Obama. She published *Social Media and Integrated Marketing Communication: A Rhetorical Approach* (Lexington Books, 2013) and has published in *Review of Communication* and *The Journal of the Association for Communication Administration.* Dr. Persuit is the conference planner for the biennial Integrated Marketing Communication Conference held at UNCW and has taught short courses in IMC pedagogy at the Eastern Communication Association and National Communication Association Conventions.

Chip Rouse, associate professor in the Business Communication department at Stevenson University, serves as department chair of the major and faculty advisor to the student newspaper at the university. She is one of three co-authors of *Event Planning: Communicating Theory and Practice* (Kendall Hunt) with Leeanne Bell McManus and Stephanie Verni, due out in 2015. Professor Rouse oversees all of the student interns in the department, and is a member of the College Media Association, the Associated Collegiate Press, the Journalism Education Association, and the Eastern Communication Association. She has Masters degrees from the University of Maryland and Loyola University of Maryland.

Cassandra Vinhateiro completed her BA degree in Communication Studies, University of North Carolina Wilmington in 2015. Her degree was focused on systemic approaches to communication in organizations and philosophy of communication. She intends to continue her education at the graduate level. Currently, she applies her interest and background in the organizations and aesthetics of communication as Planning and Purchasing Coordinator at Davis Rains Design.

David E. Weber, Ph.D., is an associate professor of communication studies at University of North Carolina Wilmington (UNCW). He earned his Ph.D. in organizational and intercultural communication at University of Denver, his master's degree in instructional design at University of Southern California, and his B.A. in English and Film Studies at University of California at Santa Barbara. Prior to entering the academic world in 1999, David was an organizational development specialist for two decades, including almost six years on expatriate assignments in Asia and the Middle East. At UNCW, David teaches courses in applied organizational communication (e.g., communication consulting, communication training and development), rhetorical theory, and qualitative research methods; he also teaches organizational development for the university's master's programs in conflict resolution and public administration. David's research interests concern communication as it occurs at and constructs the intersection of culture, identity, and organization.

CPSIA information can be obtained
at www.ICGtesting.com
Printed in the USA
LVHW111457050420
652284LV00007B/114

9 781498 540025